MAMMALS IN WYOMING

University of Kansas
Museum of Natural History

Public Education Series No. 10
Joseph T. Collins, Editor

MAMMALS IN WYOMING

Tim W. Clark
and
Mark R. Stromberg

University of Kansas
Museum of Natural History

The Public Education Series, initiated in 1974, is intended to provide publications on natural history for the people of Kansas and surrounding states. This volume is the result of studies sponsored, in part, by various conservation organizations and is published by the Museum of Natural History, The University of Kansas, to provide a deeper understanding of our nation's natural fauna.

Distributed by the University Press of Kansas
Lawrence, Kansas 66045

Library of Congress Cataloging-in-Publication Data

Clark, Tim W.
Mammals in Wyoming.
(Public education series; no. 10)
Bibliography: p.
Includes index.
1. Mammals—Wyoming.   I. Stromberg, Mark R., 1951–
II. Title.   III. Series.
QL719.W8G55   1987   599'.09787   86-33210
ISBN 0-89338-026-1
ISBN 0-89338-025-3 (pbk)

Printed in the United States of America
10   9   8   7   6   5   4   3   2   1

Photographs on pp. 29, 34, 47, 49, 53, 116, 127, 161, 176, 186, 219, and 245 appeared originally in J. Knox Jones, Jr., David M. Armstrong, Robert S. Hoffmann, and Clyde Jones, *Mammals of the Northern Great Plains* (Lincoln and London: University of Nebraska Press, 1983), and are reproduced here courtesy of the photographers.

PREFACE

Mammals in Wyoming is an update of Charles A. Long's *Mammals of Wyoming* (1965). Since then, 16 new species of mammals (nine of them from Long's hypothetical list) have been added to the mammalian fauna of Wyoming. This volume is based on our own studies and the work of many other mammalogists and other interested people. It is due to this collective effort that we know as much as we do about Wyoming mammals. The recent foundation of our knowledge is Long's (1965) excellent publication.

Mammalogists have published accounts of the species that occur in several states surrounding Wyoming, and these references were invaluable in preparing our volume. We encourage readers, especially those interested in areas along state boundaries, to refer to these other state accounts. These accounts describe mammals in Colorado (Lechleitner 1969, Armstrong 1972), Montana (Hoffmann and Pattie 1968), the Black Hills region of South Dakota (Turner 1974), Nebraska (Jones 1964), Utah (Durrant 1952), and Idaho (Larrison and Johnson 1981). In addition, Hall (1981) listed and described all North American mammals. Several regional or site-specific accounts of mammals are available: Jones et al. (1983) for the northern Great Plains, Larrison and Johnson (1976) dealing with the northwestern United States, Olin (1971, 1975) on mammals of the southwestern United States, and Armstrong (1975) for Rocky Mountain National Park.

Much of the newer information on Wyoming mammals deals with species distributions and conservation. The impetus behind the compilation of much of this new information is the energy "boom" and the obvious need to mitigate its negative effects. Since 1965, there have been several near extirpations or losses of a species of Wyoming mammal. The black-footed ferret and pygmy shrew may be extinct in Wyoming. A subspecies of the thirteen-lined ground squirrel near the Bighorns may also have become extinct. Great Basin pocket mice are also extremely rare recently. Flaming Gorge reservoir destroyed most populations of canyon mice, piñon mice and cliff chipmunks in Wyoming. There are many serious conservation problems because of overgrazing and large increases in numbers of humans and the consequent destruction of mammalian habitats. This human "strain" is placing significant pressure on some native populations.

Several species have become quite rare in recent times. Since 1965, major progress has been made legislatively via the 1973 Federal Endangered Species Act and recognition of certain species of special concern by state authorities. Only three Wyoming species are federally listed—the Northern Rocky Mountain gray wolf and black-footed ferret as endangered and the grizzly bear as threatened.

Authorship of this book was a cooperative project. Mark Stromberg started working with Wyoming mammals with Clark in 1974 on a prairie dog project and in searches for the black-footed ferret. In 1979, Stromberg coordinated a natural history data base for The Nature Conservancy from Cheyenne, and until 1982, compiled data on Wyoming's vertebrates from many sources and carried out field surveys. As a result, he added or confirmed to the state list the least weasel, red bat, California myotis, Yuma myotis, pallid bat, and Brazilian free-tailed bat. The status of the swift fox was dramatically updated by Stromberg. He revised the keys and wrote the species accounts for the shrews, bats, rabbits, voles, pocket mice, rats, chipmunks, mice, and pocket gophers. Stromberg's regional responsibilities with The Nature Conservancy included Wyoming, Colorado, and New Mexico, especially with regard to rare and endangered species. Stromberg is now a research scientist and land manager with the National Audubon Society. Tim Clark began studies of Wyoming mammals in 1966, and his field work has centered on conservation-related problems. These ecological and behavioral studies included more than 30 representative species of shrews, various native mice and voles, ground squirrels, prairie dogs, pygmy rabbits, martens, black-footed ferrets, coyotes, grizzly bears, and mule deer. Additionally, he co-edited two editions of a volume on Wyoming's rare and endangered vascular plants and vertebrates (1981). He wrote the species accounts for the squirrels, carnivores, and ungulates and introductory material of this book.

Work on this book began five years ago, and in the process of completing it numerous people have contributed their time, money, observations, expertise, and cooperation. We are indebted to them all. Charles Long encouraged our work and provided early assistance in this project. Denise Casey and Deanne Winkler read and typed the manuscript. The Nature Conservancy and National Audubon Sociey provided logistic and word-processing assistance. Charles Thaeler provided unpublished data on pocket gophers. Dick Randall took many of the excellent photographs, and Wendy Morgan provided the black-and-white line drawings. The Grand Teton Natural History Association provided a grant to cover a portion of the typing costs.

The assistance in providing information is acknowledged to John Weaver, Bob Wood, Mike Bogan, Bob Finley, Bret Riddle, Bob Hoffmann, E. R. Hall, Greg Blair, Dave Armstrong, Bruce Wunder, Jim Halfpenny, Jim Findley, Mark Boyce, Harry Harju, Barry Floyd, Dave Belistsky, Doug Crowe, Steve Coy, Mike Karl, Dennis Flath, Mary Meagher, Howard Hunt, Dean Biggins, Tom Campbell, Craig Groves, Bruce Bury, Glen Clemmer, George Baxter, Mike O'Farrell, Roger Barbour, Conrad

Hillman, Bob Kiesling, Phil White, Steve Minta, Denise Casey, Margi Schroth, and Barbara Stromberg.

To all the students of mammalogy, both lay and professional, we appreciate your assistance for the long-term commitment in building up state collections and data bases and in adding to the general knowledge of mammal information and in providing us directly with information. We dedicate this book to you and to all who have curiosity and imagination, and who cannot live without wild things.

Lastly, we sincerely thank Joe Collins and the reviewers who assisted in this project. Without their support and financial commitment, this volume would have been impossible.

Tim W. Clark
Mark R. Stromberg
23 July 1986

CONTENTS

INTRODUCTION

Mammals are among the most fascinating forms of wildlife to laymen and professionals alike. Wyoming's mammals include the magnificent elk and Bighorn sheep, the rare black-footed ferret, and the elegant spotted bat. Wyoming still has species that were important to the early fur trade, such as beaver, marten, mink, and river otter. Although grizzly bears, wolves, and mountain lions are still present, their numbers are much lower than in presettlement times. To date, 117 native or naturalized mammal species have been identified in Wyoming. A few other native species will be found with additional study. Our knowledge of the natural history of each species varies considerably—from almost nothing to long and detailed accounts. Some common mammals are unknown to many people. Few have seen a flying squirrel or observed shrews or bats closely. The economically important game species (ungulates or hoofed animals especially) and fur-bearers are best known.

Wyoming's natural heritage is diverse and abundant. This treasure is accompanied by responsibilities of stewardship by private landowners individually and by our representatives—state and federal wildlife and land managers and elected officials. Foremost among our responsibilities is learning about our natural heritage and preserving or conserving mammal species and the communities and ecosystems of which they are a part. We cannot overemphasize this.

Wildlife conservation is a matter of science, ethics, and politics. Mammal conservation in Wyoming and elsewhere ultimately depends upon a large and vocal citizen constituency. Historically, states began by establishing fish and game departments to prevent over hunting of certain species about 90 years ago. Wyoming was no exception. Departments were set up principally to enforce wildlife laws and otherwise protect the greatly diminished herds of large mammals, fur-bearers, and other game animals. This successful early phase of wildlife conservation, still under way, is a large reason why so much wildlife still exists—especially the pronghorn and elk herds. Wyoming's hunters have long supported strong conservation laws. Today, in addition to those who hunt or otherwise directly utilize mammals economically, there is a growing segment of our population that utilizes native mammals and other wildlife in a non-consumptive way—viewing, photography, as artistic subjects, and so on.

Mammalogists, whether they work with universities, conservation groups, private enterprise, or state or federal agencies, are often requested to place dollar values on mammals. This is easier for hunted species than for the great majority of species, called "non-game," which are not hunted. A 1976 estimate by the Wyoming Game and Fish Department of the

1

minimum value of wildlife to the economy of Wyoming was $94,930,333. About $44 million was derived from big-game hunting and $44 million from fishing. Small game, birds, and waterfowl made up the rest. Since that time, the economic value of Wyoming's mammals has increased.

A 1975 National Survey of Hunting, Fishing and Wildlife Associated Recreation estimated that 4,546,000 person-days were spent in Wyoming for the purpose of wildlife observation and photography alone. This is 770,000 more days than were spent hunting and fishing. Altogether, the Wyoming Game and Fish Department estimated that $643 million in economic activity is generated annually by wildlife-related recreational pursuits. A large percentage of this is focused on Wyoming's wild mammals.

Wild mammals provide many valuable services, but these cannot always be easily measured in dollars. These other non-economic values include: 1) aesthetic values, 2) undiscovered or undeveloped values, 3) ecosystem stability values, 4) examples of survival, 5) environmental baseline and monitoring values, 6) scientific values, 7) teaching values, 8) habitat reconstruction values, and 9) conservation values (Ehrenfeld 1978). Recent studies throughout the United States, including the North American Wildlife Policy study, have shown that non-consumptive values of wildlife are growing rapidly. Aesthetic and nonconsumptive enjoyment of wildlife is by far the greatest value of this resource. State authorities are aware of this fact and are developing a "non-game" program. We whole-heartedly support this concept. Inventories of all "non-game" mammals are being planned. With these new data and a growing demand from the public, all of Wyoming's mammalian species can be given the conservation attention they deserve. Special attention must be given the rare, threatened, and endangered mammals. About two dozen species are so rare or so little known that we do not know the status of their populations.

As economic pressure on mammalian habitats and populations increases, it is imperative that a majority of citizens understand the need for healthy ecosystems. Education is the only road to this understanding. There is a need to shift the emphasis in wildlife-conservation education, research, and training to new areas such as conservation biology, ecosystems, and "non-game" species. Our academic institutions and the state and federal wildlife agencies need to keep pace with the broader appreciation of wildlife values by the public.

A great deal can be learned about mammals simply by watching them or examining their signs and making detailed notes. Some species, such as ground squirrels, can be observed easily, and data on habitat, foods, and home ranges thus obtained. But species like the grizzly bear require a team effort and much specialized equipment to obtain the same kind of information.

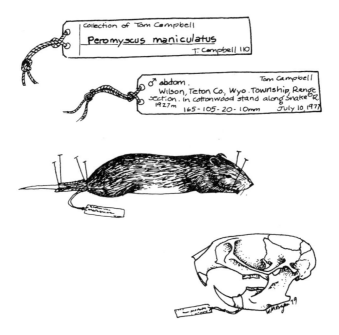

Figure 1. Typical field tag for specimen showing date, location, collector's name, habitat, scientific name (if known) and measurements. Measurements follow a standard order: total length, tail length, hind foot length and ear length.

Many aspects of the study of mammals require that the animals be collected in live-traps, examined, marked, and released. Marked mammals can later be recognized in further trapping or from direct observations. Other mammal studies on reproduction, taxonomy, and anatomy require that the animals be killed and preserved. In order to collect mammals, a state permit is required, and some species are totally protected. When mammals are collected, certain information must be recorded (Fig. 1) and attached to the specimen. Such specialized studies should be conducted only under the direction of professionals.

A PARTIAL HISTORY OF WYOMING MAMMALOGY

Knowledge of Wyoming's mammalian fauna has changed in kind and degree over the millennia. The earliest native Americans, belonging to unknown tribes, hunted many mammals and sought protection from others. Archeological investigations in the Shoshone Basin near Casper and in the Upper Green River Basin near Farson, for example, provide abundant evidence that Paleo-Indians hunted pronghorn, bison, and other mammals. Obviously, to hunt these mammal successfully using spears and bows and arrows, a great deal of information on each species' ecology and behavior was essential. Mastodons 4.5 m high were taken by Paleo-Indians near Worland more than 11,200 years ago. A major kill site of prehistoric bison dated at least 10,000 years ago is located near Casper. Northwestern Wyoming is still dotted with bighorn sheep traps made by modern Indians.

The first Europeans in Wyoming were the fur trappers of the early 1800s. They came to know well the country and the habits of beaver, marten, mink, river otter, wolves, grizzly and black bears, and others. John Colter stands out in this lot. The fur trade, widespread in areas like Jackson Hole, lasted only a few decades, into the 1840s.

Numerous explorers and naturalists visited the state after the 1840s. Their journals and expedition records sometimes give specific information about mammals. For example, Captain Benjamin Bonneville in Washington Irving's *The Adventures of Captain Bonneville USA* (1837) noted that bison "absolutely blackened" the prairies near the north fork of the Platte River in 1832. One of today's rarest mammals, the black-footed ferret, was first described from a skin obtained in Wyoming in the late 1840s by John James Audubon and a colleague, the Reverend John Bachman.

Yellowstone National Park was established in 1872 and in the following decades was visited by numerous naturalists and scientists. By 1940, more than 100 scientists in all fields of natural history had produced more than 2,000 publications on Yellowstone National Park. Of these, about 400 dealt specifically with mammals. One of the first major publications was Ernest Thompson Seton's *Mammals of Yellowstone National Park* (1898). Nearly all these 400 mammal papers dealt with the larger species—ungulates and carnivores.

The first really systematic mammal survey in Wyoming, covering a large part of the state (Fig. 2), was done just after the turn of the century by the U.S. Biological Survey. Mammalogists included C. H. Merriam, V. Bailey, B. H. Dutcher, J. A. Loring, E. A. Preble, A. Wetmore, H. E. Anthony, S. G. Jewett, and D. D. Streeter, Jr. Results were published in M. Cary's *Life Zones in Wyoming* (1917). Cary listed the many species they had collected or observed by life zone.

Since that time, professional mammalogists, some at the University of Wyoming and many from universities in other states, and more recently personnel in state and federal agencies—Wyoming Game and Fish Department, Bureau of Land Management, U.S. Fish and Wildlife Service, National Park Service, Soil Conservation Service—have conducted studies of Wyoming's mammals.

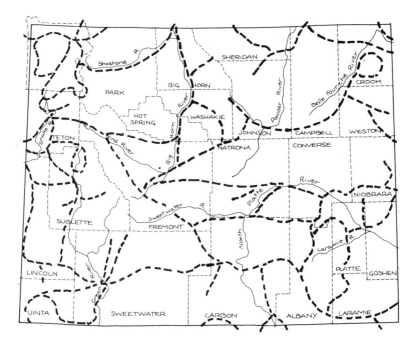

Figure 2. Map of Wyoming showing routes along which mammals were collected by Merritt Cary and other members of the U.S. Biological Survey, mainly from 1909 to 1915.

Charles Long's (1965) study on Wyoming mammals, conducted through the University of Kansas, focused on the identification of species and subspecies and their distribution in the state, and it listed 101 species. In the intervening 21 years, 16 additional species have been found. Taxonomic reassessments and documentation of a few other expected species also probably will occur in the next decade. Because Long's work was so comprehensive, all mammal research since then, including the present volume, has relied heavily on it.

A recent survey of the scientific journal literature on Wyoming's mammals found that only 57 of the state's native species had been studied through 1975 (Clark et al. 1978). Half of the 130 published articles found were less than two pages long. Elk, moose, bighorn sheep, deer mice, and western jumping mice were the mammals most frequently studied. Ecology and habitat, behavior, reproduction and genetics, and distributions were the most frequent subjects. Three of the 96 authors produced one-quarter of the papers. Half of all the studies were made in Yellowstone National Park and Teton County, which contains Grand Teton National Park. Many counties had never had any mammal research conducted. This study concluded that much needs to be learned about most Wyoming mammal species.

Both the University of Kansas and University of Wyoming have figured prominently in mammal study in Wyoming. Most of the more active collectors were affiliated with these two universities. E. Walker (1911–1917) donated skins and collected widely over the state. From 1945 to 1961 E. R. Hall and later his students from Kansas collected throughout the state. From 1934 to 1966, A. B. Mickey of the University of Wyoming collected and collaborated with E. R. Hall. The majority of Mickey's extensive collection was given to the University of Kansas. From 1947 to 1951, J. Getz also collected for A. B. Mickey. L. R. Brown was at Laramie from 1964 to 1969, and R. Fautin was present from the late 1940's till mid 1970's. C. McLaughlin was the mammalogist at Laramie from 1967 to 1972. J. Turner was the mammalogist from 1972 to 1978. In 1978, M. Boyce joined the University as a mammalogist and ecologist. Boyce reorganized and catalogued specimens in the museum of verterbrate biology and actively sought support for the museum. In 1982, B. M. Gilbert became part-time curator at the University of Wyoming. We hope Wyoming will continue to recognize the need for a well maintained mammal collection at the museum.

A number of helpful publications including three bibliographies have been produced in the last 5 years. Clark et al. (1980) listed 316 studies done in Wyoming up to 1976, and Rothwell et al. (no date) repeated many of these and also listed studies related to Wyoming mammals from adjacent states. Whelan and Riggs (no date) listed more than 800 references, including studies from similar habitats in adjacent Rocky Mountain states and elsewhere. Clark and Dorn (1981) reported on rare and endangered mammals in the state giving primary references for each. The Wyoming Game and Fish Department has collected data on species presence and habitats by latitude and longitude blocks (1982). We have cited other more recent literature. A detailed account of the history of Wyoming mammalogy remains to be written.

BIOTIC REGIONS

Wyoming includes 250,695 square kilometers and is about 600 km east-west and 440 km north-south. Surface features include major mountain ranges, mostly lying in a general north-south orientation, which are separated by broad, intermountain plains and basins (Porter 1962) (Fig. 3). Several smaller east-west oriented ranges, such as the Owl Creek, Green, Rattlesnake, Ferris, Seminoe, and Shirley Mountains, are located near the center of the state. Elevation ranges from 930 to 4207 meters above sea level, but the plains and basins are generally between 1200 and 2100 and meters. The highest point in Wyoming is Gannett Peak in the Wind River Range.

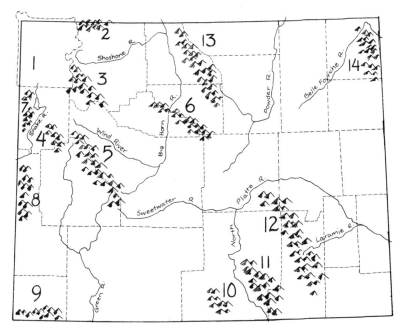

Figure 3. Map of Wyoming showing rivers, mountain ranges and county outlines. Number 1 designates Yellowstone National Park. The remaining numbers designate mountain ranges as follows: 2. Beartooth Mountains; 3. Absaroka Mountains; 4. Gros Ventre Mountains; 5. Wind River Mountains; 6. Owl Creek Mountains; 7. Teton Mountains; 8. Wyoming Mountains; 9. Uinta Mountains; 10. Sierra Madre Mountains; 11. Medicine Bow Mountains; 12. Laramie Mountains; 13. Big Horn Mountains; and 14. Black Hills.

Interior basins and eastern plains are essentially rolling to flat. The eastern plains are part of the Great Plains. The major basins include Powder River Basin, Big Horn Basin, and Wind River Basin, all in the north, and Great Divide Basin in the south, an extension of the Red Desert.

Salt River, Wyoming, Absaroka, Beartooth, Gros Ventre, Teton, and Wind River Mountain Ranges are in the northwest of Wyoming. The Big Horn Range is located in the north central of the state. The Sierra Madre, Medicine Bow, and Laramie Ranges are in the southeast. The Black Hills, mainly the Bear Lodge Mountains, are in the northeast. The Continental Divide runs northwest to southeast from the Yellowstone Plateau through the Wind River Range, across the Red Desert, and down the Sierra Madres.

The region east of the Continental Divide is drained by the Belle Fourche, Cheyenne, Powder, Big Horn, and North Platte rivers and west by the Yellowstone, Snake, and Green rivers.

Wyoming's climate varies considerably, from semiarid in the lower to middle elevations to wetter, colder conditions in the mountains. Lows of

−51 °C and highs of 46 °C have been recorded. Winds are sometimes severe.

A dominant feature comprising the habitat of Wyoming mammals is vegetation. Vegetation types have been described in a general way and a map of the vegetation of Wyoming is available from the U.S. Fish and Wildlife Service–Cooperative Research Station, University of Wyoming. The natural communities have been divided into several major zones generally following Porter (1962): 1) alpine, 2) timbered mountain slopes, 3) foothill scrub, 4) grassland, 5) desert and basin, and 6) river bottoms. The following is taken directly from Porter (1962):

1. ALPINE. This zone extends from the upper limit of trees to the crests of the high mountain ranges, and in Wyoming it is mostly above 3200 m in elevation. It is composed of alpine tundra, rocky summits, scree slopes, alpine lakes, meadows, stream channels, permanent or temporary snowbanks, and in some places glaciers. The vegetation is chiefly herbaceous, with a few low or dwarf shrubs. Woody species found here include Common Juniper *(Juniperus communis)*, dwarf or shrubby willows *(Salix arctica, S. brachycarpa, S. glauca, S. cascadensis, S. dodgeana, and S. planifolia)*, Shrubby Cinquefoil *(Potentilla fruticosa)*, and Currant *(Ribes montigenum)*. Some of the grasses represented include Bluegrass *(Poa alpina, P. lettermanii, and P. pattersonii)*, Oatgrasses *(Deschampsia caespitosa and Trisetum spicatum)*, and Wheatgrasses *(Agropyron latiglume and A. scribneri)*. Sedges include *Carex atrata, C. capillaris, C. capitata, C. chalciolepis, C. elynoides, C. engelmanii, C. misandra, C. nigricans, C. pyrenaica, C. rupestris,* and *C. scopulorum, Eriophorum callitrix* and *E. scheuchzeri,* and *Kobresia* spp. Rushes include *Juncus albescens, J. biglumis,* and *Luzula spicata.* Common cushion plants or mat formers are *Silene acaulis, Arenaria obtusiloba, Paronychia pulvinata, Phlox pulvinata,* and *Eritrichium elongatum.* Bistorts *(Polygonum bistortoides* and *P. viviparum)* occur almost everywhere. Showy-flowered plants include Cowslip *(Caltha leptosepala)*, Globeflower *(Trollius laxus)*, various mustards *(Draba* spp., *Thlaspi alpestre,* and *Smelowskia calycina* var. *americana), rosaceous plants (Dryas octopetala, Geum rossii, Potentilla diversifolia,* and *P. nivea)*, Clover *(Trifolium dasyphyllum* and *T. parryi)*, Stonecrop *(Sedum rhodanthum* and *S. lanceolatum)*, Dwarf Bitterroot *(Lewisia pygmaea)*, Gentian *(Gentiana detonsa* var. *unicaulis* and *G. romanzovii)*, Primrose *(Primula parryi)*, Jacob's Ladder *(Polemonium viscosum)*, Lousewort *(Pedicularis* spp.), Daisy *(Erigeron* spp.), and Rydbergia *(Hymenoxys grandiflora)*.

Many of these plants are found in all the alpine zones of Wyoming, but some of them have thus far been observed only in northwestern Wyoming, where the best development of this zone occurs in the Wind River Range and on the Beartooth Plateau.

2. TIMBERED MOUNTAIN SLOPES. This zone includes the flanks of the mountain ranges that are covered by trees. Elevational limits are highly variable, but in general these are bewteen 1850 and 3200 m but may extend lower in many places, particularly in northeastern Wyoming. Most of the trees are conifers, but Aspen occurs as a common interspersed element. Included also are numerous meadows and parks, where trees are only scattered or entirely lacking, many of these parks being at or near the 2770 m contour. Lakes are frequenty and often quite productive of a variety of aquatic plants. Streams are somewhat larger than in the alpine zone and are often dammed by beaver to form highly productive ponds and marshes. Three major divisions may be recognized in this category.

a. *Spruce/Fir Forest.* This is the characteristic element at the upper limit of trees, but may extend downward along streams into lower valleys. Near its upper limit the trees are scattered, but the main belt is almost continuous forest. The chief trees are Engelmann Spruce *(Picea engelmannii)* and Subalpine Fir *(Abies lasiocarpa),* but in northwestern Wyoming Whitebark Pine *Pinus albicaulis)* is a frequent constituent, particularly on rocky or exposed sites. In mature stands the understory is frequently composed of Huckleberry *(Vaccinium scoparium).* At the upper limit of this forest the trees become dwarfed, forming characteristic wind-timber islands of trees contorted by high winds and blowing snow. Within the forest, in more open situations or along streams, we find numerous willows and Aspen *(Populus tremuloides).*

b. *Lodgepole Pine Forest.* Occupying the middle part of the timbered mountain slopes there is usually present a broad and dense forest of Lodgepole Pine *(Pinus contorta* ssp. *latifolia).* This belt of coniferous forest is often the most conspicuous part of the mountain slopes. Occasional mature stands occur, with well-spaced trees and an understory of shrubs such as Canadian Buffaloberry *(Shepherdia canadensis)* and Common Juniper *(Juniperus communis).* But commercial logging, as well as fire, have resulted in most of the stands being less mature and more dense. After fire, particularly, this forest returns as a very dense and slowly maturing stand of closely spaced, slender trees, with very little development of an understory. Here, also, we find numerous streams, ponds, and lakes that are highly productive of plant life. There are frequent openings or parks that are grassy or are occupied by Sagebrush *(Artemisia tridentata).* Aspen occurs as a conspicuous element around the edges of the forest, and in moist situations along streams are numerous willows.

c. *Ponderosa Pine/Douglas Fir Forest.* This forest type marks the lower limit of the tree-clad mountain slopes, occurring below the Lodgepole Pine forest and extending downward in a rather narrow belt to the open foothills. In northeastern Wyoming, however, and in scattered areas in eastern Wyoming generally, this is often a broad belt extending out onto the plains. The chief trees are Ponderosa Pine *(Pinus ponderosa* var. *scopulorum)* and Douglas Fir *(Pseudotsuga menziesii* var. *glauca),* but we find Limber Pine *(Pinus flexilis)* and Aspen *(Populus tremuloides)* associated with them in many places. The forest is more open than the Lodgepole Pine forest, the trees often being widely spaced. The common understory is Sagebrush *(Artemisia tridentata)* and Bitterbrush *(Purshia tridentata).* On the more sheltered and moister slopes there is sometimes an almost pure stand of Douglas Fir. Limber Pine is usually associated with exposed, rocky sites. Along the lower streams Balsam Poplar *(Populus balsamifera)* may occur as scattered individuals or as a nearly pure stand.

3. FOOTHILLS SCRUB. On the lower slopes of the mountains there is often a zone of shrubs and small trees. In some places, particularly in limestone areas, this consists mainly of Mountain Mahogany *(Cercocarpus montanus* in eastern Wyoming and *C. ledifolius* to the west), while Sagebrush *(Artemisia tridentata)* is a characteristic and often dominant element where there is good soil development and adequate moisture from snow accumulation in the winter. Juniper *(Juniperus scopulorum* in eastern Wyoming and *J. osteosperma* in central and western Wyoming) may occur as scattered small trees or shrubs along with the preceding species, but it often forms an extensive woodland. Pinyon Pine *(Pinus edulis),* a common associate of Juniper in the Southwest, occurs only in extreme southern Wyoming near the Green River, associated with Utah Juniper *(Juniperus osteosperma).* In valleys, along major streams, a streamside forest, or sometimes only scattered trees, of Narrowleaf Cottonwood *(Populus angustifolia)* may be found, as well as shrubs such as willows *(Salix* spp.), roses *(Rosa* spp.), and Dogwood *(Cornus stolonifera).* A common, conspicuous, tall grass of these sites is Giant Ryegrass *(Elymus cinereus).*

4. GRASSLAND. On the plains and foothills there are some extensive grasslands. Such areas are almost devoid of shrubs, and no trees are present except along water courses. These grasslands may be divided into two types.

a. *The Eastern Plains and Foothills.* This is a broad belt of grassland extending from southeastern Wyoming, east of the Laramie Range, northward toward the Black Hills. These rolling hills and plains, lying at an elevation bewteen 1380 and 1850 m, are covered with a rather uniform stand of relatively tall grasses and forbs, the belt constituting an extension westward of the Nebraska sandhills flora and that of the Great Plains. Characteristic here are several species of tall grasses, such as Needlegrass *(Stipa* spp.), Little Bluestem *(Andropogon scoparius)*, Big Bluestem *(Andropogon gerardi)*, and Sand Bluestem *(Andropogon hallii)*. Characteristic also are patches of lower grasses such as Buffalograss *(Buchloë dactyloides)* and Blue Grama *(Bouteloua gracilis)*, together with other grasses of more general distribution. Soapweed *(Yucca glauca)* is often common on exposed, arid sites, along with Prickly Pear *(Opuntia polyacantha* and *O. fragilis)*. Lupines *(Lupinus* spp.), Purple Loco *(Oxytropis lambertii)*, and a white-flowered Beardtongue *(Penstemon albidus)* are showy forbs, and in sandy soils there is abundance of Psoralea *(Psoralea tenuiflora)*.

b. *The Interior Grassland Plains.* The extensive Laramie Plains and similar grasslands of the interior of Wyoming are of a somewhat different character than the eastern plains, being shortgrass plains. Dominant grasses here are Blue Grama *(Bouteloua gracilis)*, several species of Bluegrass *(Poa* spp.), Junegrass *(Koeleria cristata)*, Needlegrass *(Stipa* spp.), and several species of Wheatgrass *(Agrophyron* spp., especially *A. smithii)*. A low, caespitose species of Vetch *(Astragalus spatulatus)* is abundant, and low species of Rabbitbrush *(Chrysothamnus* spp.) are fairly common here and there. Another element in this zone is found in alkaline depressions, where there are extensive stands of Greasewood *(Sarcobatus vermiculatus)*, Saltsage *(Atriplex* spp.), and Alkali Spikegrass *(Distichlis stricta)*. Along streams are willows and occasional cottonwoods.

5. DESERT AND BASIN. Extensive areas of flat or undulating desert occur in Wyoming, certain parts having been designated as named basins, such as the Great Divide Basin in the south, and the Big Horn and Powder River basins in the north. This arid land has an elevational range of about 1230 to 1850 m, and it has a xerophytic flora composed of plants such as Prickly Pear *(Opuntia polyacantha)*, Hop Sage *(Grayia spinosa)*, several species of Saltbush *(Atriplex* spp.), Low Sagebrush *(Artemisia arbusula)*, and Rabbitbrush *(Chrysothamnus* spp.), together with several grasses and forbs. In highly alkaline places, which are common here, are large communities dominated by Greasewood *(Sarcobatus vermiculatus)* and Sea Blite *(Suaeda* spp.). Bud Sage *(Artemisia spinescens)*, Shadscale *(Atriplex confertifolia)*, and Kochia *(Kochia americana)* are common elements. Dry or intermittent stream courses are often marked by large clumps of Giant Ryegrass *(Elymus cinereus)*.

6. RIVER BOTTOMS. Along major drainages, such as those of the North Platte, Powder, Big Horn, and Green rivers, the bottom land is usually wooded, the chief tree being Plains Cottonwood *(Populus sargentii)*, often associated with Boxelder *(Acer negundo)* and Peach-leaved Willow *(Salix amygdaloides)*. In northeastern Wyoming there are also

Bur Oak *(Quercus macrocarpa)*, Elm *(Ulmus americana)*, and Green Ash *(Fraxinus pennsylvanica)*. In many places thickets of lower trees and shrubs occur, composed largely of Silverberry *(Elaeagnus commutata)*, Buffaloberry *(Shepherdia argentea)*, Rose *(Rosa* spp.), Sandbar Willow *(Salix exigua)*, and Rabbitbrush *(Chrysothamnus nauseosus)*. In many places the introduced and weedy Salt Cedar *(Tamarix pentandra)* occurs in stream channels or along sandbars. In some places there are extensive swampy areas occupied by Cattail *(Typha latifolia)* and various rushes and sedges. Numerous large reservoirs and a few natural lakes occur here, containing beds of Elodea *(Elodea canadensis)* and Pondweed (chiefly *Potamogeton pectinatus)*. The ground cover of the bottoms is largely grassland where there is sufficient moisture, but in drier areas the desert flora extends right up to the stream margins.

Dorn (1986) reviewed all available descriptions of the vegetation of Wyoming before grazing by Europeans dominated the landscape. Much of Wyoming's sage-grassland probably was well developed before grazing. Other plant communities, particularly stream-side vegetation, have been radically changed by domestic grazing in many places.

The first attempt in Wyoming to group mammals according to the types of environments they occupy was done by Cary (1917). Such groupings, it was thought, would aid in understanding the patterns and causes of mammal distributions. He used a popular system of his day, "Life Zones." Wyoming contains five Life Zones and Cary listed mammals by which zone they occupied. They are: Upper Sonoran, zone of broad-leafed cottonwood, juniper and saltbush, in most valleys and low plains; Transition, yellow pine, narrow-leafed cottonwood and sage-grassland in the high plains and lower slopes of mountains; Canadian, forest of spruce, fir, lodgepole pine, and aspen covering the middle mountain slopes and highest foothill ranges; Hudsonian, narrow zone of white-barked pine and dwarfed spruce and fir in the timberline region; and Arctic-Alpine, treeless zone on mountain crests and peaks above timberline.

More recent examination of mammal distributions and Life Zones led Long to conclude that the Life Zone concept is useful only in a very general way. Life Zone descriptions are an over-simplification of complex patterns of vegetation, mammal distributions, elevations, and climatic correlates. We agree with Long that the distributional limits of mammalian species should be studied in their own right to shed light on the general patterns of factors in nature which limit the distribution of mammals. When the species and subspecies ranges were overlaid, a moderately clear pattern emerged—faunal divisions, marked by the large number of range limits that coincided (Fig. 4). Indeed some of the Life Zones did coincide with the faunal zones, but many did not. Udvardy (1969) discussed reasons why the range limits do not always agree.

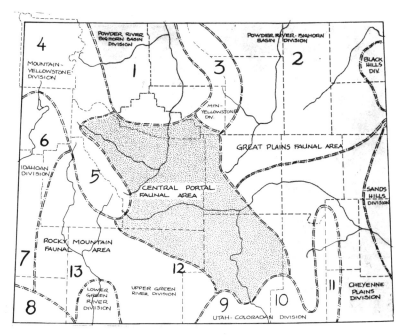

Figure 4. Faunal areas and Faunal Divisions in Wyoming (after Long, 1965). Numbers designate the following faunal subdivisions: 1. Big Horn Basin; 2. Powder River 3. Big Horn Mountains; 4. Yellowstone Plateau; 5. Wind River Mountains; 6. Snake River; 7. Bear River; 8. Uinta Mountains; 9. Sierra Madre Mountains; 10. Medicine Bow Mountains; 1. Laramie Mountains; 12. Red Desert; and 13. Upper Green River.

A widespread popular system of environmental classification is "habitat typing" (Pfister 1982). Much of the forested mountains of Wyoming have been classified by this system (Reed 1969, Cooper 1975, Wirsing and Alexander 1975, Hoffman and Alexander 1977, Steele et al. 1979).

The distribution of Wyoming's mammals should not be considered a fixed pattern. Rather, the distributional limits change slowly with time. The remains of at least 60 mammal species have been found in Little Box Elder Cave in Converse County, Wyoming, and research on them has produced great insights into the history of mammals in this region. This cave, first reported in 1946, contains one of North America's largest deposits of late Pleistocene (Ice Age) mammal remains as well as evidence of early humans. Analysis of the remains shows that coniferous forests occurred several thousand years ago in what now are arid lowlands of eastern Wyoming. The presence of several cold-adapted species indicates that the climate was formerly colder. As the climate has warmed over the last few thousand years, the mammals tolerant of cold climates have been replaced by species adapted to a warmer climate. The process of environmental change followed by mammalian adaptation and movement goes on.

EXPLANATION OF SPECIES ACCOUNTS

There are seven orders and 117 species of mammals in Wyoming; this represents only a small fraction of the 18 orders and about 4,200 species of living mammals in the world. Only about one-third of all the mammal species that ever lived are living today. Modern mammals "branched" off from early mammal-like reptiles (Lillegraven et al. 1979). Mammals emerged as the dominant terrestrial life forms after the periods of great dinosaur extinctions. They currently occupy almost all major habitats on land, and in the water and air.

Mammals are grouped together because they share certain derived characteristics of morphology and behavior. They can regulate their body temperature and do so through a high metabolic rate and partly by the insulation value of their fur. Most mammals possess a placenta by which young are nourished within the female's body. All mammals have mammary glands, which produce milk for the young after birth. Mammals are more highly evolved than reptiles or birds in their mode of reproduction, in parental care, and suckling of young and in greater brain development. Mammals in general are larger than most other living vertebrates. Hair or pelage is present at some stage in the development of all mammals. Most mammals have an ear opening surrounded by a well-developed pinna (except in aquatic or fossorial taxa). Mammals have a muscular diaphragm. Also, many have elaborate and complex social groupings. Each species account in this volume includes sections on names, description, size, range and habitat, reproduction, habits, food, and remarks.

Common Names: Each Wyoming mammal species may have one, or more, or no common names. Because of this and because names may be used locally only common names need standardization. Jones et al. (1982) produced a checklist of standardized common names which we follow and it is available from The Museum, Texas Tech University, Lubbock, Texas.

Scientific Names: Each mammal species possesses a unique, standard name accepted worldwide. Names are governed by the International Code of Zoological Nomenclature. Each name is comprised of two or three Greek, Latin, or Latinized modern words, followed by the name of the person(s) who first described it. The first word in the full scientific name is its genus, which is capitalized, followed by species and subspecies, which are not capitalized. If the currently recognized generic name is different from the one the author first assigned in the original description, then the author's name is in parentheses.

Scientific names show the relationship among species. The zoological classification system is in the form of a hierarchy with species of similar structure related at different levels. For example, in Wyoming, the Order

Carnivora (meat eaters) includes the families of dogs (Canidae), bears (Ursidae), procyonids (Procyonidae), weasels (Mustelidae), and cats (Felidae). Within the dog family, you can see that the coyote and gray wolf, which both have the same generic name, are more closely related to each other than either is to the red fox or swift fox, both of which have the same generic name.

Description: This section gives the normal external and structural characteristics, including color. The descriptions we provide are of live animals as they would be observed in the field. External descriptions are essential in field identification. Skull characteristics are not given because of their technical nature; a glossary of many of the terms used in keys and in mammalogy in general is provided.

Size: Measurements and weights of each mammal are presented as: 1) total length, in a straight line when the mammal is placed on its back, exclusive of hair at the end of its tail, 2) length of tail, exclusive of hair at the tip, 3) length of hind foot, from edge of heel to end of the longest nails when foot is straight, 4) length of ear, from bottom of notch to the top exclusive of hair on edge of ear, 5) weight. All measurements are metric, length in millimeters and weight in grams or kilograms. Because each mammalian species exhibits variation in size of individuals, our measurements are only a general guide. We present measurements from Wyoming specimens (Long 1965 and recent collections). Measurements presented elsewhere in the account (Hall 1981) include specimens from a larger geographic range, and so may differ from measurements presented here.

Range and Habitat: Here we give a brief statement of the continental and Wyoming ranges of the species, the major ecosystem needed for its habitat, and a list of Wyoming subspecies. The subspecies concept came into general usage in taxonomy during the nineteenth century. It was considered a taxonomic unit similar to the concept of species, but on a lower taxonomic level. Subspecies were defined as a taxonomic unit made up of individuals conforming to the type of the subspecies. That is, individuals generally conforming in size, shades or patterns of color, or other features that are consistent for a relatively isolated geographic locality. Using various attributes (sometimes combining several at once mathematically), between 80–90 percent of the individuals can be correctly classified into a given subspecies. In Wyoming and elsewhere, this concept has often been difficult to apply. Barriers and boundaries between populations which have been differentiated as subspecies remain to be clearly defined. A Wyoming map shows the distribution of the species or subspecies. Map symbols mean that a specimen of that species has been photographed or collected; most evidence is in a museum collection. Shaded areas show the range that we feel is currently occupied.

Reproduction: This section presents data on the reproductive biology of the species. This includes stages in the reproductive cycle, breeding, gestation, parturition, early development, weaning, and growth.

Habits: Various behavioral and ecological characteristics of each species included here: general activities, home ranges, territoriality, nests, runways, social organization, and noteworthy characteristics.

Food: This section gives food habits and may list key food items or species.

Remarks: Interesting details from Wyoming about the species are given. Some notes on longevity, predation, legal status, and any unusual observations may be listed. In general, if any of these subjects are not treated, it indicates that we do not have adequate natural history observations about that trait.

KEY TO THE ORDERS AND FAMILIES
OF WYOMING MAMMALS

1A. Tail prehensile, clawless apposable thumb (inside digit) on hind foot, marsupium present on abdomen of female; 10 upper incisor teeth, 50 teeth total ....
.... Order Marsupialia; Family Didelphidae, Opossum

1B. Tail not prehensile, no apposable thumb on hind foot, marsupium absent; upper incisor teeth 8 or less, 48 total teeth of less 2

2A. Flight-membrane present, fingers elongated, some longer than forearm and without claws, except thumb ....
Order Chiroptera; Families Vespertillionidae and Mollosidae, Bats

2B. Flight-membrane absent, fingers with either claws or hooves, not modified for flight 3

3A. Pointed, flexible muzzle projecting well over the mouth; canine teeth always present, but same size as other adjacent teeth (unicusps)
.... Order Insectivora; Families Soricidae (Shrews) and Talpidae (Moles)

3B. Muzzle not projecting forward over mouth; canine teeth, when present, conspicuously larger than adjacent teeth 4

4A. Feet with hooves, canines small or absent .... Order Artiodactyla; Families Cervidae (Deer), Antilocapridae (Pronghorns), and Bovidae (Sheep, Bison, Goat)

4B. Feet not ending in hooves 5

5A. Canine teeth enlarged and conspicuous .... Order Carnivora; Families Canidae (Dogs), Ursidae (Bears), Procyonidae (Raccoon), Mustelidae (Weasels), Felidae (Cats)

5B. Canine teeth absent 6

6A. Tail short and "powder puff-like" and shorter than ears; 4 incisor teeth above and 2 below, 10–12 cheek teeth above and 10 below .... Order Lagomorpha; Families Ochotonidae (Pika) and Leporidae (Rabbits and Hares)

6B. Tail not "powder puff-like" and longer than ears, 2 incisor teeth above and 2 below, 10 or less cheek teeth above and 8 or less below ..... Order Rodentia; Families Sciuridae (Squirrels), Geomyidae (Pocket Gophers), Heteromyidae (Pocket Mice and Kangaroo Rats), Castoridae (Beaver), Cricetidae (New World Rats and Mice), Muridae (Old World Rats and Mice), Zapodidae (Jumping Mice), Erethizontidae (Porcupine)

An adult Virginia opossum *(Didelphus virginiana)*. Photograph by Larry C. Watkins.

Virginia Opossum
Didelphis virginiana virginiana Kerr

Description: The Virginia opossum can be identified immediately by its prehensile, grasping tail. It is also unique in having 50 teeth, a white, grizzled face, and hind feet without claws but rather flat toenails. The "thumb" (first toe) on the hind foot is apposable to the hind toes. Because it is a marsupial, the opossum has a pouch where in young cling to nipples. No fossils of opossums have been found in Wyoming, and the fossil record elsewhere clearly suggests they are a southern animal that recently arrived in Wyoming.

Size: Adults may attain the following dimensions: total length 643–900 mm; tail 250–440 mm; hind foot 53–80 mm; weight 1.9–2.8 kilograms. Adult males are larger than adult females.

Range and Habitat: Opossums occur on eastern riparian areas along the Platte River, Cheyenne River and its tributaries. In these areas, they have been seen in cottonwood galleries, cattail wetlands and in agricultural lands. They use a wide range of habitats but typically live near water.

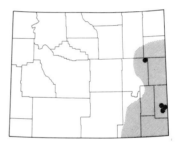

Reproduction: In Wyoming, little is known of opossum's breeding. Elsewhere, the opossum produces many young, rapidly. Up to 40 young emerge and crawl to the 9–13 nipples available. There, an average of seven young survive about 100 days and are abandoned by the mother at this time. Mating occurs from January to July, and a second litter is often born in May or June. Females breed in the first summer after birth.

Habits: The opossum walks, swims, and climbs trees. It can be found in nests under logs or boulders or in trees. Opossums hiss, growl, and screech. When threatened, they bluff with exposed teeth and growls. They also "play dead" when they lie immobile, their mouth open and body curled slightly. While in this catatonic state, they do not respond to stimulation. Although active year-round, these generally nocturnal animals are less active in cold weather. Opossums are not social and generally avoid each other.

Food: Opossums eat just about anything edible. Fruits, berries, carrion, bird eggs, frogs, crayfish, worms, and insects are included in their diet.

Remarks: Several Wyoming observers have reported opossums with rag-
ged ears and partial tails and suggest that frostbite may occur during
unusually cold winters. These primitive relatives of the kangaroos may
be limited to Wyoming's warmer river bottoms.

SHREWS (FAMILY SORICIDAE)
Hayden's Shrew
Sorex haydeni Baird

Description: Like other Wyoming shrews, Hayden's shrews have small bodies, long pointed snouts, and tiny eyes, and the tips of the teeth are pigmented-dark red to black. The ears barely emerge from the fur. Van Zyll de Jong (1980) recognized this shrew as distinctly different from the masked shrew.

Wyoming has nine kinds of shrews. The differences between shrews are often based on small body parts, usually differences in teeth which are small. A dissecting microscope or good hand lens is needed for identification, and an expert should be consulted for positive identification. A key to the shrews of Wyoming is provided on page 278, and is based on dental differences.

Size: Adults may attain the following dimensions: total length 88–99 mm; tail 34–40 mm; hind foot 10.6–11.8 mm; weight 3–5 grams. Sexes do not differ in size.

Range and Habitat: Hayden's shrew in Wyoming may be restricted to the Black Hills region in the northeastern corner of the state. This shrew lives in Canada, Montana, through the Dakotas to Nebraska, Kansas, and Iowa. In the Black Hills, it occurs in montane habitats and is locally abundant in wet areas (bogs, willow flats). 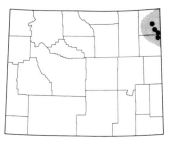 It is sometimes found in rocky, drier pine habitats, and appears to favor areas with at least some open grassland.

Reproduction: Turner (1974) observed that only half of the females trapped through mid-July were reproductively active. Pregnancy and lactation were observed from mid-June through July. Studies elsewhere suggest that neither sex reproduces until its second year, reproduction starts in early spring and 4-10 are produced in a litter. Gestation requires from 19 to 22 days. Young reach adult size in 20-30 days and leave the nest. Nests are under logs or rocks or in crevices and resemble miniature bird nests. Occasionally, two or three litters are produced in one year.

Habits: Like other shrews in Wyoming, Hayden's shrew lives on small prey. The shrew is very active, running rapidly along runways and scurrying under leaves and other debris. Hearing is acute and eyesight is poor. The long vibrissae or whiskers and the snout provide tactile cues on prey. Young

21

often play gregariously and "caravan" when moving from place to place. That is, each shrew puts its nose into the fur on the rump of the shrew in front, the entire litter moves in a train. Little else is known of their social behavior, but they are believed to live solitarily as adults. Pitfall traps (cans buried with tops flush to the ground) will capture shrews when other methods fail.

Food: Shrews have among the greatest food requirement per gram of all mammals. Thus, they must be active year-round, eating virtually all day. High protein, wet food is required and includes beetles, grasshoppers, spiders, earthworms, insect larvae, and even other small vertebrates. Availability of open ground water appears to be important to this shrew.

Remarks: Weasels, hawks and owls feed on shrews, and they may be eaten by snakes, foxes and even large frogs. Additional specimens of shrews in the isolated Bear Lodge Montains (Black Hills) and the Laramie Peak areas would help clarify the taxonomic status in Wyoming of *Sorex haydeni,* now considered distinct from *S. cinereus.*

An adult masked shrew *(Sorex cinereus)*. Photograph by Robert S. Hoffmann.

Masked Shrew
Sorex cinereus cinereus Kerr

Description: Contrary to the name, this shrew does not have an obvious facial mask. The face is uniformly colored dark gray. In general aspect, this shrew looks like Hayden's shrew. The fur is fine, soft and silky and of various colors, generally darker brown than Hayden's shrew. Again, a key based on dental characteristics is provided on page 278. Each cusp on the lower incisor usually has distinct pigmentation.

Size: Adults may grow to the following sizes: total length 87–109 mm; tail 35–39 mm; hind foot 10–11 mm; weight 3.5–6 grams. As far as known, there is no difference in size between the sexes.

Range and Habitat: Masked shrews occur widely over Canada, the northern states, and down the Rocky Mountains to New Mexico. They occur throughout Wyoming in wetter habitats. Open water may not be necessary, but damp coniferous or deciduous areas with dense overhead plant cover are favored. Bogs in aspen, lodgepole and

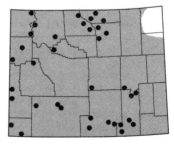

spruce-fir forests support higher densities of the masked shrew, yet they occur in sagebrush communities as well.

23

Reproduction: In general, the masked shrew's reproduction is similar to that of Hayden's shrew. Studies in Jackson have shown a mean litter size of 4.6 (range 3–12) and one or two litters are produced each year. Young are born in early July. Elsewhere, young are born from March to September. The male stays with the female during pregnancy and early growth of the young.

Habits: In other parts of its range, the activities of the masked shrew have been well studied. Masked shrews are active year-round, all day. They do not hibernate or migrate. Home ranges are small, less than 0.02 hectares. Masked shrews are also almost entirely terrestrial, rapidly running under litter, over logs and hunting continually. They can swim and can jump 15–20 cm. Masked shrews appear to live solitarily and are not gregarious. If two or three are placed together in a small cage, only one may survive, having killed and eaten the others within a few hours.

Food: Like other shrews, masked shrews are voracious, with relatively high metabolic rates. High energy, easily digested food is the rule: bugs, beetles, moths, flies, insect larvae, crickets, spiders, small vertebrates, and only rarely vegetable matter.

Remarks: This is one of Wyoming's most widespread shrews. Although frequently killed by many carnivores, masked shrews are rarely eaten. Glands along the side of the shrew produce an odor that may make them unpalatable.

Preble's Shrew
Sorex preblei Jackson

Description: This shrew is one of the rarest Wyoming shrews. It is only identified through careful skull measurements and dental characteristics (see key, p. 278). Preble's shrew outwardly resembles all the other long-tailed Wyoming shrews. The tail is bicolored-dark above and pale below. Dorsal fur is brownish.

Size: Adults may grow to the following sizes: total length 85-95 mm; tail 35-36 mm; hind foot 11 mm. Sexes are not known to differ in size.

Range and Habitat: Preble's shrew is known to occur only in extreme northwestern Wyoming (Lamar Ranger Station, Yellowstone). It has been trapped in a wide area, from western Oregon across Idaho to eastern Montana, and is known to occupy a wide range of habitats, from sage-bunchgrass to alpine tundra. Fewer than 100 specimens of this animal have ever been collected. Only one specimen is known in Wyoming. Little is known of its biology. It may be more common than we know. However, extensive pitfall trapping over two years by us in upland and wet habitats near Lamar Ranger Station did not result in any captures of Preble's shrew.

Reproduction: Nothing is known of its reproduction. Because it is similar to *Sorex cinereus*, breeding biology is probably similar.

Habits: Little is known of the behavior of this shrew.

Food: Preble's shrew has an unknown diet, but is probably similar to that of other shrews.

Remarks: This shrew is listed as rare in Montana (Flath 1981). Pitfall trapping in northwestern Wyoming for Preble's shrew could add significantly to our meager knowledge of this mammal. Specimens from Montana (Thompson 1982) suggest that Preble's shrew may occur in the Bighorn Montains of Wyoming.

Vagrant Shrew
Sorex vagrans vagrans Baird

Description: Vagrant shrews closely resemble dusky shrews. The matching notches on the inner sides of the upper incisors meet at the start of the pigmentation, which extends down to the tips of the incisors. The middle toes on the hind feet may have only four pairs of fleshy pads (van Zyll de Jong 1982). The fur is brownish-red.

Size: Adults may grow to the following dimensions: total length 95–108 mm; tail 36–41 mm; hind foot 8–13 mm. Adult males and females are of similar size.

Range and Habitat: Vagrant shrews live in the arid interior basins of western Washington, Idaho, Nevada and Utah. In Wyoming, this shrew is only present in the extreme western edge of Lincoln County and may occur west of the Bear River Divide in Uintah County. These shrews live in and around riparian habitats, where moist soil, leaf litter, and rotting logs are available.

Reproduction: Vagrant shrews breed from January to August, with young born from March to July. Litters range from two to nine with an average of six. Sometimes two litters are produced in one year.

Habits: Like other shrews, the vagrant shrew is active year-round and active any time of the day and night. They live solitarily as adults with home ranges of from .06–.4 hectares. These home ranges vary with the breeding season—as do the dusky shrew's. Further, home ranges are variable in shape and follow riparian areas. This shrew forages through ground litter, under vegetation and rocks and beneath logs. As with most shrews, it is not known to climb. Vagrant shrews use echolocation to locate prey.

Food: Vagrant shrews eat insects, spiders, earthworms, and some plants.

Remarks: In Wyoming, this shrew is known from only 25 specimens. However, it is abundant throughout its total range. Characters suggested by van Zyll de Jong (1982) may help differentiate between the vagrant shrew and dusky shrew. Unfortunately, the few specimens preserved in alcohol of these shrews from Wyoming do not allow a good comparison of the pattern reported by van Zyll de Jong.

An adult dusky shrew *(Sorex monticolus).* Photograph by D. L. Pattie.

Dusky Shrew
Sorex monticolus obscurus Merriam

Description: Dusky shrews are impossible to identify without study of the upper tooth row. The third unicuspid tooth on the upper jaw is smaller than the fourth. Also, from a front view, a notch can be seen in each upper first incisor where the two meet and pigmentation extends well above this notch. These two features are illustrated on page 279. Vagrant shrews are similar, but smaller, than the dusky shrew.

Size: Adults may grow to the following dimensions: total length 99–119 mm; tail 41–48 mm; hind foot 8–14 mm. Adult males and females are of similar size. Dusky shrews show an extremely wide variation in size between different populations.

Range and Habitat: Dusky shrews oc- 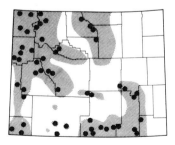 cur from Alaska, down the Rocky Mountains through Idaho, northwestern Wyoming, central Colorado, and New Mexico into the mountains of northern Mexico. The usual habitat in Wyoming is moist montane deciduous or spruce-fir forests, or alpine tundra. Dusky shrews may descend into lodgepole pine or Douglas fir forests and may inhabit also the wet riparian streamsides extending across eastern Wyoming.

Reproduction: Studies elsewhere show that young are born in the spring, mature during the summer, but wait until their next winter to breed. Males show signs of reproductive activity by mid-winter. Females become receptive in March. Near Douglas, Wyoming, a female was pregnant with eight pups in June. Females can produce up to three litters each year.

By autumn, virtually all overwintering adults die. Total lifespan for this mammal usually does not exceed 16 months. Young are weaned within 3 weeks. In the Sierra Madres (26 km SW Saratoga), we collected a pregnant female with six pups on 5 August 1980.

Habits: No doubt the dusky shrew maintains a typical frantic shrew lifestyle. Studies in British Columbia have shown that these animals have non-overlapping home ranges. Non-breeding home ranges average 1227 square meters, whereas breeding home ranges average 4000 square meters. Males had larger home ranges during breeding, and each male could include the home ranges of four to five females. This larger home range probably results from the three- to four-fold increase in food requirements due to raising young.

Food: Diets of Wyoming's dusky shrew have not been studied, but probably include animal material similar to that eaten by other shrews.

Remarks: Evidently the Star River, Smiths Fork, and Bear River form a western boundary for the distribution of the dusky shrew in Wyoming. To the west, the similar vagrant shrew exists. The actual ecological boundaries between these species are unknown. The dusky shrew is curiously absent from the east side of the Bighorn Mountains.

Sweetwater County has several mountains that rise out of the sage steppe and support small pockets of spruce, pine, and aspen along riparian corridors. Small, isolated populations of several small mammals occur on these low peaks. Dusky shrews have been found on Aspen Mountain, Sand Hill and Pine Mountain, and may occur on Little Mountain and Steamboat Mountain.

An adult dwarf shrew *(Sorex nanus)*. Photograph by D. L. Pattie.

Dwarf Shrew
Sorex nanus Merriam

Description: This small shrew's third unicuspid tooth on the upper tooth row is smaller than the fourth. Both the third and fifth upper unicuspid (single-pointed) teeth are easily visible and the average tail length is 38 mm. Consult the key (p. 278) to distinguish this shrew from the pygmy shrew. Fur is olive-brown on the back and a silky silver below.

Size: Adults may grow to the following dimensions: total length 83–105 mm; tail 27–40 mm; hind foot 10–10.5 mm; weight 1.8–3.2 grams; condylobasal length of skull less than 15.2 mm. Sexes do not differ with regard to size.

Range and Habitat: Dwarf shrews have a fossil record suggesting that they inhabited rubble slopes and coniferous forests in Kansas and southern New Mexico when glaciers covered much of the Rocky Mountains. Now, dwarf shrews are present as relatively small, isolated populations where suitable "relict" habitats remain. Their habitat 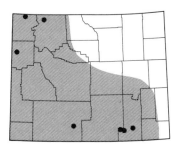 includes alpine rubble above 4240 meters, yet dwarf shrews are sometimes found in arid habitats such as shortgrass prairie, dry stubble fields, and pinyon-juniper at lower elevations.

Reproduction: Breeding probably begins in the mountain populations by late June or early July. By late July or early August, litters are born and the females become pregnant again. Second litters thus are born in late August or early September, and may face problems with early snowfalls. Females breed in their second year, producing litters of six to seven young. At lower elevations, breeding probably starts earlier in the spring and litter size and numbers of litters may be greater.

Habits: Dwarf shrews are enigmatic. They escape snap traps and thus formerly were rarely collected. From 1895 to 1960, only 18 specimens were known from their entire range. Now that pitfall traps are being used, the dwarf shrew has been captured in such different places as the alpine, high altitude Beartooth Plateau on the Montana-Wyoming border and the alkaline sage flats of Sweetwater County. Fewer than 25 specimens are known from Wyoming, so it is extremely difficult to generalize about their behavior or lifestyle. We can safely presume they lead an active life, involving a continuous hunt for food.

Food: Captive dwarf shrews have been observed to eat carrion of several species of small mammals, ignore slugs, and prefer soft-bodied spiders and insects. Captive individuals cache extra prey.

Remarks: In 1979 and 1980 we repaired the pitfall traps used by Brown (1967) on a talus slope near Centennial, Wyoming. A series of 13 dwarf shrews was taken, and although the range of tail lengths was smaller (33–40 mm), the mean length (37.5 mm) is similar to measurements reported by Hoffmann and Owen (1980). Spiders were extremely abundant in the talus slope, often virtually filling the pitfall traps. Dwarf shrews are classified as rare in Montana and Utah, and until more data show otherwise, should be considered rare in Wyoming.

Water Shrew
Sorex palustris navigator (Baird)

Description: The water shrew is the largest shrew in the state. It can also be identified by its relatively large hind foot with a very obvious fringe of stiff hairs along the edge. The third and fourth toes of the hind feet are joined by a thin web for more than half their length. Water shrews are nearly black above with a silvery sheen and the underfur is silvery white to smoke gray. They have pointed snouts and tiny eyes, and the tail is about half as long as the body and bicolored.

Size: Adults may grow to the following dimensions: total length 139–168 mm; tail 69–85 mm; hind foot 19–21 mm. There are no sexual variations in color, size or proportion.

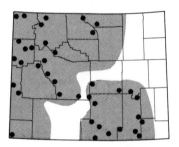

Range and Habitat: Water shrews occur over most of Canada, across the upper midwestern states, and south in the Rocky and Appalachian mountains. In the west, they occur as far south as New Mexico. In Wyoming, they occur in the western, Bighorn, and southeastern mountains. Curiously, they are not known from the Black Hills. Water shrews can be found where there are cold, clear streams with wet meadows nearby.

Reproduction: Breeding apparently goes on from January to August. Pregnant females have been observed in March, young are nursed in early June and are adult-size by July. Sometimes two litters are produced in a year. Litter sizes vary from five to eight young. In Montana, water shrews live to only 18 months of age.

Habits: Water shrews are sedentary, are active all winter and can be active day or night. When seen in the field, they are often escaping to a stream. They can swim, dive, walk on the bottom of a creek, and even run on the surface of the water! While fly fishing in the Lamar Valley in Yellowstone, we have seen them rush across a meadow, splash across a pond and disappear into the grass. In Wisconsin, extensive fat deposits on the shoulders of males were observed. Although no physiological studies of Wyoming's water shrews have been done, this may suggest that "brown fat" (heat-producing fat) is used by water shrews to live in icy water and be active all winter under the snow. Nests are built in stream banks and are lined with moss or grass.

Food: Water shrews eat beetles, bugs, flies, caddisflies, and mayflies. Reflecting an aquatic lifestyle, snails, leaches, planarians, tadpoles, and small fish are also consumed by these small mammals.

Remarks: Weasels and garter snakes prey on the water shrew. Hawks, owls, mink, coyotes, foxes and other predators probably prey on them as well. Larger trout can take these shrews.

Merriam's Shrew
Sorex merriami Dobson

Description: Merriam's shrew is the only Wyoming shrew without medial notches on the first upper incisors. Rather, the incisors form a smooth curve on the edges where they meet when viewed from the front. Also the third unicuspid tooth on the upper tooth row is larger (or about the same size) as the fourth unicuspid tooth.

Size: Adults may grow to the following dimensions: total length 84–105 mm; tail 32–39 mm; hind foot 11–13 mm; weight 4.2–6.8 grams. There appears to be no variation in size, color or proportion with sex.

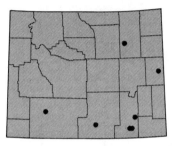

Range and Habitat: Merriam's shrew occurs in each of the western United States, and appears to be the best adapted member of the genus in arid regions. It occupies grasslands, sage steppes, pinyon-juniper, mountain mahogany, and mixed woodlands. This shrew often uses runways of other small rodents *(Microtus, Lemmiscus)* where it hunts for food. In Wyoming, it has only been collected below 2300 meters and is known only from about 10 specimens.

Reproduction: In other states, pregnant females were observed from mid-March to early July. From five to seven young are in a litter. Very little is known of the reproductive biology of Merriam's shrew.

Habits: Population levels of these shrews seem to be extremely low. Virtually nothing is known of their behavior, physiology, or genetics.

Food: Merriam's shrews probably use tactile senses to locate prey, which includes spiders, adult and larval beetles, crickets, larval moths, butterflies, and wasps. During warmer months, caterpillars appear to be common food items.

Remarks: Most specimens of this mammal have been captured with sunken cans or unbaited snap traps. Montana and North Dakota officially list this shrew as rare or uncommon, and until shown otherwise, it should be so listed in Wyoming. We follow Diersing and Hoffmeister (1977) in not recognizing subspecies for Merriam's shrew.

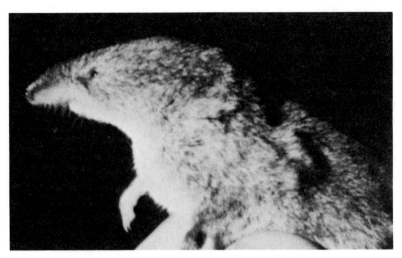

An adult pygmy shrew *(Sorex hoyi)*. Photograph by R. E. Wrigley.

Pygmy Shrew
Sorex hoyi montanus (Brown)

Description: This shrew is the smallest Wyoming mammal. In general, it resemble the dusky shrew. Pygmy shrews are gray-brown above and gray below. The third and fifth unicuspid on the upper tooth row are so tiny they are often difficult to see.

Size: Wyoming adults may grow to the following dimensions: total length 75–87 mm; tail 25–31 mm; hind foot 9–10.5 mm; weight 2.2–3.8 grams. Pygmy shrews show no significant differences in external or cranial measurements based on sex. One of the smallest subspecies occurs in Wyoming.

Range and Habitat: There are five recognized subspecies of pygmy shrews. They range all across Canada, the northern United States, and in scattered populations southward in the Appalachian Mountains and the Rocky Mountains. The populations in the Southern Rockies start at the Medicine Bow Mountains in Wyoming and ex-

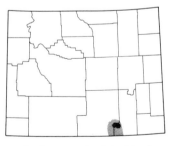

tend south to central Colorado. These populations are isolated by hundreds of kilometers from any other population to the northwest. The wood frog is similarly isolated. This isolated, disjunct distribution is thought to reflect the effects of recent glaciation. Fossils from Little Box Elder

Cave, near Douglas, indicate the pygmy shrew had a wider range when coniferous forests were more widespread. As the glaciers retreated and the climate warmed, pygmy shrews persisted in the cool, wet mountains. Here, their habitat is sphagnum moss on edges of small ponds in Engelmann Spruce and alpine fir at 3000 meters above sea level. In other parts of its range, the pygmy shrew occupies some different habitats— heavy woods, clearings, dry sandy ridges, closely grazed pasture, and edges of cold sphagnum bogs.

Reproduction: Pygmy shrews living at high elevations, where summers are short and cool, probably have a breeding season that starts much later than observed elsewhere in early June. Nothing is known of the breeding habits of this montane shrew.

Habits: In Ontario, a pygmy shrew was observed briefly to run, climb, and jump up to 11 cm. Running speed was often actually difficult for the eye to follow. Its snout was continuously in motion, suggesting a great dependence on a sense of smell. The shrew rarely slept and was active day and night. Audible short, high-pitched squeaks were emitted as it moved about. Others nave noticed whispering or whistling noises made by the pygmy shrew at night.

Food: Food habits are not known in detail. The pygmy shrew eats mostly insects. A captive was observed to eat about ten grams of animal material (wet weight) each day, or about three to five times its body weight each day. Captive pygmy shrews ate other shrews, beetles, grasshoppers, dead voles *(Microtus, Clethrionomys)* and deer mice *(Peromyscus).*

Remarks: Pygmy shrews are known in Wyoming only from eight specimens. Seven were taken from Trails Divide Pond, above the old University of Wyoming Science Camp. Extensive pitfall trapping at this locality in 1979-1980 revealed no pygmy shrews. Further, the once-abundant wood frog is no longer at that pond and has disappeared from most of its former range in the Medicine Bow Mountains. No causes for these declines are known. Montana officially lists this shrew as rare, and North Dakota lists it as uncommon. Until more is known about this creature in Wyoming, it should be considered a rare species in the state.

An adult eastern mole *(Scalopus aquaticus)*. Photograph by Robert R. Patterson.

MOLES (FAMILY TALPIDAE)
Eastern Mole
Scalopus aquaticus caryi Jackson

Description: Eastern moles are virtually never seen above ground. Moles have a stocky body, about the size of a rat, without much of a neck. They have a short, naked tail, lack external ears, and have tiny eyes that are concealed in fur. Their front feet resemble paddles with disproportionately large toenails or claws. Mole noses are long and pointed with a naked tip. Their fur is dense, soft and silky, and resembles a light brown velvet.

Size: Adults may grow to the following dimensions: total length 136-187 mm; tail 19–38 mm; hind foot 19–27 mm; weight 54–99 grams. Males are slightly (5 percent) larger than females.

Range and Habitat: The eastern mole is found outside of Wyoming as far south as Texas and northern Mexico, and northeast to Massachusetts. In Wyoming, it has been captured at Lingle and on Horse Creek in Laramie County, and can be expected in southeastern Wyoming where soils are soft and deep or where moisture loosens soil periodically.

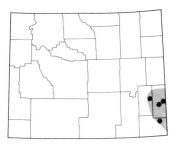

Reproduction: Eastern moles live alone except for the breeding season, which starts in early spring. The gestation period is about 40 to 45 days. One litter of from two to five young is born each year, usually in March or April. Young are born naked, but are well-developed and relatively large. Young moles reach independence in five to six weeks and can breed at 10 months. Nests are built in its tunnel system and are lined with dry leaves.

Habits: Eastern moles are specialized to dig. They have unique, short, strong bones, powerful muscles, and the shoulder bones (pectoral girdle) are greatly modified for digging. Moles walk with difficulty on flat surfaces but they can dig 5.4 meters an hour in garden soil. Home ranges of 0.5–1.0 hectares consist of a complex of burrows. Many burrows are just below the surface of the soil, dug as the mole searches for food. Soil is pushed up from below as the mole digs and thus it forms a surface ridge. These ridges may radiate from small mounds and should not be confused with similar ridges of soil produced by the activity of pocket gophers *(Thomomys* and *Geomys)*. Moles also dig deeper burrows where they rest. They are active year-round and at any time of the day, spending virtually all of their time in burrow systems. Floods in riparian areas often kill many of them, if they are unable to escape from their tunnels.

Food: Eastern moles eat insects and soil invertebrates, but little plant material. Like shrews, they are very active foragers with a high metabolic rate.

Remarks: Eastern moles may live up to 3 years Their aeration of the soil is beneficial to its natural development. Moles may make ridges in lawns (cemeteries, golf courses) but are generally harmless. Special traps which fit in their burrows are needed to capture moles. Because of their subterranean, secretive life, distribution in southeastern Wyoming is poorly known.

An adult California myotis *(Myotis californicus)*. Photograph by Roger W. Barbour.

COMMON BATS (FAMILY VESPERTILIONIDAE)
California Myotis
Myotis californicus californicus (Audubon and Bachman)

Description: This is one of eight known little "mouse-eared" bats *(Myotis)* in Wyoming. The illustrated key (p. 280–282) to all of Wyoming's bats should be consulted when attempting to identify these mammals. This bat has a tiny foot, a forearm of less than 34 mm, and a keel on the calcar. California myotis fur is variably light tan to nearly black. The small-footed myotis is similar to this bat, but its skull is comparatively flattened. Without considerable experience, it is virtually impossible to distinguish live specimens of these two bats.

Size: Adults may grow to the following sizes: total length 73–90 mm; tail 29–45 mm; hind foot 5–8 mm; ear 11–15 mm; forearm 30–35 mm. Males are slightly smaller than females but in some populations the sexes are the same size.

Range and Habitat: California myotis live in western North America, from Alaska to southern Mexico. It is a bat of the western lowlands, ranging from sea level to about 1800 meters. These bats live from low desert to oak-juniper woodlands and often occur in rock-walled canyons where water is available. Virtually any shelter is used for 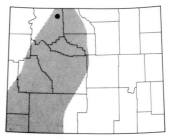 roosting. In Wyoming, they are known from Powell and may occur throughout the Bighorn Basin.

Reproduction: Studies elsewhere indicate that males become reproductively active in the fall. They breed in September and October, and a single young is born in late May or June. Young are able to fly after about 2 months.

Habits: This is one of the few western bats that may hibernate only briefly. They are able to fly at cold temperatures (− 5 to 33 °C) and have been observed flying intermittently throughout the winter. Interscapular brown fat masses probably warm these bats enough to allow flight. Amazingly, their pectoral muscles resemble frog muscles in being able to contract strongly down to 0 °C. Needs for water and food probably arouse the California myotis from their brief hibernations. They have a slow, erratic flight pattern and usually feed within 2-30 meters above ground. These bats start trips for feeding and drinking at sunset, and their peak activity is about 1 hour after sunset. A wide variety of buildings are used for day roosts.

Food: California myotis take only flying insects, including beetles and moths. Their flight is relatively slow and they give a buzz or burst of sonar at each abrupt turn in the air; the buzz is associated with zeroing in on, and capturing, an insect. California myotis feed along the edges of trees at the canopy height. Apparently they do not forage in groups and do not appear to be territorial.

An adult small-footed myotis *(Myotis ciliolabrum)*. Photograph by Roger W. Barbour.

Small-Footed Myotis
Myotis ciliolabrum ciliolabrum (Merriam)

Description: The small-footed myotis closely resembles *Myotis californicus,* and can be distinguished from it based on the skull. The skull of the California myotis has a braincase that rises abruptly in comparison to the flattened skull of this bat. The ratio of height of coronoid process to cranial depth is less than 0.59 in *M. ciliolabrum* and greater than 0.61 m *M. californicus.* Further, the ratio of cranial depth to rostral breadth is less than 0.85 and greater than 0.87 for these species, respectively. Wings and interfemoral membrane (uropatagium) are black, whereas the fur is brown to light tan. The palest subspecies occurs in Wyoming.

Size: Adults may grow to the following dimensions: total length 68–86 mm; tail 25–37 mm; hind foot 5–8 mm; ear 11–14 mm; weight 4–6 grams. Males and females are the same size.

Range and Habitat: This species is common and widespread in the western half of the United States and into Mexico. it has been captured throughout Wyoming, and apparently can be expected from montane forests to sage steppes or shortgrass prairie near rock outcrops.

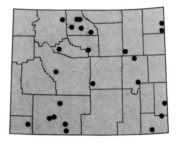

Reproduction: Like many other bats, the female mates in the fall and holds sperm over winter hibernation. In spring, females ovulate and fertilization occurs. This species produces one young each year in June or July. No nest is made and the babies are born into the tail membrane. Well-developed young attach to the mother's nipple and cling to the fur. Females roost together in nursing colonies and leave their young hanging in clusters while they forage. They recognize their young on return and pick them out to nurse. Within 3 weeks, young are able to fly and forage on their own.

Habits: This bat is often captured with mist nets as it approaches water. It forages on the wing using sonar to locate insects, and is an agile flier able to hover. It rests all day and generally only forages for about an hour after sunset. Small-footed myotis hibernate in caves and mines. Like all hibernating bats, they have only enough fat reserve to make it through the winter resting quietly. If disturbed and forced to fly during winter these precious fat reserves are used up and the bats may not survive the rest of the hibernation period. We urge that observers not disturb these or other hibernating bats.

Food: In New Mexico, a study was made of the food habits of several bats, including this species. Food resources available as flying insects included 10 orders of insects. Two orders, Lepidoptera (moths) and Coleoptera (beetles), accounted for 95 percent and 4 percent respectively of the biomass available. Although this species took moths, it selected a disproportionaly large percentage of beetles compared to the percentage available.

Remarks: Recent electronic developments have created relatively inexpensive devices to translate the high frequency of bat's sonar to lower frequencies within the range of human hearing. With experience, a person can recognize the echolocation calls of Wyoming bats. As use of these bat detectors increases, we should be able to learn more of Wyoming bat distributions.

An adult Yuma myotis *(Myotis yumanensis)*. Photograph by Roger W. Barbour.

Yuma Myotis
Myotis yumanensis yumanensis (H. Allen)

Description: This is a rather small *Myotis* with relatively large feet, lacking a keel on the calcar (visible to the naked eye), and having relatively short ears. It closely resembles *Myotis lucifugus* and can be distinguished by the matte color of the dorsal fur (brassy sheen in *Myotis lucifugus*) and the narrower skull (mastoid breadth 7.4 mm or less).

Size: Adults may grow to the following dimensions: total length 85–88 mm; tail 37–39 mm; hind foot 10–11 mm; ear 14–15 mm. Apparently, sexes do not differ in size.

Range and Habitat: The Yuma myotis occurs throughout the western coastal states and is found in Idaho on the north, through Arizona to central Utah, and across New Mexico. Historically, its range approached Wyoming from the south and west borders. This bat has been collected at Sheridan. Yuma myotis probably occur in drier

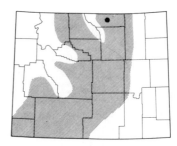

basins of the Green, Wind, and Bighorn rivers, which connect the Wyoming populations to those farther south. Elsewhere, it is limited to riparian communities in desert, woodland, and grassland, usually below the coniferous forest life zone.

Reproduction: Females give birth to a single offspring each year. Young are born from May to July. Females form maternity colonies away from males, which live alone during this time. These bats are extremely sensitive to disturbance of nursery colonies, and they abandon colonies rather frequently.

Habits: Streams are important to Yuma myotis. They feed almost exclusively over the surface of the water, usually just a few centimeters above it. Within a few minutes after sunset they fly out from their day roosts and almost all return within 2 hours. Some individuals have full stomachs after only 15 minutes of foraging. They land briefly to drink water. Because there are few winter records of this bat, it is surmised to migrate to an unknown location by September. Yuma myotis often roost in man-made structures, frequently using bridges and occasionally mines and caves.

Food: Moths and beetles are eaten by the Yuma myotis, but unlike many western bats, they specialize on neither. Rather, a wide variety of the relatively rarely taken insects are consumed — flies, bugs, stoneflies, and mayflies.

Remarks: Disturbance of the daytime roosts of this species should be minimized to keep this agent of natural insect control around. Although only known from one record, several factors contribute to their apparent rarity in Wyoming. First, comparatively little mist-netting for bats has been done in Wyoming. Second, these bats are easily confused with *Myotis lucifugus.* Third, they fly under mist nets set over streams. More work with ultrasonic listening devices could help clarify this bat's status in Wyoming.

An adult little brown myotis *(Myotis lucifugus)*. Photograph by Thomas H. Kunz.

Little Brown Myotis
Myotis lucifugus carissima Thomas

Description: Little brown myotis are so similar to many other Wyoming myotis that some care must be taken to identify this bat. First, *Myotis lucifugus* only rarely has a slight keel and generally has hairs on the hind foot that extend beyond the toes. This bat's underwing is not furred as in *Myotis volans,* and *Myotis ciliolabrum* has a much smaller (8 mm) foot. *Myotis yumanensis* has a smaller skull (less than 14 mm) and its fur lacks the brassy sheen of *Myotis lucifugus. Myotis keenii* has a longer ear (17–19 mm) and a longer, more pointed tragus inside the ear.

Size: Adults may grow to the following dimensions: total length 83–103 mm; tail 31–44 mm; hind foot 8–10 mm; ear 12.5–15.5 mm; forearm 33–41 mm; greatest length of skull 14–15.9 mm; weight 5.5–8.5 grams. Females average slightly larger than males.

Range and Habitat: The little brown myotis occurs over virtually all of North America except the southern Great Plains. It occurs throughout Wyoming and is probably the most abundant bat in the state. This bat uses a wide variety of habitats but is always close to water. Day roosts include suitable humid caves where air

45

temperatures do not generally drop below freezing. After feeding in the early evening, these bats pack together in night roosts formed in confined spaces. Night roosts are frequently in buildings.

Reproduction: Breeding occurs in the fall or winter and the sperm are stored by the female during hibernation. Fertilization occurs after the females leave hibernation, gestation is 50-60 days, and young are born in July. A single young is born. Females live in separate maternity colonies where warmer temperatures are selected to speed growth of young. Young are weaned and can fly by their third week. When the young bats are dispersing, they commonly roost in buildings no usually occupied by bats or in very exposed places — tree trunks, porches, etc. This leads to most human encounters with these befuddled youngsters. Little brown myotis live long lives (up to 31 years is known) but most individuals do not exceed 10 years of age.

Habits: Little brown myotis are specialists in feeding over water. Their flight can be slow and erratic. Their rapid clicking noise is relatively unique and can be recognized quickly with bat detectors. During an evening, their feeding includes a variety of techniques; zipping in and out of vegetation edges from 1.5–6 meters above ground, flying over water, and flying along edges of streams or ponds. They show no evidence of territoriality. Their echolocation allows them to detect insects at short range. They "honk" at each other when on collision courses. This bat may migrate a few hundred kilometers to hibernate, but it hibernates throughout its range. When hibernation sites are disturbed, these bats lose weight and fewer survive the winter. After feeding in early evening, night roosts provide a place for the bats to cluster and thus raise their body temperature to aid in digestion. Little brown myotis have a keen sense of smell and their eyesight in dim light is quite good.

Food: Little brown myotis usually eat aquatic insects. They select prey by size (3–10 mm in length) but are otherwise non-selective in their choice of prey. Young have a more variable diet than adults, probably due to inexperience. Lactating females eat larger insects, but still select some small items like midges.

Remarks: When they fly during the day, these bats (and others) are easy prey for raptors. However, hawks and owls only rarely take bats. A wide variety of small terrestrial carnivores take these bats, as do mice, snakes, and birds.

Misguided human efforts to control these bats have included a long list of chemicals that are largely ineffective. These chemicals are often toxic to people as well as bats. This widespread western subspecies was named in 1909 from specimens taken at the Lake Hotel in Yellowstone National Park.

An adult long-legged myotis *(Myotis volans)*. Photograph by Roger W. Barbour.

Long-Legged Myotis
Myotis volans interior Miller

Description: This mouse-eared bat has furred underwings from the knee to the elbow. It is the only large-footed Wyoming myotis with an obvious keel on the calcar. The big brown bat *(Eptesicus fuscus)* has a keeled calcar also, but its body is much larger. Long-legged myotis have dorsal fur that varies from tawny to dark brown.

Size: Adults may grow to the following dimensions: total length 95–103 mm; tail 43–48 mm; hind foot 8.5–11 mm; ear 11–14 mm; forearm 34–41.2 mm; weight 4.8–10 grams. Sexual variation in body size is not known.

Range and Habitat: Long-legged myotis live throughout the western half of North America. They can be expected anywhere in Wyoming in suitable habitats and are the most abundant *Myotis* in the West.

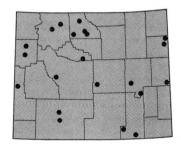

Their habitat in other areas includes oak, ponderosa pine, and mixed deciduous-coniferous forests above 1300 meters. Roosts include tree crevices, snags, buildings, and rock crevices.

Reproduction: Long-legged myotis assemble in nursery colonies. Here, in groups of 100 or more, females each give birth to a single young sometime from late June or July to mid-August. Altough they probably resemble other *Myotis* in their breeding biology, few details are known.

Habits: These bats fly in direct, fast routes, often at treetop level. When passing through a clump of insects, evidently only one is singled out and taken. They detect their prey at a distance of 5 to 10 meters. These bats do not appear to be territorial but are solitary foragers. Long-legged myotis also forage under the canopy of deciduous trees. They emerge early at dusk and are often one of the earliest foragers visible before sunset.

Food: Long-legged myotis are moth specialists. As they approach a moth, they give a burst of rapid echolocation clicks and make rapid, elaborate maneuvers for capture. These bats only take flying insects.

Remarks: This bat is readily identified by its echolocation vocalizations. It is also captured over water with mist nets. Long-legged myotis are officially designated as uncommon in North Dakota, but are probably abundant in Wyoming.

An adult fringed myotis *(Myotis thysanodes)*. Photograph by Roger W. Barbour.

Fringed Myotis
Myotis thysanodes pahasapensis Jones and Genoways

Description: This is the only Wyoming myotis with long ears and a conspicuous fringe of hair along the center posterior margin of the uropatagium. This fringe is *not* just a few scattered hairs but several hundred hairs, clearly visible, each 1–2 mm long, and usually much lighter in color than the tail membrane.

Size: Adults may grow to the following dimensions: total length 77–104 mm; tail 34–54 mm; hind foot 7–9 mm; ear 16–20 mm; forearm 40–47 mm. Females are slightly larger than males.

Range and Habitat: This bat occurs from British Columbia through the western states to southern Mexico. Fringed myotis skirt Wyoming to the west and south, yet occur as isolated populations on the Black Hills south to Laramie. Fringed myotis generally occurs in middle elevations in grasslands, deserts and woodlands, and are occasionally observed as high as spruce-fir habitats.

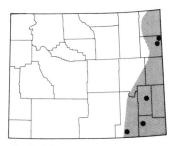

Reproduction: Studies in New Mexico provide some details on the reproduction of this bat. Females copulate in the fall, but ovulation and fertilization don't occur until April or May. Gestation is about 60 days and a single young is born by early July. Young may fly at 17 days of age and are good fliers at 21 days of age. Maternity colonies form rapidly in the spring and females leave the maternity colonies as soon as the young are independent in late summer.

Habits: Females segregate from males into maternity colonies of several hundred bats. Caves, mine tunnels, and buildings are used as roosts. Fringed myotis are known to migrate, but hibernation sites are poorly known. They are known to hibernate in caves in the Black Hills of South Dakota.

During the summer, they forage just after dusk for 1 or 2 hours. Fringed myotis mostly eat flying beetles taken with slow, highly complex maneuvers at canopy height. Over their entire range, they take a wide variety of prey.

While in roosts, these bats move about to stay in comfortable air temperatures. They cluster when cold and seek warm places. These bats may lose up to 20 percent of their body weight overnight in the roost. Much of this loss is water evaporated from the skin or from the lungs during breathing.

Food: Evidently, fringed myotis have developed behavior which allows them to specialize in feeding on beetles. Their food habits in Wyoming are unknown.

Remarks: The Sioux name for the Black Hills is Paha Sapa, thus the subspecific name. The agility of fringed myotis is exemplified by a captive bat in New Mexico able to hover in circles within a 0.6-meter diameter sink and sip water from a pool in the bottom.

Colorado and Montana officially listed the fringed bat as rare, and until additional evidence is gathered it should be so considered in Wyoming as well.

An adult Keen's myotis *(Myotis keenii)*. Photograph by Thomas H. Kunz.

Keen's Myotis
Myotis keenii septentrionalis (Trouessart)

Description: This bat is a medium-sized member of the "mouse-eared" genus *Myotis*. Fur is matte brown, the ear is long, reaching 4 mm beyond the tip of the nose when gently laid forward. There is no obvious keel on the calcar. The tragus inside the ear is long and pointed.

Size: Adults may reach the following dimensions: total length 84–92 mm; tail 38–41 mm; hind foot 9 mm; ear 15–19 mm; weight 5.2–8.4 grams. Adult males and females are of similar body size.

Range and Habitat: Keen's myotis lives throughout the northern, central, and eastern United States and it extends through the Dakotas into northwestern Canada. It appears to be isolated in the Black Hills of Wyoming and South Dakota, and perhaps Bear Lodge Mountains in Wyoming.

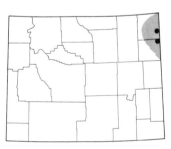

Keen's myotis is probably resident year-round in the ponderosa pine and mixed deciduous-pine habitats. In South Dakota, it is restricted to elevations between 1200 and 1900 meters. This bat roosts in caves and tree cavities. It can occupy dense forests. Keen's myotis forages in hillside and ridgetop vegetation rather than riparian areas.

Reproduction: Keen's myotis has not been well studied with regard to breeding. Sperm are stored in the uterus over winter. Probably only a single young is born. In the Black Hills of South Dakota, lactation was observed from late July to late August. Adults may live as long as 18 years.

Habits: Females segregate in maternity colonies of up to 30 bats. Maternity colonies are usually apart from summer roosting sites of males. Sometimes, Keen's myotis live in association with other bats including *Myotis lucifugus, Myotis ciliolabrum,* and *Eptesicus fuscus.* Hibernation sites are cool (1–5 °C), humid (relative humidity 70 percent) and calm.

Keen's myotis forages on the wing at shrub level. It emerges at dusk and sometimes makes another brief foraging trip at dawn.

Food: Presumably, Keen's myotis takes flying insects. Its diet is poorly known.

Remarks: The Black Hills of Wyoming have a large number of isolated populations of species that are otherwise found in the central and eastern United States. This bat is one such "disjunct" species. In addition, there are about 30 plant species with similar disjunct distribution. About 10,000 years ago Wyoming's Black Hills probably resembled the natural communities now found in states to the north and east.

Keen's myotis is listed as rare or uncommon in Alabama, Mississippi, Missouri, and North Dakota. Its rarity in Wyoming is largely due to the peripheral, disjunct nature of its populations in the state.

An adult long-eared myotis *(Myotis evotis)*. Photograph by Thomas H. Kunz.

Long-Eared Myotis
Myotis evotis evotis (H. Allen)

Description: The ears of this bat are heavily pigmented and are the longest ears of any American myotis. Ears of long-eared myotis are black in Wyoming and are virtually opaque. Fur is long, glossy and brown above, and paler below.

Size: Adults may grow to the following dimensions: total length 87–96 mm; tail 39–43 mm; hind foot 9–11 mm; ear 17–25 mm; forearm 36–41 mm.

Range and Habitat: Long-eared myotis occur throughout the western part of North America south to Baja California. These bats occur throughout Wyoming in suitable habitat.

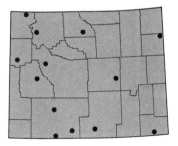

The favorite habitat of long-eared myotis is the coniferous forests. Especially common in ponderosa pine, they have been taken up to spruce-fir forests. This bat roosts in caves, buildings, and mine tunnels. Although almost always taken over water holes, three were captured on Steamboat

Mountain in Sweetwater County in an opening in a dry coniferous woodland. In addition, two were taken foraging over a temporary pond in the sand dunes at the base of Steamboat Mountain where spadefoot toads, sage, and rushes were thriving. In Alkali Draw, also in Sweetwater County, we captured one over water in a greasewood flat with occasional juniper along sandy bluffs.

Reproduction: A single young is produced and small maternity colonies of up to 30 bats are formed. Pregnancy has been observed from mid-June to mid-July. In South Dakota, nearly adult-sized young were captured in early August. Breeding probably occurs in August or September. Little else is known about the breeding of this bat.

Habits: Long-eared myotis emerge well after sunset and forage among trees and over open water. Only a few are taken at any given locality suggesting low natural densities. This bat is rarely taken above the ponderosa pine life zone. Little is known about the habits of this bat.

Food: Long-eared myotis are evidently beetle specialists in New Mexico. The diet of this bat is poorly known.

Remarks: Once again, the coniferous islands in the sea of sage steppe in Sweetwater County provide refugia for a small mammal. Because scattered "islands" of pine forests occur throughout Wyoming, this bat could be expected anywhere in the state.

An adult silver-haired bat *(Lasionycteris noctivagans)*. Photograph by Thomas H. Kunz.

Silver-Haired Bat
Lasionycteris noctivagans (Le Conte)

Description: Silver-haired bats can be distinguished at once by their unique silver-tipped fur. A few Wyoming specimens are blond with silver tips, but generally the fur on the body has black bases or is entirely black with only frosted silver-white tips. In all cases, the silvery-white tips of the hair, especially on the back, are diagnostic. The interfemoral membrane (uropatagium) is furred above. Generally, the fur around the face is not silver-tipped.

Size: Adults may grow to the following dimensions: total length 92–115 mm; tail 35–45 mm; hind foot 7–10 mm; ear 12–17 mm; forearm 38–43 mm; weight 8.1–10 grams. Males and females are about the same size.

Range and Habitat: Silver-haired bats occur throughout central North America south to central California, across Arizona to southern Texas and northern Mexico, and then to the eastern coast. It occurs throughout Wyoming in warm months.

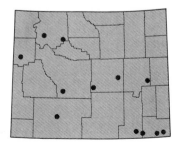

Silver-haired bats in Wyoming are known from a wide variety of habitats.

Records from the State Veterinary Laboratory indicate relatively few occurrences in human habitations until August and September when many encounters have been reported from Casper, Douglas, and Cheyenne. This may be associated with a fall migration to the south.

Reproduction: Copulation occurs in the fall and sperm remains viable in the female over winter. Ovulation peaks in April and May, and gestation requires 50–60 days. Usually two babies are born and the sex ratio at birth is equal. Lactation is about 36 days and young can fly by 3 or 4 weeks of age. In Alberta, the mean age was 2 years with some bats as old as 12 years. Maternity colonies have not been verified, but probably are formed. These bats can breed during their first summer.

Habits: Silver-haired bats are relatively late fliers, often appearing 2 to 3 hours after sunset. They may also forage again 6 to 8 hours after sunset. Apparently this temporal pattern allows the silver-haired bat to forage when other similar bats are roosting. Flight is slow and erratic with many short glides. Silver-haired bats forage in or near deciduous forests and/or mixed coniferous forests, often adjacent to water. Individual bats seem to have exclusive feeding routes of about 50–90 meters. Echolocation by this bat has not been studied, but occasional audible high-pitched buzzes are known. This bat is not known from any large aggregations. It roosts in tree foliage, hollow trees, mines, caves, houses, and under loose bark.

Food: In Montana, silver-haired bats consumed a wide variety of insects including moths, bugs, carab beetles, flies, and caddisflies. In the Southwest, it appears to eat only moths. Spiders are occasionally taken. In general, the silver-haired bat appears to be an opportunistic feeder.

Remarks: The name of this bat, *noctivagans,* means night flying. These bats are probably abundant in Wyoming.

An adult big brown bat *(Eptesicus fuscus)*. Photograph by Thomas H. Kunz.

Big Brown Bat
Eptesicus fuscus pallidus Young

Description: The big brown bat is the largest bat in Wyoming with uniformly brown fur. Ears are black, and when gently laid forward do not extend beyond the nose. The calcar has a keel. The only species of *Myotis* with an obvious keel is much smaller. Other Wyoming bats this large do not have uniformly dark fur.

Size: Adults may grow to the following dimensions: total length 109–118 mm; tail 41–50 mm; hind foot 10–13 mm; ear 14–19 mm; forearm 42–51 mm.

Range and Habitat: Big brown bats occur throughout North America and throughout Wyoming. They are probably one of the most abundant bats in the state. Big brown bats are frequently found in buildings. Occasionally rock crevices, caves, hollow trees, or crevices in bark are used. This bat is frequently seen in flight around

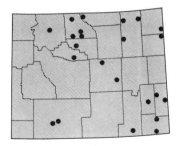

57

city lights and isolated ranch yard lights. Buildings are used as both summer day roosts and winter hibernation sites. These bats forage over open meadows, along tree-lined city streets, above corrals, and around farms or ranches.

Reproduction: Breeding occurs from late summer to fall. Ovulation occurs in early spring and by May maternity colonies of 20–300 females are formed. Pregnant females have been observed as late as July. Elsewhere, the birth of twins is the rule, but in Wyoming probably only a single young is produced.

Young are sheltered under their mother's wing and cling tenaciously to her fur. Generally young are left hanging alone for up to an hour. Females can pick up young that fall, and evidently recognize their own. Young are born at the unusually large body size of 10 percent of that of their parent, and can fly at 3 to 4 weeks of age. Females can reproduce as yearlings. Adults have been known to live up to 18 years.

Habits: Big brown bats are efficient feeders, eating 2.7 grams per hour, and are able to fill their stomachs within an hour. Throughout their range, these bats specialize on beetles, but take many other insects harmful to humans. A colony of 500 in a typical barn could take hundreds of kilograms of insects in a summer. Big brown bats take relatively few moths. It is curious that they are evidently fooled by moths which hear them and "jam" the bat's echolocation with their own imitations.

These bats hibernate, sometimes storing and using a third of their body weight in fat. Hibernation sites are cool but dry. If the air temperature drops below freezing, the bats arouse and stay active until it warms or they find warmer shelter.

Big brown bats can return home when displaced up to 720 kilometers, but they are not migratory. When they fly, they emit an audible, high-pitched chatter. Their ultrasonic vocalizations are heard on detectors as loud, distinctive chirps. They drink by flying over open water and scooping sips while in flight.

Food: Big brown bats specialize on flying beetles, but take house flies, ants, caddisflies, stoneflies, mayflies, moths, and a few crickets.

Remarks: Hawks and great horned owls have been observed to prey on these bats, hawks having captured bats which were released during the day. Other predators are not known.

An adult red bat *(Lasiurus borealis).* Photograph by Thomas H. Kunz.

Red Bat
Lasiurus borealis borealis (Müller)

Description: Red bats are the only Wyoming bats with fur that is brick red to rusty red washed with white. The uropatagium is well furred, and in flight the long tail membrane is characteristically extended straight behind the body.

Size: Adults may grow to the following dimensions: total length 90–120 mm; tail 36–65 mm; hind foot 6–9 mm; ear 9–11 mm; forearm 38–41 mm; weight 7–13 grams. Females are about 8 percent larger than males.

Range and Habitat: Red bats occur over most of North America except the Rocky Mountains, and south through Central America. They are known from the Black Hills of South Dakota and occur in southeastern Wyoming.

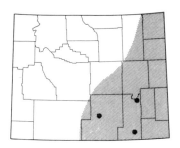

Red bats are recorded from Wyoming on the basis of three specimens. In 1861, the U.S. National Museum catalogued a specimen for Dr. Hayden taken from "Laramie Peak, Nebraska," but the specimen cannot now be located (Stromberg, 1982). Eastern Wyoming was once part of Nebraska Territory. A specimen from near Rawlins was found in cottonwood trees growing along an isolated water pond south of town. This red bat and another from Laramie were brought to a veterinarian.

Elsewhere in their range red bats are solitary (0.4 per hectare) and roost singly or in female-litter groups. Trees or shrubs are used almost exclusively for roosts. Roosting red bats cling to leaf petioles or twigs in clumps of vegetation, shielded from view except from below. Deciduous trees, sunflower plants, hedges, and leafy crop plants are all used. Generally, red bats use the south side of the object they select as a roost.

Evidently, any area with some trees or leafy shrubs is potential habitat. These bats virtually never use buildings.

Reproduction: Red bats mate in August and September, initiating copulation in the air. Sperm is stored in the uterus over winter and fertilization occurs in the spring. A female taken in Rawlins on 28 May 1981 had four 15 mm embryos. Gestation is about 80-90 days and, although an average of three to four embryos develop, only two or three young are born. Young cling to their mother and grow rapidly. After 4 to 6 weeks, they can fly. During lactation, young are left behind while the female forages. Males and females seem to have different summer ranges. Males may migrate to higher elevations or latitudes.

Habits: Red bats are strong fliers (65 kph) and can migrate long distances. Once in an area, they maintain feeding territories within 900 meters of their roost. Red bats drop straight down out of their day roost early in the evening. Foraging flights are straight and fast at treetop level, with occasional arcs down to ground level. Roost sites and feeding territories often are used by different individuals on different days. An area with good roosts may attract several bats, and individuals probably are attracted to good roosting sites by sounds made by other red bats already present.

Most red bats migrate to warmer winter climates, but they can hibernate in trees even where air temperatures drop below freezing. They wrap their well-furred tail membrane over themselves like a blanket. Red bats drop their heart rates to 10-16 beats per minute and their body temperature just above $-5\,°C$ while they hibernate. These adaptations allow them to minimize energy requirements when food is not available. Only when air temperatures rise above $19\,°C$ do red bats rouse from their slumber. In the summer, red bats forage during the peak activity of flying insects, 1–2 hours after sunset. They often feed under street lights.

Food: Red bats probably select food according to size. Bugs, beetles, ants, flies, and moths are eaten.

Remarks: When roosting in a tree, red bats resemble a dead leaf. A person picking fruit once mistook a female and her young for a peach. Sometimes females or their flightless young fall from daytime roosts. Most encounters with people occur in such situations. If you should find this beautiful bat in such a predicament, take its photograph and then place the bat in a partly enclosed shelter. The female can then carry her young at night back to a roost.

This bat is rarely seen. In Colorado, it is listed as rare. Any observations of this bat would be appreciated.

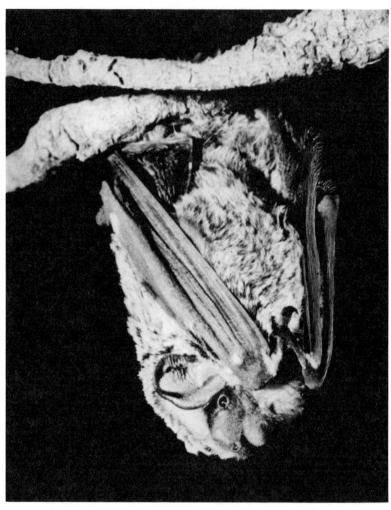

An adult hoary bat *(Lasiurus cinereus)*. Photograph by Thomas H. Kunz.

Hoary Bat
Lasiurus cinereus cinereus (Palisot de Beauvois)

Description: Hoary bats are huge, compared to most other Wyoming bats. Their fur is dark with white tips, or white, especially around the face. Hoary bats have thick, rounded, short ears edged with black, bare skin.

Size: Adults may grow to the following dimensions: total length 130–145 mm; tail 55–58 mm; hind foot 9–11 mm; ear 17–19 mm; forearm 48–52 mm; weight 20–35 grams. Females are about 4 percent larger than males.

Range and Habitat: Hoary bats range over all of North America. They are such strong fliers that they made it to Hawaii where they are the only native bat. Hoary bats have been found throughout Wyoming.

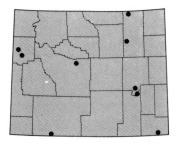

These bats are solitary and roost in deciduous trees. Roosting sites are generally open only from below and are 3–4 meters above the ground. Hoary bats rarely enter houses or other man-made structures. In Wyoming, they inhabit greasewood flats, short-grass prairies, and aspen-pine forests.

In August, we have seen swarms of hoary bats flying above hay meadows and riparian areas of the upper Roaring Fork near Laramie Peak. They circle and climb to high altitudes, disappearing from sight. Hoary bats are migratory through Wyoming in spring and fall.

Reproduction: Both sexes appear to have broadly different summer ranges in North America. In Nebraska, Montana, Wyoming, and the Dakotas, both have been collected in summer months.

Copulation probably occurs in the fall migration and pregnancy starts in early spring. Litter size is usually two (range one to four) in hoary bats, and young are born from mid-May to July. Young can fly by 3 to 4 weeks of age. Females can carry young until they are 6 or 7 days old. During lactation, females leave their young while foraging.

Habits: Hoary bats are distinctive in flight because they are large and emit a high-pitched chatter. During the summer, these bats often fly late in the evening, 2 to 5 hours after sunset. During migration, they can be seen flying in late afternoon and early evening. Their thick body fur and well-furred uropatagium allow these bats to tolerate air temperatures from 0-22 °C, and minimizes water loss. These bats can lose up to 28 percent of their weight in water loss without ill effect.

Food: What little is known about feeding in hoary bats indicates they have a strong preference for moths. Moths are approached from the rear and the sheared head and wings are dropped to the ground. These bats also eat beetles, flies, grasshoppers, and wasps.

Remarks: The biology of hoary bats is poorly known because they are rarely observed. In Wyoming, these bats are known from fewer than a dozen specimens collected in the last 120 years.

An adult spotted bat *(Euderma maculatum)*. Photograph by Roger W. Barbour.

Spotted Bat
Euderma maculatum H. Allen

Description: Spotted bats are magnificent mammals. Their faces are black and their large eyes give them a typical carnivore appearance. Sweeping back from their brows are spectacular ears almost as long as their body. Each shoulder and the rump have a white patch surrounded by dark black fur. Their belly fur is black with white tips, and their naked ears, wings and tail membranes are pinkish-red. No other American bat has such large ears or resplendent pelage.

Size: Adults may grow to the following dimensions: total length 107–115 mm; tail 47–50 mm; hindfoot 9–10 mm; ear 45–50 mm; forearm 48–51 mm.

Range and Habitat: Spotted bats occur in western North America from Mexico to the southern border of British Columbia. In Wyoming, only one specimen and a recent photograph document this species from near Byron and the Bighorn National Recreation Area headquarters, respectively. Collections of spotted bats in Montana,

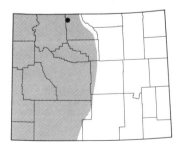

Utah, and Colorado suggest that these bats may be expected throughout western Wyoming. Although widespread, local distribution is patchy. There is evidence from New Mexico that spotted bats are transient in the Rocky Mountains over the summer.

Spotted bats are known from only a few specimens and many of these were associated with accidental encounters in man-made structures. Because spotted bats have been found over a large geographic area, they are associated with many different habitats, ranging from low deserts (Big Bend, Texas) to evergreen forest (Okanagun Valley, British Columbia). Cliffs over perennial water are frequently reported as part of the spotted bat's habitat.

Reproduction: Scant evidence suggests that breeding occurs in the fall. Assuming the spotted bat is similar to other members of this bat family, fertilization occurs in spring. A single young is born from late May (Texas) to July (Utah). Lactation has been observed as late as mid-August. Although the young are born well developed, the rate of growth or how long the young remain with the female are unknown. Maternity roosts are formed, but are vacated if disturbed.

Habits: There is evidence that spotted bats migrate south in winter, but in southern Utah, they are active the entire year. While torpid or resting, the ears are folded like ram's horns but in flight they are unfurled and held forward. Spotted bats can run quickly over the ground, and have been observed to scramble with agility in crevices on a cliff. These bats use both echolocation and sight to fly. They emit loud vocalizations easily heard by humans and described as metallic squeaks. Spotted bats probably capture insects both on the ground and in the air.

Food: Moths make up virtually all of the spotted bat's diet, but occasionally grasshoppers and beetles are eaten. Moths from 5–11 mm are most frequently taken.

Remarks: From 1891 to 1965, only 35 specimens of this bat were known from throughout its entire range. As mist nets have become more widely used to study bats, more specimens are found. However, this bat remains a mystery in many ways and is only available for year to year observation at a few places in the West. Nevada and Wyoming list it as rare and Utah lists the spotted bat as endangered. A "status report" for the spotted bat was prepared for the Office of Endangered Species, U.S. Fish and Wildlife Service (Clark and Dorn, 1981; O'Farrell, 1982).

An adult Townsend's big-eared bat *(Plecotus townsendii)*. Photograph by John P. Farney.

Townsend's Big-Eared Bat
Plecotus townsendii pallescens (Miller)

Description: A pale brown bat of medium size with large ears. Townsend's big-eared bat is the only long-eared, brown bat in Wyoming possessing two fleshy lumps on its nose.

Size: Adults may grow to the following dimensions: total length 90–112 mm; tail 35–54 mm; hind foot 10–12 mm; ear 30–39 mm; forearm 39.2–47.6 mm; weight 5–13 grams. Females are slightly larger than males.

Range and Habitat: This bat is most common throughout the western half of North America and south into central Mexico. It occurs throughout Wyoming.

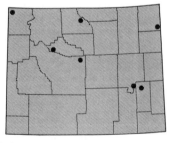

Townsend's big-eared bat is a cave dweller for both day roosts and hibernation sites. It is frequently found in abandoned mines. Big-eared bats also commonly use buildings, but only as night roosts. Most typical western habitats for this bat are desert shrub lands, pinyon-juniper woodlands or dry coniferous forests.

Reproduction: Pearson et al. (1952) conducted a study of reproduction in this bat. Copulation occurs from November to February and young females of the year mate. Sperm are stored over winter, and in spring ovulation, fertilization and pregnancy begin. A single embryo takes 56–100 days to develop. Young are large (25 percent of their mother's weight), can fly at 3 weeks, and are weaned by 6 weeks. Females form separate maternity colonies in warm parts of caves or mines. Maternity colonies generally break up by August or September. These bats may live up to 16 years.

Habits: Big-eared bats are gentle. They fly slowly, their ears extended forward and tail held down. Their wings provide extremely high lift and allow slow wing-beats and hovering.

Barbour and Davis (1969) reported that Vernon Bailey's field notes from Sundance, Wyoming, include descriptions of this bat beginning its flight late in the afternoon near sundown so that the ears were still visible. However, other recent studies show that this bat flies 4 to 5 hours after sunset. Big-eared bats are extremely agile fliers.

Solitary Townsend's big-eared bats live in densities of from 0.25 to 1.0 per hectare. No long distance migrations by them have been reported. They have been observed hibernating on Copper Mountain (Fremont County) and in the Black Hills of South Dakota. Hibernation sites are generally cold (1–12 °C) and often near well-ventilated parts of caves and mines. These bats may lose one-half of their fall weight over hibernation. During hibernation, they coil their ears up like a ram's horn. Disturbance of winter hibernation is particularly devastating to big-eared bats. Forced to wake up, they use too much of their budgeted fat reserve and often die before spring arrives.

Food: These bats are moth specialists, selecting prey 3–10 mm in length. Big-eared bats can glean moths from leaves, but most of their feeding is on flying moths. Flies and beetles are occasionally eaten.

Remarks: Like other bats, some populations of this species are threatened. Habitat loss, vandalism and increased disturbance by cavers of maternity and hibernation roosts combine to reduce numbers of this gentle mammal.

An adult pallid bat *(Antrozous pallidus)*. Photograph by Thomas H. Kunz.

Pallid Bat
Antrozous pallidus pallidus (Le Conte)

Description: Pallid bats have pale yellow fur tipped with gray or brown. Their belly fur is creamy yellow to almost white. With their large size, pale brown wing membranes, long broad ears, large eyes, and pig-like snouts, they are unique. In flight, their ears are clearly visible in profile.

Size: Adults may grow to the following dimensions: total length 92–135 mm; tail 40–45 mm; hind foot 11.5–16 mm; ear 23–37 mm; forearm 48–60 mm. Females are slightly larger than males.

Range and Habitat: Pallid bats occur in the western and southwestern states from British Columbia to western Texas, and range south to Baja California and central Mexico.

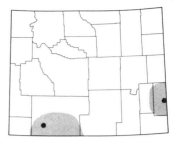

The distribution of pallid bats in Wyoming is not clear. They have been taken at Green River and Torrington. Collections in Utah and Colorado suggest also that they occur in the Green River drainage in Wyoming. The specimens from Torrington are disjunct by hundreds of kilometers from other collections in Colorado, and are a significant range extension to the northeast. Suitable habitat probably exists from Green River across the Oregon Trail in Wyoming to Torrington.

Pallid bats are generally desert and grassland species. They use cottonwood bottomlands in these habitats. Although they have been taken in ponderosa pine as high as 2100 meters, they are most common at lower elevations. In Torrington, they were collected in an old county highway maintenance shop. These bats are non-migratory, and winter from California to Kansas.

Reproduction: Mating generally occurs in October and probably continues through February. Fertilization occurs in spring and gestation takes about 9 weeks. Maternity colonies are formed, often in rock crevices and buildings. Two young are usually born to a female, but occasionally only one. Newborn weigh about 3 grams, and nurse for about 6 to 8 weeks before reaching independence. By late summer, young of the year are indistinguishable from adults. Females breed in the winter following their birth.

Habits: Unique among Wyoming's bats, the pallid bat forages almost entirely on the ground. When capturing its prey, it runs and hops on its hind feet with its wings folded.

During the day, pallid bats roost in small crevices where they can retreat from sight. They are intolerant of disturbance and may abandon a roost for years if molested. About an hour after sunset, they emerge to feed, moving about 3 kilometers from day roosts. After feeding they hang in night roosts, where most of their digestion (and defecation) occur. Open buildings, natural rock overhangs, porches and other similarly exposed places are thus often littered with droppings. However, the bats are rarely seen, retreating to their day roosts about an hour before dawn.

Food: Prey includes a long list of terrestrial vertebrates and invertebrates, including crickets, grasshoppers, scorpions, June beetles, ground beetles, lizards, and pocket mice. These bats use both echolocation and vision to capture relatively large prey and may perch to eat it. Their kidneys are well developed to concentrate urine, and this suggests that Pallid bats may need to drink only rarely.

Remarks: Great horned owls eat this bat. Because pallid bats frequently forage on the ground, they are often injured or captured by predators. It is not listed anywhere as rare. Breeding status and abundance in Wyoming remain poorly known. Hermanson and O'Shea (1983) provided a synopsis of the biology of the pallid bat.

An adult Brazilian free-tailed bat *(Tadarida brasiliensis)*. Photograph by Thomas H. Kunz.

FREE-TAILED BATS (FAMILY MOLOSSIDAE)
Brazilian Free-Tailed Bat
Tadarida brasiliensis mexicana (Saussure)

Description: This bat is small, dark brown to dark gray and uniformly colored. It is unique among Wyoming bats in having the lower one half of the tail protruding free from the interfemoral (tail) membrane. The face and ears are sparsely haired, and long, hooked hairs (as long as the foot) protrude from the toes. This bat has long, narrow wings.

Size: Adults may grow to the following dimensions: total length 90–105 mm; tail 32–38 mm; hind foot 9–11 mm; ear 42–44 mm; forearm 36–46 mm; weight 9–16 grams. Males are slightly larger than females.

Range and Habitat: Brazilian free-tailed bats occur across central North America south through Mexico and Cuba to northern South America. This strong-flying migrant occupies a large range, but has a spotty distribution and is limited to selected caves. In winter, this bat migrates south, probably to Central America and  southern Mexico. In Wyoming, this bat is known from one record in Laramie County taken in the first week of July. The nearest known breeding colony is in north-central Colorado.

71

Reproduction: Mating occurs from February through April. Males become more solitary and females form large nursery colonies. A single young is born each year and gestation periods of 75-100 days have been recorded. Most young are born in mid-summer and are left in the cave while females forage at night. Upon their return, females select their young from among, perhaps, millions, and nurse. Young can fly by 5 weeks of age. Sexual maturity is reached in the spring following their birth. Brazilian free-tailed bats may live as long as 8 years.

Habits: Colonial life is the rule for this bat. Colonies of 12-14 million have been reported. These bats feed on insects over agricultural fields and have suffered massive declines in numbers from exposure to DDT. Huge swarms emerge at dusk and fly in columns over long distances. A variety of flying insects are taken in flight. Brief hibernation (2-3 weeks) is possible because these bats become torpid if cooled. Evidently warmer climates and frequent feeding sessions are needed through the winter. Migration from their southern range starts in February, and they reach their summer homes by April and stay until August or September. When displaced, they can find their way home from up to 200 kilometers away. During the day, they may fly at altitudes as high as 3000 meters. In New Mexico, hawks routinely feed on these bats as they emerge in huge, twisting torrents in late afternoon.

Food: Brazilian free-tailed bats feed largely on small moths (5–9 mm) taken on the wing. They may fly up to 64 km to foraging sites. Woodlands, open fields and riparian areas are used by this bat for feeding. They may eat over half their body weight in insects during a night.

Remarks: Caves with large colonies of this bat should not be entered because it has been known to transmit rabies to humans.

An adult pika *(Ochotona princeps).* Photograph by Dick Randall.

PIKAS (FAMILY OCHOTONIDAE)
Pika
Ochotona princeps Bangs

Description: Pikas are somewhat larger than a guinea pig, have short legs, lack an external tail, and have almost circular, prominent external ears. Their fur varies from chalky gray to brown. Pikas have two pairs of upper incisors — the obvious anterior pair, and a small, peg-like pair tucked just behind the first pair.

Size: Adults may grow to the following dimensions: total length 170–204 mm; hind foot 30–33 mm; ear 22–29 mm; weight 150–175 grams. Sexes are of the same size.

Range and Habitat: Seventeen species of pika live in Siberia and the USSR. North American pikas are distinct from their Siberian relatives (Weston, 1982). Pikas occur throughout the Rocky Mountains and western coastal ranges of North America. In Wyoming, pikas live in the northwest mountain ranges (*Ochotona princeps*

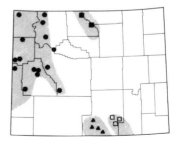

ventorum A.H. Howell-(circles); the Bighorn Mountains (*Ochotona princeps obscura* Long-(squares); the Sierra Madre Mountains (*Ochotona princeps figginsi* J.A. Allen-(triangles) and the Medicine Bow Range (*Ochotona princeps saxatilis* Bangs-(open squares). Long (1965) discussed the minor differences between these subspecies. Studies of the genetics of these pikas suggest that all but the Bighorn Mountain subspecies are perhaps not justified (Glover et al. 1977).

Pikas are never found far from talus slopes or outcrops of shattered rock. They live from the sides of 3600-meter Medicine Bow Peak down to isolated rocky hillsides at 2500 meters. Tundra, spruce-fir, subalpine fir and Douglas fir forests often surround pikas. Generally, some nearby patch of grass or forbs is required.

Reproduction: Pikas breed in late winter and first births are observed as early as April. From one to five young are born after a pregnancy of 30 days. Nests are made in between rocks or in burrows beneath the talus slopes. Young are weaned in 3–4 weeks, and two or three litters may be produced each year.

Habits: The unique, shrill whistle of the pika has been described as a high-pitched "hneee" or the "beep-beep" of a child's toy horn. We have noticed considerable variation between subspecies and populations in this alarm call. Often the call first draws attention to these small mammals.

Pikas are active all year, usually in the morning. During the summer, food is cut and piled in "haystacks" where it can dry in the sun. This hay is stored and eaten during the winter. Pikas do not hibernate and are not active at night. They often perch on prominent rocks. During the summer, pikas are territorial around haypile sites (0.04–0.30 hectares). Home ranges follow the edge of rockpiles and include adjacent meadow areas.

Food: Pikas eat grass, sedges, leaves of forbs, conifer twigs, aspen and lichen. Like other mammals, pikas themselves cannot digest cellulose, which forms the bulk of their vegetarian diet. They have a caecum or large sac in their hind gut where microorganisms digest the cellulose in their diet. In order to give the microorganisms enough time to digest the cellulose, pikas pass "soft" pellets and later re-ingest these partially digested food packets.

Remarks: The extreme isolation of the various Wyoming populations strongly suggests that local races may be maintained.

Overgrazing of meadows adjacent to talus slopes probably has severe impacts on pika populations. Pikas are not rare in Wyoming, but recolonization of their isolated talus slopes may take many years if they become locally extinct.

HARES AND RABBITS (FAMILY LEPORIDAE)
Pygmy Rabbit
Sylvilagus idahoensis (Merriam)

Description: Pygmy rabbits are strikingly small. They are buffy gray to slate gray, and their bellies are not white. Their tails are small and, unlike cottontails, inconspicuous because of the buff color underneath.

Size: Adults may grow to the following dimensions: total length 250–290 mm; tail 20–30 mm; hind foot 65–72 mm; ear 36–48 mm; weight (males) 375–435 grams; (females) 246–458 grams. Females are slightly larger than males.

Range and Habitat: Pygmy rabbits occur through the Great Basin of northern Nevada, eastern Oregon, western Utah, and southern Idaho. The population in southwestern Wyoming may be isolated by many kilometers from populations in Utah (Campbell et al. 1982).

Pygmy rabbits are limited to areas where big sagebrush grows in dense, tall stands. In southwestern Wyoming, big sage only reaches adequate height along intermittent streams and occasional riparian areas.

Reproduction: Breeding starts in late December and January and may continue through March. Gestation is from 27 to 30 days and from four to eight young are born during early spring. Young are naked and helpless at birth, and grow to adult size by 10 weeks. Pygmy rabbits begin to breed during their second spring. Presumably young are protected in nests but no specifics are known.

Habits: Dense, tall thickets of sage where these rabbits live are laced with runways and burrows. Pygmy rabbits dig their own, multiple-entrance burrows. Burrow openings are often at the base of a large sage plant.

Social behavior of pygmy rabbits is poorly known. They occur in aggregations (0.7 to 1.4 rabbits/ha), but probably because their habitat is patchy. Individuals usually rest during the day in their burrows and feed at night. They can run 24 kph and generally stay within 30 meters of their burrow. Pygmy rabbits have a pika-like chirp "alarm call." They are active year-round and burrow under the snow.

Food: Pygmy rabbits specialize on sage. Even when other nutritious shrubs are equally available, up to 99 percent of their diet is sage. During middle to late summer, grasses become important (30–40 percent of diet). Pygmy rabbits have been observed climbing sage to eat.

Remarks: Overgrazing, which has increased the sage-grass ratio, may decrease populations of pygmy rabbits. A variety of predators (foxes, weasels, coyotes, owls and hawks) take pygmy rabbits. These rabbits are known from only a few small, isolated populations in Wyoming, and should be considered rare in the state.

An adult eastern cottontail *(Sylvilagus floridanus)*. Photograph by Ken Stiebben, courtesy of the Kansas Fish and Game Commission.

Eastern Cottontail
Sylvilagus floridanus similis Nelson

Description: Eastern cottontails are small rabbits. The similar desert cottontail has much larger ears, and the auditory bullae of desert and eastern cottontail are of different size and shape. Nuttall's cottontail is slightly larger than the eastern cottontail, which is darker than the other two Wyoming cottontails. Jackrabbits are larger. Eastern cottontail fur is cinnamon intermixed with black on the upper parts; underparts are white with a patch of brown on the chest. Like pikas and all other rabbits, this cottontail has two pairs of upper incisors. Front feet have five toes and the hind feet have only four toes.

Size: Adults may attain the following dimensions: total length 375–463 mm; tail 39–65 mm; hind foot 87–101 mm; ear 48–60 mm; weight 1–1.5 kilograms. Sexes are about the same size.

Range and Habitat: Eastern cotton-tails live throughout the central and eastern United States. In other places they appear to be generalists occupy-ing a wide range of habitats. In Wyo-ming, they apparently are restricted to riparian or brushy habitats in the ex-treme southeastern counties. Eastern cottontails occur in brushy draws and 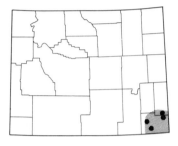 the forest edges of valley streams with thickets that extend down from the Black Hills of northwestern South Dakota. However, no specimens have been collected yet from the Wyoming side of the Black Hills.

Reproduction: Breeding starts in early spring and continues through fall. Gestation is about 30 days, and three to five young are in a litter. Young are born naked and helpless but grow rapidly. By 14 days of age, they can leave the nest. Females can produce five to seven litters in a year depending on weather, food and day length. Young reach independence after 4 to 5 weeks, but generally do not breed until their next summer. Although eastern cottontails can live to 10 years, they generally survive only about 15 months.

Habits: Behavior of eastern cottontails is well known and is summarized by Chapman et al. (1980). These rabbits feed in the early morning and at sunset. They rest in burrows abandoned by other animals or in shallow depressions in dense thickets. Eastern cottontails are not territorial and have home ranges of 0.95 hectares to 2.8 hectares. Densities vary from year to year but can reach 9 per ha in the fall. These cottontails are ac-tive all year.

Like other rabbits, partially digested "soft" pellets are re-ingested. Fur-ther digestion extracts more nutrients before "hard" pellets, which com-prise about 60 percent of the total fecal material, are voided.

Food: Eastern cottontails eat a wide variety of foods and will take vir-tually all green vegetation. In winter, buds and bark of woody vegetation are eaten.

Remarks: Many predators eat eastern cottontails: owls, hawks, eagles, coyotes, house cats, skunks, snakes, weasels, red fox and crows.

Nuttall's Cottontail
Sylvilagus nuttallii grangeri (J. A. Allen)

Description: This rabbit is the medium-sized member of Wyoming's three cottontails. Nuttall's cottontail co-occurs in Wyoming with the desert cottontail, which is larger, has longer ears, and has a larger bulla and ear opening in the skull. Nuttall's cottontail has olive to light brown dorsal fur, and is white below. Where Nuttall's and the desert cottontail co-occur, Nuttall's cottontail occurs in higher elevations in wooded or brushy habitat while the latter occurs in open, grassy habitats at lower elevations.

Size: Adults may attain the following dimensions: total length 350–415 mm; tail 44–57 mm; hind foot 88–100 mm; ear 55–65 mm; weight 630–830 grams. Females are slightly larger than males.

Range and Habitat: Nuttall's cottontail is the mountain cottontail of Wyoming. This rabbit occurs in rocky, wooded or brushy areas of the interior western United States, and throughout Wyoming except for the extreme southeastern counties. It lives in sagebrush, juniper, pine and fir from about 1200 to over 2700 meters in elevation.

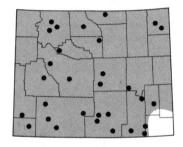

Reproduction: Nuttall's cottontail begins to breed in early spring. Gestation is 28 to 30 days. Litter size varies from one to eight, and females may produce three to five litters a year starting in May. Young are placed in a fur-lined, covered nest. They are probably independent by 4 or 5 weeks of age. These cottontails occasionally breed during their first summer, but reproduction generally begins in the spring following birth.

Habits: These mountain cottontails live solitarily, but may form groups in patches of abundant food. Frequently they run about 10 m when disturbed, then stop and look back through heavy brush. Nuttall's cottontail feeds near or under shrubs, frequently in openings along streams. Feeding occurs in the early morning and early evening. This cottontail has not been reported to dig its own burrows.

Food: Grasses are eaten when green and available. During winter, sagebrush, juniper and other woody shrubs (bark, buds) are eaten.

Remarks: Nuttall's cottontail is an important prey item for many predators including bobcats, owls, hawks and eagles.

An adult desert cottontail *(Sylvilagus audubonii).* Photograph by J. Knox Jones, Jr.

Desert Cottontail
Sylvilagus audubonii baileyi (Merriam)

Description: This is the largest of the three Wyoming cottontail rabbits. In general, it resembles the other cottontails. However, the ears are larger, the auditory bulla and ear opening in the skull are larger, and the bony plate above the eye is turned up. Fur is olive-buff above and white below, but much paler than other cottontails in Wyoming.

Size: Adults may attain the following dimensions: total length 390–420 mm; tail 45–60 mm; hind foot 83–94 mm; ear 62–78 mm; weight (males) 835–988 grams; (females) 1096–1191 grams. Females are slightly larger than males.

Range and Habitat: Desert cottontails occur throughout the the low, arid regions of North America. In Wyoming, they live throughout the state, and occur in grasslands, shrublands, and juniper woodlands. These rabbits require some shrubs or brush for hiding and resting.

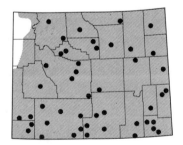

Reproduction: Desert cottontails breed from late winter through the summer. The gestation period is 28 days. Nests are placed on the ground and are lined with fur. Females crouch over the shallow nest depression to nurse. Three or four are born in a litter. Females may have two to six litters a year. Young leave the nest by 2 weeks of age and are weaned by 3 or 4 weeks. Young are sexually mature at 80 days of age. Few desert cottontails live longer than 18 months.

Habits: Desert cottontails are usually active in the cool early morning and evenings. They can climb trees and brush, and can swim. When alarmed, they run to dense brush. Desert cottontails tolerate high temperatures and cool themselves by evaporation through skin and lungs, and by staying in cooler, shady places. Home ranges are 3–4 hectares, but rarely may be as large as 6 hectares. Densities of 16.3 per hectare are reported from Colorado, but vary with season and habitat. These cottontails are active year-round, and are apparently not territorial.

Food: Grasses, herbaceous vegetation and occasionally bark or buds from shrubs are all eaten by desert cottontails. These rabbits feed under cover of shrubs, but may venture up to 100 m from shelter in open grassy fields.

Remarks: Like the other Wyoming cottontails, the desert cottontail is food for many predators. In general, the three cottontail rabbits found in Wyoming are difficult to distinguish from each other.

An adult snowshoe hare *(Lepus americanus)*. Photograph by Roger A. Powell.

Snowshoe Hare
Lepus americanus (Erxleben)

Description: Snowshoe hares differ from cottontails in having much larger hind feet, while possessing shorter ears than either Wyoming jackrabbit. These rabbits are white in the winter with black-tipped ears. During the summer, their fur is dark flecked with patches of buff and their tails are blackish or brownish all around.

Size: Adults may grow to the following dimensions: total length 360–520 mm; tail 25–55 mm; hind foot 112–150 mm; ear 62–70 mm; weight 1.4–1.8 kilogram. Females are significantly larger than males.

Range and Habitat: Snowshoe hares live from Alaska, across Canada and extend as far south as New Mexico along the major mountain ranges in North America. In Wyoming, snowshoe hares occupy the mountain ranges, except the Black Hills, and select high elevation riparian or shrubby habitats including aspen, willow and brushy conifers.

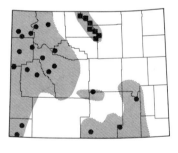

Wyoming has two subspecies of snowshoe hares. *Lepus americanus bairdi* Hayden (circles) occurs in the northwest mountains, and the Uinta,

Sierra Madre, and Medicine Bow ranges. *Lepus americanus seclusus* Baker and Hawkins (squares) occurs in the Bighorn Range.

Reproduction: Births begin in April and continue into August. Most young are born in June and July, with one to six in a litter. Females may have two to four litters a year. Young reach independence in about 6 weeks. Nests are made in dense thickets (frequently in willows) and are shallow, fur lined depressions. Populations appear to fluctuate widely in density, perhaps on about a 10-year cycle.

Habits: Snowshoe hares forage on the ground during the night. During the day they may occasionally be active, but generally rest in dense thickets. When disturbed, snowshoe hares hop or creep slowly into brush where their cryptic pelage often makes them difficult to see. They often remain motionless until approached closely. Elsewhere, home ranges averaged from 2–16 hectares, but it is not known if these hares are territorial. Densities may be as high as 2–5 per hectare. Snowshoe hares sometimes thump the ground with their hind feet. The function of this loud thumping is not known.

Food: During the summer, grasses, other herbs and willows are eaten. In the winter, bark and twigs of deciduous trees and shrubs are eaten. Occasionally buds and bark of conifers are eaten.

Remarks: Overgrazing of high elevation willow flats along riparian corridors in the mountains may decrease snowshoe hare populations.

An adult white-tailed jackrabbit *(Lepus townsendii)*. Photograph by Dick Randall.

White-Tailed Jackrabbit
Lepus townsendii (Bachman)

Description: White-tailed jackrabbits are large-footed, long-eared hares. Their tails are all white except for those white-tailed jackrabbits from southwestern Wyoming which often have a light brown strip on the upperside of the tail. This hare turns white in winter and is gray, tinged with brown and black in summer. Black-tailed jackrabbits have a different tail pattern and a longer hind foot which is less furry in the winter. Both kinds of jackrabbits have black-tipped ears.

Size: Adults may attain the following dimensions: total length 565–655 mm; tail 66–112 mm; hind foot 145–172 mm; ear 96–113 mm; weight 3–6 kilograms. Adult females are larger than males.

Range and Habitat: White-tailed jackrabbits live throughout interior North America. In Wyoming, two subspecies are known. *Lepus townsendii campanius* Hollister (circles) lives in most of the state. *Lepus townsendii townsendii* Bachman (squares) is found in southwestern Wyoming. Both subspecies occupy a wide range of open habi-

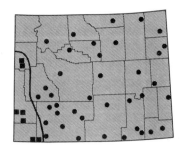

tats from shrub grasslands to openings in foothill, montane coniferous forest and alpine tundra.

Reproduction: Breeding starts in March and young may be born as late as August. From one to nine are born in a litter and apparently females have at least two litters a year. Like other hares, the well-developed young are born with hair and open eyes, and grów rapidly to independence. They are born in shallow nests lined with fur and dry leaves. Nests are well hidden in dense vegetation. Young can forage at 15 days and leave the female after about 2 months. They probably reach sexual maturity in the breeding season following their birth.

Habits: White-tailed jackrabbits are nocturnal. These hares feed all night but are particularly active at dusk and dawn. Although they sometimes drink, they obtain much of the moisture they require from vegetation. In Wyoming, runoff from paved roads creates unusually lush roadside vegetation and this attracts jackrabbits from surrounding areas. Many jackrabbits (up to 3–7/km/night) are killed by cars as they cross roads while foraging.

The cryptic color of this hare allows it to remain motionless, and frequently it goes unseen until virtually tread upon. Then it explodes into long (3-meter) leaps, ears upright as it quarters away from the startled observer. Daytime "hides" are frequently low shrubs, depressions behind rocks or abandoned burrows of badgers and ground squirrels.

Social behavior of white-tailed jackrabbits is poorly known. Both in winter and summer these hares sometimes assemble in groups of up to 60 or 80 per hectare. Home ranges vary from 4–777 hectares. In Colorado, densities of 8 per square kilometer were observed. These hares, active all year, have keen eyesight, excellent hearing and a good sense of smell.

Food: In the summer, white-tailed jackrabbits feed on virtually all green, succulent vegetation. They feed by hopping slowly or walking and grazing, looking up frequently. They lick their fur and wipe their ears after feeding. During the winter, bark and buds of vegetation above the snow are eaten.

Remarks: The sage grassland steppe of southern Wyoming supports many of these hares. White-tailed jackrabbits are abundant and are hunted in Wyoming by humans and a wide variety of other predators, including hawks, owls, coyotes, foxes, badgers and eagles.

An adult black-tailed jackrabbit *(Lepus californicus)*. Photograph by Ken Stiebben, courtesy of the Kansas Fish and Game Commission.

Black-Tailed Jackrabbit
Lepus californicus melanotis (Mearns)

Description: Wyoming's jackrabbits are really "hares" because all hares have long ears, long hind feet, and precocial young. Black-tailed jackrabbits have black hair on the top of the tail which continues as a black strip on the rump. All the ventral fur is white. Their dorsal fur is brown with streaks of black and remains dark during winter. Black-tailed jackrabbits are smaller then white-tailed jackrabbits.

Size: Adults may attain the following dimensions: total length 465–630 mm; tail 59–112 mm; hind foot 112–145 mm; ear 110–130 mm; weight 2.4–4.0 kilograms.

Range and Habitat: Black-tailed jackrabbits occur in dry grasslands of central North America, and shrub grasslands and interior basins of western
North America. In Wyoming, black-
tailed jackrabbits live in the shortgrass
prairies of the eastern counties, below
the ponderosa pine forest zone. They
also live in open greasewood or sage-

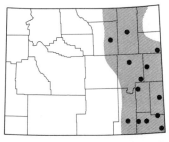

brush grasslands, often resting during the day in small depressions at the
base of prickly pear cactus.

Reproduction: As with Wyoming's other jackrabbit, breeding starts in
late winter or early spring. About four (range one to eight) young are
born in a litter. Elsewhere, as many as four litters a year are born. Gestation is about 40–45 days. Young are born fully furred and able to move
about within a few hours. Nests are not used for long and are simple
depressions sometimes lined with fur. Young are weaned in 2 to 4 weeks,
and disperse at about 1 month of age. They reach adult size in about
2 months, but do not breed until the spring following their birth.

Habits: Black-tailed jackrabbits are active all year, and are usually active daily at sunset and early morning, foraging on open ground. During
the heat of a summer day, this hare rests in shade, sitting upright with
ears erect. When approached, it crouches in hiding and has caused some
near heart attacks when it erupts from underfoot undetected. As it escapes
in leaps and bounds, it will sometimes spring almost straight up
presumably to monitor its route and the cause of its disturbance.

Roadside vegetation also attracts this jackrabbit, and many are killed
by cars at night. While it grazes, it keeps it ears upright and follows any
sounds closely, pausing frequently. This hare is not territorial but lives
solitarily. Home ranges vary from 4 to 75 hectares. Higher densities up
to 100 per square kilometer that have been observed elsewhere that may
be short-term aggregations based on local patches of abundant food.

Food: Grasses and small forbs are preferred but virtually all green plants
are taken as available. During winter any exposed vegetation is taken,
including cactus, bark and buds of trees and shrubs.

Remarks: Black-tailed jackrabbits vary greatly in abundance over the
years. A wide variety of vertebrate predators take this hare. Many records
now available have increased its range of occurrence in Wyoming since
Long (1965) provided a map. Perhaps its range is expanding, as has been
noted in states to the east of Wyoming.

An adult least chipmunk *(Tamias minimus)*. Photograph by Dick Randall.

SQUIRRELS (FAMILY SCIURIDAE)
Least Chipmunk
Tamias minimus (Bachman)

Description: This is Wyoming's smallest chipmunk. It has multiple stripes down the back and the outermost dark one is quite distinct. The outermost side stripe is white. The underside of the body is usually white. The tail is carried straight up when this species runs.

Size: Adults may attain the following dimensions: total length 190–212 mm; tail 74–91 mm; hind foot 26–33 mm; ear 15–16 mm; weight 29–53 grams.

Range and Habitat: The least chipmunk occurs across Canada and in the
interior northern Rocky Mountains. In
Wyoming, it is found statewide. This
chipmunk lives in arid situations such
as sagebrush and dry rocky hillsides.
It inhabits more biotic communities
and has a greater altitudinal range
than other chipmunk species.

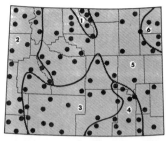

Representatives of six subspecies are found in the state: (1) *Tamias minimus confinis* (Howell) is in the Big Horn Mountains; (2) *Tamias minimus
consobrinus* J. A. Allen is in the western one-fifth and Wind River Mountains; (3) *Tamias minimus minimus* Bachman is in the Great Divide Basin
and Red Desert including all of Sweetwater County and southern Sublette
and Fremont Counties and north to Natrona County; (4) *Tamias minimus
operarius* (Merriam) is in the Sierra Madre and Medicine Bow Mountains; (5) *Tamias minimus pallidus* J. A. Allen is in Big Horn Basin south
to the Lander area and Powder River Basin and south including Platte,
Goshen, and Laramie counties; and (6) *Tamias minimus silvaticus* (White)
is in the Black Hills.

Reproduction: Breeding occurs in late March through mid-May. Gestation is about 29 days, and young are born in May or early June. Litters
average 5.5 (range three to nine). A single litter is produced annually
in Wyoming.

At birth, the newborns are blind, helpless, and devoid of fur. Their
weight is about 2 grams. Juvenile pelage is obtained by 40 days of age,
and weaning begins at that time. At 60 days of age, young chipmunks
are independent and nearly adult size.

Habits: This chipmunk ceases above-ground activity in winter. In areas
of deep, persistent snow cover, it hibernates. Social organization is partly
maintained through a series of "chirping" vocalizations. Home ranges
overlap considerably. Commonly, several chipmunks are seen foraging
close to one another. Least chipmunks frequently climb shrubs and trees.
Density of these chipmunks varies seasonally, but in late summer, highs
of 20 per hectare in quality habitat are common.

Food: Food is largely plant matter: green parts, roots, nuts, fruits, berries, and fungus. In addition, arthropods such as beetles, grasshoppers,
and caterpillars are consumed.

Remarks: Chief predators on chipmunks are long-tailed weasels, mink,
red foxes, marsh hawks, and red-tailed hawks.

An adult yellow-pine chipmunk *(Tamias amoenus)*. Photograph by Tim W. Clark.

Yellow-Pine Chipmunk
Tamias amoenus luteiventris J. A. Allen

Description: This chipmunk is similar to the least chipmunk, but the belly is usually buffy instead of white. The head is cinnamon mixed with smoke gray. The upper two facial stripes are black. The rump and thigh are gray.

Size: Adults may attain the following dimensions: total length 203–225 mm; tail 81–100 mm; hind foot 32–33 mm; ear 17–19 mm; weight 29–62 grams.

Range and Habitat: This species occurs in parts of northwestern United States. In Wyoming, it occurs in the mountains of western and northwestern counties. It is most abundant in aspen and lodgepole pine forests, especially where these forests are open and support a ground cover of shrubs and forbs. Occasionally, it occupies sage-

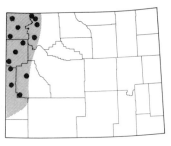

brush and open grass meadows, but always when these are near aspen or lodgepole pine.

Reproduction: A single litter of about five (range two to nine) is produced annually in May or June. Breeding occurs immediately after this chipmunk emerges from hibernation in March or April, depending on altitude. Gestation is 28 to 30 days. Early growth and development of young is similar that of *Tamius minimus.*

Habits: This chipmunk hibernates from about November to April. Yellow-pine chipmunks are diurnal in daily activity. Population density is controlled by territorial behavior of individual chipmunks, which spaces them about 20 meters apart, and by predation from long-tailed weasels, badgers, coyotes, goshawks, and kestrels. Mortality among young chipmunks during their first few weeks above ground is high. Annual survival is about 29 percent. Only 10 percent reach 3 years of age. Densities of 7–10 per hectare are reported.

Food: Foods consumed are mostly seeds, nuts, buds, roots and bulbs, and fungi. Insects such as larvae, grasshoppers, and beetles are also eaten.

Remarks: This species often lives in close association with least chipmunks, red squirrels, and golden-mantled ground squirrels. Competition may occur among these squirrels.

Cliff Chipmunk
Tamias dorsalis utahensis (Merriam)

Description: Cliff chipmunks are unique among Wyoming's small chipmunks in having a gray back with only indistinct dorsal stripes. Generally, the dorsal stripes are not visible at a distance. Cliff chipmunks have a long gray, bushy tail, a stocky body with short legs, white stripes on a pointed, brown face, a white underbelly and brown feet.

Size: Adults may attain the following dimensions: total length 208–240 mm; tail 81–110 mm; hind foot 30–33 mm; ear 17–21 mm; weight 55–90 grams.

Range and Habitat: Cliff chipmunks occur in the dry interior basins of Utah, Nevada, Arizona, New Mexico, and central Mexico. They live, as their name suggests, on rocky, steep hillsides. In Wyoming, cliff chipmunks were formerly abundant along the Green River north of the presently inundated Linwood, Utah. Cliff chipmunks are now restricted to an extremely small area of rock outcrops along the Flaming Gorge at Sage Creek (Belitsky 1981).

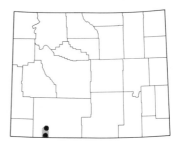

Reproduction: Cliff chipmunks copulate soon after emerging from hibernation in early March. Gestation of 28–31 days follows. Only one litter of four to six is born each year to adult females. Young are nursed about 30 days and they begin to leave their nest at that age. Nests are deep in crevices of cliffs. Adults probably live only 1 or 2 years in the wild.

Habits: Cliff chipmunks in Wyoming are not very well known. From limited observations in Utah, the following natural history sketch emerges. Cliff chipmunks hibernate from early winter to mid-May. They sometimes emerge when snow is still on the ground in spring. In Arizona, cliff chipmunks may be active all year. In Utah, they molt into a thick winter pelt. When active, they have been observed to forage in areas close to cliffs. Home ranges may be only 100 meters across. Cliff chipmunks climb trees and forage on the ground in clearings. Each night they return to sleep in nests deep in the cliff. Food is stored for use in the winter. Unlike other hibernators, cliff chipmunks do not live on body fat but rather wake up briefly to eat stored food. They appear to be relatively tolerant of other chipmunks. Social behavior, territoriality and ecology in their northern range are not well studied.

Food: Cliff chipmunks eat blossoms, stems and seeds of a wide variety of plants.

Remarks: Cliff chipmunks are prey for red-tailed hawks, badgers, rattlesnakes and long-tailed weasels. Although abundant elsewhere, these small mammals are rare in Wyoming due to habitat destruction by humans.

An adult uinta chipmunk *(Tamias umbrinus)*. Photograph by B. J. Bergstrom.

Uinta Chipmunk
Tamias umbrinus (J. A. Allen)

Description: The Uinta chipmunk's outermost stripe along its side is white and below the strips the fur is dark brown. On all other Wyoming chipmunks with stripes on their backs and sides, the outermost stripe is black. Underparts are white. Uinta chipmunks have long bushy tails, large heads with facial stripes, and their skull is longer than 34 mm.

Size: Adults may attain the following dimensions: total length 200–243 mm; tail 90–115 mm; hind foot 30–35 mm; ear 16–19 mm; weight 55–80 grams. Sexes do not differ in size.

Range and Habitat: Uinta chipmunks occur from California to Wyoming and northern Colorado in seven isolated populations. The three Wyoming populations probably have been separated for a long time and are considered distinct subspecies. *Tamias umbrinus umbrinus* J. A. Allen occurs from spruce-fir forests at about 2600 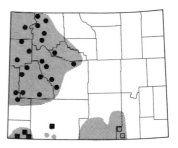 meters in the Uinta Mountains, along the upper Black's Fork, and east to the isolated mountains in southern Sweetwater County (squares). *Tamias umbrinus montanus* (White) (open squares) is most abundant in lodgepole pine to Douglas fir where the habitat has a closed tree canopy and open understory. However, it occurs in open rocky habitat from ponderosa pine to subalpine fir in the Medicine Bow and Sierra Madre Mountains, and perhaps north along the Laramie Range. *Tamias umbrinus fremonti* (White) (circles) lives in the northwestern mountains along edges of clearings in dense spruce-fir forests.

Reproduction: Uinta chipmunks probably mate as soon as they emerge from hibernation. Gestation is probably about 30 days and up to seven embryos are carried. On Togwotee Pass, lactation was observed from early to mid-July (Negus and Findley 1959). Probably only one litter is born each year by an adult female, and sexual maturity is probably reached the summer after birth. Reproductive studies of Wyoming's Uinta chipmunks are lacking.

Habits: Life history of Uinta chipmunks is poorly known. In Colorado, where they co-occur with least chipmunks, Uinta chipmunks use the open-canopy/closed-understory habitats avoided by least chipmunks (Telleen 1975). Female Uinta chipmunks defend a small area around their nest and otherwise there is only a linear dominance order and no territoriality (Gorden 1936). Uinta chipmunks are active only during the day. They climb frequently to feed on the tips of branches of conifers and brush. When alarmed, they flatten their body on larger branches. Before young emerge, Uinta chipmunks are solitary. They are probably partial hibernators, occasionally awaking to eat stored food. Hibernation dates are probably October to May but are not well known (Long and Cronkite 1970).

Food: Uinta chipmunks eat seeds of a wide variety of plants. When seeds are not available, buds and tender green shoots are consumed.

Remarks: The three subspecies of Wyoming Uinta chipmunks deserve careful study to determine their specific status. Interbreeding is clearly impossible because the arid, sage lowlands are effective barriers between isolated populations. These populations were perhaps isolated even during the open arctic grassland/tundra environment of the last glacial period 18,000–11,000 years ago (Walker 1983). At that time the boreal coniferous forests probably extended down along drainages well across these arid lowlands. As these forests receded and the arctic grasslands gradually became the arid sage-grasslands of today, Uinta chipmunks were left in isolated coniferous habitats.

An adult yellow-bellied marmot *(Marmota flaviventris)*. Photograph by Tim W. Clark.

Yellow-Bellied Marmot
Marmota flaviventris (Audubon and Bachman)

Description: Marmots are large, heavy-bodied rodents. The upper pelage is brown to yellowish, and the belly is yellow to orangish. Their fur is generally coarse. There is considerable variation in color and fur texture. The ears are small and well-furred, and the tail is relatively long.

Size: Adults may attain the following dimensions: total length 470–700 mm; tail 130–220 mm; hind foot 70–92 mm; ear 29–34 mm; weight 2.3–4.5 kilograms.

Range and Habitat: This marmot is widely distributed through western North America from British Columbia to Utah and northern New Mexico. Rock outcrops are an important habitat. Marmots occur at all altitudes from tundra to forest clearings to foothills, and to nearby plains.

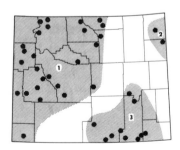

Three subspecies are recognized in Wyoming: (1) *Marmota flaviventris nosophora* A. H. Howell; (2) *Marmota flaviventris dacota* (Merriam); and (3) *Marmota flaviventris luteola* A. H. Howell.

Reproduction: Reproduction mostly occurs the first 2 weeks after emergence from hibernation. Gestation is about 30 days and litter sizes range from three to eight. Young weigh about 3 grams at birth. They stay in the nest burrow about 25 days, by which time they are weaned.

Habits: Marmots are colonial and live in complex tunnel systems. Burrows usually are located on well-drained slopes, and function as nurseries, shelters from inclement weather and predators, and as hibernacula. Colonies are typically comprised of a territorial adult male, several adult females, and their offspring. Peripheral habitats may be occupied by a single marmot or a pair. Hibernation lasts about 8 months, from early September until May. This indicates that about 60 percent of a marmot's time is spent underground. Daily activity is most frequent in the morning and late afternoon. Communication is mainly by sight and hearing, and sometimes by smell.

Food: Marmots are herbivorous, and eat a wide variety of foods, including grasses, flowers, and forbs.

Remarks: Overgrazing of meadows by domestic livestock may adversely affect marmot survival. Coyotes, badgers, bobcats, owls, eagles, and hawks all prey on marmots. In Wyoming, marmots are often called "rock chucks," or woodchucks. The true woodchuck is a distinct, but related species, living in the eastern half of the United States.

An adult Wyoming ground squirrel *(Spermophilus elegans)*. Photograph by Dick Randall.

Wyoming Ground Squirrel
Spermophilus elegans elegans Kennicott

Description: This ground squirrel is a medium sized rodent with buff brownish sides. The nose is cinnamon, and the underside of the tail is buff. This ground squirrel closely resembles the Uinta ground squirrel.

Size: Adults may attain the following dimensions: total length 243–337 mm; tail 65–100 mm; hind foot 34–49 mm; ear 11–18 mm; weight 210–315 grams.

Range and Habitat: This species' range is centered in Wyoming, but it occurs elsewhere. There are three subspecies of Wyoming ground squirrels: *Spermophilus elegans elegans* Kennicott occurs throughout southern Wyoming and south to parts of Colorado; *Spermophilus elegans nevadensis* (Howell) occurs in Nevada; and 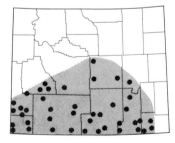 *Spermophilus elegans aureau* (Davis) is found in Idaho and Montana. Wyoming ground squirrels live in open habitats, from sage grasslands to alpine meadows.

Reproduction: Females pass through a well-defined cycle of seasonal changes in reproductive organs similar to those in other ground squirrels. Breeding begins in late March and ends in mid-April. The number of embryos that females carry range from four to nine. Juveniles emerge from their nest burrows by June (Clark 1970a).

Early growth, development, and behavior of young Wyoming ground squirrels is well known (Clark 1970b). At two days after birth, young are reddish in color, their ears are evidenced only by slight irregularities in the skins, and they emit audible squeaks. Weight is about 5.9 grams and their total length is 53 mm at this time. At two weeks of age, the hair at the base of the nose has the characteristic adult rust-reddish color. Teeth begin to erupt at 21 days. At four weeks, young have adult coloration. At five weeks, young are passing dark fecal pellets, apparently indicating a change from milk to a solid diet at the time of weaning. At this time, they begin appearing above ground.

Habits: This small mammal has been well studied in the Laramie Basin. It is completely diurnal. Patterns in daily activity are dependent on prevailing weather. On cool days, it may be active all day, but in hot weather the Wyoming ground squirrel is active only in morning and late afternoon.

Wyoming ground squirrels emerge from hibernation over a three week period beginning in early March. By early July, squirrels begin disappearing below ground. By mid-September, all squirrels are in hibernation.

Home ranges average 2 to 4 hectares. Densities are one squirrel per 5 hectares in June. Individual squirrels group together in areas of high quality habitat. Hawk, badger, and eagle predation eliminates some of them.

Food: Plant material comprises 73 percent of the total diet, animal tissue 14 percent, seed fragments 11 percent, and arthropods 1 percent. Grashoppers, beetles, flies, and bees are all eaten (Clark 1968).

Remarks: This species was, until recently, classed as a subspecies of the Richardson's ground squirrel, *Spermophilus richardsonii* (Sabine), which occurs from western Montana to Minnesota.

An adult Uinta ground squirrel *(Spermophilus armatus)*. Photograph by Tim W. Clark.

Uinta Ground Squirrel
Spermophilus armatus Kennicott

Description: Uinta ground squirrels are similar in size and body configuration to Wyoming ground squirrels. Pelage is usually darker and the underside of the tail is gray. The rusty-cinnamon nose and shoulder, blending into a finely spotted, gray back and rump, are distinctive.

Size: Adults may attain the following dimensions: total length 280–303 mm; tail 63–81 mm; hind foot 42–45 mm; ear 11–16 mm; weight 196–295 grams.

Range and Habitat: This species' range centers in western Wyoming, Idaho, and Utah. In Wyoming, it occupies the western one-fifth of the state. Habitats include grasslands, meadows, sage grasslands, open areas in forests, and tundras. In areas of sympatry with the Wyoming ground squirrel, the Uinta ground squirrel uses sites at higher elevations.

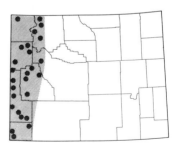

Reproduction: Reproductive patterns are similar to those of the Wyoming ground squirrel. A single litter is produced annually. Breeding occurs within 30 days after squirrels emerge from hibernation in April. Gestation is about 28 days. Litters range from six to eight. Young develop at rates similar to the Wyoming ground squirrel.

Habits: This species hibernates up to 6 months each year (late September to late March). Patterns of daily activity vary depending on temperatures. Population characteristics are similar to the Wyoming ground squirrel. Densities may become quite high (5 per hectare) in favorable meadow habitats or in alfalfa fields. Burrow systems were described by Stromberg (1975).

Uinta ground squirrels are found in aggregations where habitat quality permits high densities. Conflict or agonistic behavior, as a means of social regulation, was studied in this species in Jackson Hole. Since this species is diurnal, a large part of agonistic behavior is based on visual exchanges of information between potential opponents (Clark and Russell 1977). This study found that the complex sequence of agonistic behavior patterns served to establish or reinforce social dominance relationships with a minimum of physical contact. Balph (1984) summarized much of what is known of the social behavior of this squirrel, including how territorial females tend their "gardens" to help their young.

Food: Uinta ground squirrels consume a wide variety of food plants: grasses, forbs, shrubs, and mushrooms. Insects are also eaten. This species frequently eats carrion, and commonly can be observed eating other Uinta ground squirrels killed on highways.

Remarks: Uinta ground squirrels live up to 2 years in the wild. Usually 80 percent of the babies born each year die within twelve months. Hawks, eagles, badgers, coyotes, and long-tailed weasels are their chief predators.

An adult thirteen-lined ground squirrel *(Spermophilus tridecemlineatus)*. Photograph by J. Knox Jones, Jr.

Thirteen-Lined Ground Squirrel
Spermophilus tridecemlineatus (Mitchell)

Description: This small ground squirrel may be identified by a series of alternating dark (brownish or blackish) and light longitudinal stripes on its back with a row of nearly square white spots in each of the dark stripes. Pelage is yellowish-brown above and yellowish below. The ears are small and the eyes are large.

Size: Adults may attain the following dimensions: total length 170–297 mm; tail 60–132 mm; hind foot 27–41 mm; ear 27–41 mm; weight 135–190 grams.

Range and Habitat: This ground squirrel occurs throughout most of the central United States. In Wyoming, it occurs in grasslands and desert-grasslands, except in the western one-fifth. Four Wyoming subspecies are recognized: *Spermophilus tridecemlineatus alleni* Merriam (solid squares) occurs in the Big Horn Mountains; *Spermophilus tridecemlineatus olivaceus* J. A. Allen (triangles) occurs in the Black Hills; *Spermophilus tridecemlineatus pallidus* J. A. Allen (solid circles) occurs on the eastern prairies; and *Spermophilus tridecemlineatus parvus* J. A. Allen (open circles) occurs in the Wyoming Basin.

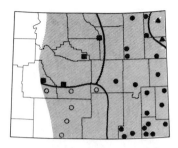

Reproduction: Both sexes are ready to copulate soon after they emerge from hibernation in late March or early April (Clark 1971). Breeding occurs over the following 6 weeks. A single litter is produced annually (average 7.5, range 1 to 10) after a gestation of 28 days. Young are born blind and helpless. Their eyes open about 21 to 31 days after birth, and they first emerge above ground in June. Adult coloration is attained during this period. Weaning is complete by the 28th day. Adult body weight is attained by 11 weeks.

Habits: Grasslands are the preferred habitat. This species hibernates from about September to March, and some estivation may occur also. Even though thirteen-lined ground squirrels occur in groups, this grouping results from use of habitat patches and not from sociality. These aggregations are mainly groups of solitary squirrels. In the Laramie Basin, densities of 0.24 to 0.35 squirrels per hectare are common (Clark 1981), but they are reported elsewhere at densities of 18/hectare.

Food: This species is highly carnivorous, eating many insects and occasionally birds, young cottontails, lizards, and snakes. Grass and seeds make up the remainder of its diet.

Remarks: The subspecies in the Big Horn Basin area is considered rare, if not extirpated, because of repeated, widespread distribution of poisoned grain by humans.

An adult spotted ground squirrel *(Spermophilus spilosoma)*. Photograph by Donald P. Streubel.

Spotted Ground Squirrel
Spermophilus spilosoma obsoletus Kennicott

Description: This ground squirrel's upper pelage is smoky gray or wood brown. Characteristic squarish whitish spots are scattered on the back. Underparts are whitish.

Size: Adults may attain the following dimensions: total length 185–253 mm; tail 55–92 mm; hind foot 28–37 mm; ear 6–8 mm; weight 166–195 grams.

Range and Habitat: Spotted ground squirrels are found from South Dakota south to central Mexico in short grass prairies and desert grasslands. In Wyoming, they are found only on the High Plains of the southeastern part of the state. They prefer deep sandy soils and little vegetation. They inhabit sand dunes, yucca-grass, and sage-grass communities.

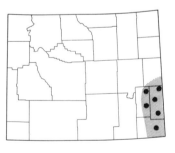

Reproduction: Breeding begins in mid-April, 2 to 3 weeks after emergence from hibernation. Most males are capable of breeding through June. Females are pregnant between early May and late July. Gestation is probably about 27 days. Litter sizes average 6.6 (range 4 to 12). Young are pink at birth, grow rapidly, and emerge above ground when 40 to 50 grams in weight.

Habits: Foraging and feeding behavior comprise about 66 percent of all above-ground activity, and alert behavior 15 percent. Daily activity varies with local weather and season. On hot days, these mammals are active in the mornings and evenings, and on days cooler than 33 °C, they may be active all day.

Home ranges during the breeding season average 1.5 hectare per female. After litters emerge from the nest burrow, they range from 0.50 to 0.52 hectares. Both male and female home ranges averaged 1.5 hectares (Streubel and Fitzgerald 1978).

Population densities of 2 to 7 per hectare have been reported. Hibernation is incomplete and begins in September. Estivation may occur in hot summer months.

Food: Spotted ground squirrels eat seeds and green plant parts, but eat some meat. Forbs are utilized heavily.

Remarks: Bull snakes are the major predator, but red-tailed hawks and carnivores also prey on this species. Other than the single study by Maxell and Brown (1968), little is known of the status or ecology of this species in Wyoming.

An adult golden-mantled ground squirrel *(Spermophilus lateralis)*. Photograph by Tim W. Clark.

Golden-Mantled Ground Squirrel
Spermophilus lateralis (Say)

Description: Golden-mantled ground squirrels are medium-sized with a single white stripe bordered by black down each side. They are often mistaken for large chipmunks. The golden-mantled ground squirrel has no stripes on the sides of its head as do chipmunks. The head and shoulders are often a deep reddish brown so that they appear to be wearing a "mantle."

Size: Adults may attain the following dimensions: total length 230–308 mm; tail 63–118 mm; hind foot 35–46 mm; ear 11–16 mm; weight 210–315 grams.

Range and Habitat: Golden-mantled ground squirrels occur throughout favorable habitats in the northwestern United States. They are found in southern and western Wyoming. Rocky outcrops are a key habitat feature. Open areas such as lowland meadows, openings in coniferous forests, and tundra are also used.

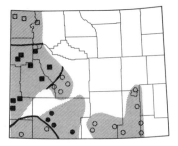

Four subspecies are recognized in the state: *Spermophilus lateralis castanurus* (Merriam) (solid squares) in western Wyoming south of Yellowstone and north of the Uinta Mountains; *Spermophilus lateralis cinerascens* (Merriam) (open squares) in the Yellowstone Plateau; *Spermophilus lateralis lateralis* (Say) (open circles) has three populations, one in the Uinta Mountains, a relict in the Wind River Mountains, and a third in the Sierra Madre and Medicine Bow Mountains; and *Spermophilus lateralis wortmani* (J. A. Allen) (solid circles) in the Green River Basin.

Reproduction: Breeding occurs in golden-mantled ground squirrels just after they emerge from hibernation each spring. Gestation is about 27 days. Two to eight young are produced in a single litter annually. Birth in Wyoming occurred between 28 May and 2 June for four pregnant females from the Laramie Mountains. Early growth and development of young shows that newborn are 6 grams at birth (2.8 percent of adult size) and about 61 mm long. By 77 days after birth, young are 90 percent of adult size.

Habits: This species may occur in small isolated colonies or as isolated individuals. Hibernation occurs from mid-fall (depending on altitude) until about April (or even May in some cases). Little is known of population dynamics. Home ranges vary from 4 to 12 hectares depending on habitat quality.

Food: Golden-mantled ground squirrels eat a wide variety of foods. Although they consume vegetation primarily, they do eat bird eggs, insects, and carrion. Plant matter consists of leaves, buds, seeds, nuts, roots, bulbs, and fruits, as well as mushrooms.

Remarks: Predators include long-tailed weasels, badgers, coyotes, hawks, and eagles. The maximum longevity is 5 years.

An adult black-tailed prairie dog *(Cynomys ludovicianus).* Photograph by E. R. Kalmbach.

Black-Tailed Prairie Dog
Cynomys ludovicianus ludovicianus (Ord)

Description: This prairie dog is a robust, stocky rodent with short legs. It is distinguished by its black-tipped tail. The overall pelage is pale brownish with a grizzled appearance. The ears are small.

Size: Adults may attain the following dimensions: total length 312–410 mm; tail 72–99 mm; hind foot 50–67 mm; ear 8–14 mm ; weight 680–1500 grams.

108

Range and Habitat: Black-tailed prairie dogs formerly lived throughout the Great Plains. In Wyoming, they now occur as isolated populations in the eastern half of the state. Black-tailed prairie dogs have probably been reduced by over 80 percent of their pre-settlement numbers (Campbell and Clark 1981). They are most abundant in overgrazed shortgrass prairies.

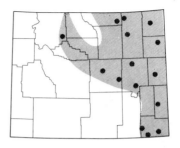

Habits: This species forms dense, large colonies, which historically covered tens of thousands of hectares. The city of Cheyenne, Wyoming, is built on a poisoned-out prairie dog town. Often this animal is arbitrarily considered a pest and destroyed. Black-tailed prairie dogs may have the most complex social organization of all rodents. Colonies are organized into "coteries" made up of 2 to 40 members. Coterie members will defend their group territory against intrusion by members of adjacent coteries. Their complex vocal and postural communication system is an effective mechanism in avoiding predation. They are active above ground year round, and have color vision. Individuals may live up to 5 years. There are about 10 burrow entrances per adult prairie dog in a colony. The burrows are scattered over the colony area, which often has distinct boundaries.

Reproduction: Copulation may occur from early March to early April. A single litter is produced annually after a gestation period of 28 to 32 days. Litters average five (range 2 to 10). Young are born with eyes and ears closed. After about 40 days, young emerge above ground and begin eating green vegetation. At this time, they are about one-fourth adult size. After 90 days, they are nearly full grown.

Food: Prairie dogs eat a variety of grasses, forbs, and shrubs as well as an occasional insect. Koford (1958) summarized food habits, and noted that, in many cases, prairie dogs preferred to eat plant species other than those consumed by livestock.

Remarks: Prairie dogs may modify the vegetation of their colonies so that the forage quality is improved, and native grazers (bison, in particular) may spend up to 90 percent of their time foraging on these colonies (Coppock et al. 1983a,b).

Adult white-tailed prairie dogs *(Cynomys leucurus)*. Photograph by Tim W. Clark.

White-Tailed Prairie Dog
Cynomys leucurus Merriam

Description: White-tailed prairie dogs, like their black-tailed cousins, are about the size of house cats. They have robust bodies with short, stout legs. Upper body parts are yellowish buff streaked with black. A dark black-brown patch extends from above the eye to a large area on the cheek. The tail is white-tipped.

Size: Adults may attain the following dimensions: total length 340–370 mm; tail 40–65 mm; hind foot 60–65 mm; ear 8–14 mm; weight 650–1130 grams.

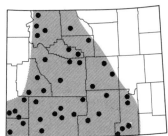

Range and Habitat: White-tailed prairie dogs occur in parts of Colorado, Utah, Wyoming, and Montana. In Wyoming, they live in the western one-half of the state. This prairie dog occupies grass, shrub-grass, and desert-grass communities.

Reproduction: The reproductive biology of white-tailed prairie dogs has been extensively investigated. Copulation occurs in late March and early April. Gestation lasts about 30 days. Parturition occurs in late April and early May, and a single litter of five (range one to eight) is produced annually. Nothing is known of the growth and development of young prior to their first appearance above ground in late May or early June. Clark (1977) described early growth and develpoment once pups have emerged. At 120 days of age, females consistently attain adult body weight more rapidly than males.

Habits: Colonies of this prairie dog may reach several hundred hectares in size, although they are usually much smaller. Burrow openings are usually low in density (fewer than 15 per hectare). Range relationships were reviewed by Clark et al. (1971). The white-tailed prairie dog is not the severe range pest as was once thought. These mammals aid in soil formation, in controlling insect eruptions, and they produce beneficial modifications to the plains landscape for other vertebrates (Clark et al. 1982).

The mean density of white-tailed prairie dogs is 3.2 per hectare (range 0.7–6.2), but this average fluctuates widely throughout the year and between years.

Immigration occurs chiefly in the spring, and movements of 2.7 km have been recorded. Mortality and emigration in combination account for the loss of over 50 percent of the young of each year.

Home ranges average about 6 hectares for adults in the Laramie Plains but may vary elsewhere. Prairie dogs hibernate from 30 to 120 days each winter depending on elevation and other factors.

Food: These rodents feed mainly on annual forbs and other plants which tolerate repeated long-term grazing. Green plant parts, seeds, roots, flowers, insects, and carrion are all consumed.

Remarks: More than 140 vertebrate species have been noted to utilize prairie dog colonies (Clark et al. 1982). These colonies are the focus for many species, especially predators such as hawks, owls, eagles, badgers, long-tailed weasels, skunks, foxes, and coyotes.

An adult fox squirrel *(Sciurus niger)*. Photograph by Tim W. Clark.

Fox Squirrel
Sciurus niger rufiventer E. Geoffroy St.-Hilaire

Description: This tree squirrel is larger than other tree squirrels, has rounded ears without an ear tuft, and has a large fluffy tail. Its color is usually reddish black to light brown above, and bright to dull rufous or light gray to dusty white below. The tail is mixed tawny rufous and black.

Size: Adults may attain the following dimensions: total length 454–698 mm; tail 200–330 mm; hind foot 51–82 mm; ear 27–32 mm; weight 696–1233 grams.

Range and Habitat: Fox squirrels occur throughout the eastern one half of the United States. In Wyoming, they occur in the cities of Cheyenne and Laramie, in the Black Hills region along certain streams, and at a few other sites. They reach a western limit of their range in Wyoming. Fox squirrels require deciduous trees, in 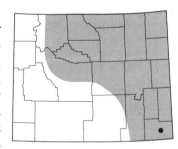 Wyoming especially elms, cottonwoods, and willows.

112

Reproduction: Breeding begins towards the end of December. Females come into estrus in early January and again in June. Gestation is about 44 days. Most births occur in mid-March and July. Litter sizes average about 2.8. Newborns weigh about 15 grams and are 50 to 60 mm long. Their color is pink, and their ears and eyes are closed. Development is slow compared to other rodents. After 4 to 5 weeks, their eyes open; the ears open at 6 weeks. Sexual maturity is attained at 10 to 11 months.

Habits: Fox squirrels are noticeably more active in September and October than in other months. During this period, young become independent from adults, and all are burying nuts and other food for later winter use. Some squirrels disperse over 64 kilometers. Home range sizes vary, but generally range from 0.4 to 16 hectares. Elsewhere effect of good or poor seed crops is reflected in the following year's reproductive success. Densities range from 0.5 to 3.5 per hectare. Leaf nests up to 0.3 meters in diameter are constructed.

Food: Buds of ornamental trees are the staple food. Their caloric content is high. This squirrel eats also the nuts and seeds of other trees, as well as corn. It is opportunistic and readily eats new foods.

Remarks: Many of the fox squirrels in Wyoming are descended from individuals introduced into cities by humans.

Abert's Squirrel
Sciurus aberti ferreus True

Description: Long ears, with a tassel or tuft of hairs as long as the ears, distinguishes Abert's squirrels. The unusually broad tail is relatively short. Upper pelage is black to gray, and underparts of the tail and body are gray with flecks of white.

Size: Adults may attain the following dimensions: total length 463–584 mm; tail 195–255 mm; hind foot 65–80 mm; ear 37–50 mm; weight 450–490 grams.

Range and Habitat: Abert's squirrel is associated with Ponderosa pine in the southwestern United States at elevations ranging from 1800 to 3000 meters. In Wyoming, it occurs only in the rocky Ponderosa pine grassland community near Harriman.

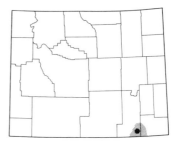

Reproduction: Little is known about this species' reproductive biology. Mating chases, in which one or more males chase a female in estrus for up to eleven hours before copulation, may occur. Young (three to five per litter) are born in April or May after a gestation of about 40 days. Young are born naked, pink, with their eyes and ears closed. Weight at birth is about 12 grams.

Habits: Nests are typically built on Ponderosa pine branches from 5 to 27 meters above the ground. The nests, from 0.3 to 1 meter in diameter, are comprised of twigs that are less than 13 mm in diameter and 0.2 to 0.6 meters in length. They may have up to three openings. Sign of Abert's squirrel activity includes extensive clipping of needle bundles often found in large piles beneath favorite trees. Tree density, tree diameter, and a grouped distribution of trees are key factors in site selection for nest construction. This squirrel is totally diurnal. Home ranges in Arizona averaged 7.3 hectares (range 4 to 10 ha) in summer and autumn and 2.0 hectares in winter (Keith 1965). Abert's squirrels are active all year and only stay in nests if it is colder than − 10 °C. On sunny winter days they bask in the sun. During summer, the tail is used as a shade (Golightly and Omhart 1978). Population fluctuations are common. Densities of 30 per square kilometer are known, but 1–5 per square kilometer also occur.

Food: Abert's squirrel uses ponderosa pine as an exclusive food source during the entire year. Many parts are eaten — inner bark, twigs, seeds, terminal buds, and flowers. Trees with minimal turpentine (monoturpene) compounds are selectively chosen for food. They also eat fungi, carrion, antlers, and bones. Food is not stored and Abert's squirrels forage all winter, sometimes during snowstorms.

Remarks: Little is known of the ecology of this species in Wyoming. Because individuals tend to select only a few trees in an area, damage to a healthy stand of pine trees is negligible.

An adult red squirrel *(Tamiasciurus hudsonicus)*. Photograph by R. B. Fischer.

Red Squirrel
Tamiasciurus hudsonicus (Erxleben)

Description: This small tree squirrel is distinctly brownish red with white underparts, and has a pronounced lateral black stripe separating the white belly from darker upper colors. There is a slight ear tuft. White eye rings are common. The tail is smaller and flatter in proportion to body size than other tree squirrels.

Size: Adults may attain the following dimensions: total length 270–385 mm; tail 95–158 mm; hind foot 35–57 mm; weight 145–260 grams.

Range and Habitat: Red squirrels occur across northern Canada, south along the Rocky Mountains to New Mexico in the upper midwest, and also south in the Appalachian Mountains in the east. They are found throughout Wyoming's conifer-covered mountains. Four subspecies are recognized in Wyoming: (1) *Tamiasciurus hudsonicus*

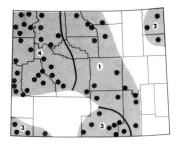

116

baileyi (J. A. Allen); (2) *Tamiasciurus hudsonicus dakotensis;* (3) *Tamiasciurus hudsonicus fremonti* (Audubon and Bachman); and (4) *Tamiasciurus hudsonicus ventorum* (J. A. Allen).

Reproduction: A single litter is produced annually between March and May. Estrous females allow males in adjacent territories to approach them. Receptivity lasts a single day. After fertilization, the females become territorial again against all other squirrels. One to 10 young (average 3.5) are born after about 36 days of gestation. Young are born pink and hairless, with ears and eyes closed. Development is slow. Weaning occurs 9 to 11 weeks after birth.

Habits: Unlike many tree squirrels, red squirrels defend territories of 1 to 2 hectares against others of their kind. Aggressive "chatter" barks are common. This species is quite vocal. It produces leaf nests or uses dens in trees, and stores food in one or more large caches, called middens (up to 0.6 m high and 2 m in diameter). During long winters with deep snow fall, this squirrel digs extensive tunnels under the snow to its middens. In snow-free areas, it uses trees frequently in winter. About 5 percent of all squirrels live more than 5 years (one in captivity lived 9 years). Mortality is highest in the first and second years. The average annual mortality is about 67 percent. Predation is considered an insignificant cause of death. In Wyoming, the American marten *(Martes americana),* often considered a major predator on red squirrels, actually takes very few of them as prey.

Food: Red squirrels eat evergreen terminal buds and seeds (pines, spruces, and firs). Fungi are also consumed. Insects, old bones, and occasionally small birds are eaten.

Remarks: This highly visible and vocal squirrel is one of the most often seen forest mammals. It is abundant throughout Wyoming's forests.

An adult northern flying squirrel *(Glaucomys sabrinus)*. Photograph by Tim W. Clark.

Northern Flying Squirrel
Glaucomys sabrinus bangsi (Rhoads)

Description: The flying squirrel is readily identified by the large furred skin folds between its legs along each side of its body. Pelage is a soft gray. It is somewhat smaller than the red squirrel, but has large eyes.

Size: Adults may attain the following dimensions: total length 290–315 mm; tail 129–142 mm; hind foot 36–46 mm; ear 16–29 mm; weight 105–170 grams.

Range and Habitat: This species occurs across northern Canada and south in the California coastal ranges, the Rocky Mountains, and the Appalachians. In Wyoming, it occurs throughout the conifer-covered mountains in the northwest. Isolated populations occur in the Black Hills and in Sweetwater County. However, this squirrel seldom is seen because it is nocturnal.

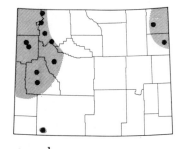

Reproduction: Both cavity nests and leaf nests are used, but cavity nests are preferred. Breeding occurs from late March through May, and a single litter is produced annually. Gestation is 37 to 42 days. About four young are produced (range two to six). At birth, young weigh about 5 grams and are blind and hairless. After about 90 days, they are gradually weaned and take their first "flights." By 120 days, they are adult size. Young become sexually mature in their second year of life.

Habits: Flying squirrels are known to be gregarious and winter aggregations of up to 20 squirrels are known. Overall, little is known of their social structure. Home ranges my be up to 15 to 20 hectares. Population dynamics are unknown. Owls, weasels, and American marten are the chief predators.

Food: This species forages both in trees and on the ground. Lichens and fungi are major food items. In addition, cones of conifers, fruits, buds, arthropods, eggs, and nestling birds are eaten.

Remarks: Flying squirrels can be located in the woods at night by pausing and carefully listening for gliding squirrels as they contact trees and then scurry up them. Once located on moonlit nights, squirrels can be glimpsed gliding overhead by looking skyward.

An adult northern pocket gopher *(Thomomys talpoides).* Photograph by W. Hadley.

POCKET GOPHERS (FAMILY GEOMYIDAE)
Northern Pocket Gopher
Thomomys talpoides (Richardson)

Description: Northern pocket gophers are medium-sized rodents with small eyes, small ears and stout, strong-clawed front feet, which are specialized for digging. The fur is soft and smooth and is brown to yellow-tan. Incisors are smooth on the anterior surface and, like pocket mice (which are much smaller) pocket gophers have fur-lined cheek pouches that open into the mouth. Pocket gophers are specialized for subterranean life.

Size: Adults may grow to the following dimensions: total length 165–253 mm; tail 40–75 mm; hind foot 25–33 mm; ear 5–6 mm; weight 75–180 grams. Females are slightly smaller than males.

Range and Habitat: Northern pocket gophers live throughout the interior of western North America and occur throughout Wyoming. Their habitat includes virtually all vegetation types with loose soil.

Pocket gophers show an astounding degree of local variation. Most of the ten Wyoming subspecies of *Thomomys*

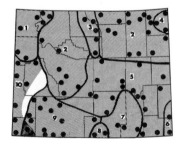

120

talpoides have 48 chromosomes, but are distinct morphologically. These subspecies probably intergrade and overlap widely; two are probably distinct species yet to be described (Charles Thaeler, pers. comm.). Boundaries of the subspecies ranges are arbitrarily drawn and often each subspecies occupies many different habitats. A great deal of work needs to be done on the Wyoming populations of this pocket gopher to clarify both species and subspecies relationships. In Wyoming, *Thomomys talpoides tenellus* Goldman (1) occurs in the Yellowstone area. *Thomomys talpoides bullatus* Bailey (2) in the Absarokas, Bighorn Basin, and Powder River basin; *Thomomys talpoides caryi* V. Bailey (3) in the Bighorn Mountains; *Thomomys talpoides nebulosus* V. Bailey (4) in the Black Hills; *Thomomys talpoides attenuatus* Hall and Montague (5) in the eastern shortgrass prairie counties westward to the shrub-grasslands of Natrona, western Carbon, and eastern Sweetwater counties; *Thomomys talpoides cheyennensis* Swenk (6) in eastern Laramie and southeastern Goshen counties; *Thomomys talpoides rostralis* Hall and Montague (7) in the Laramie and Medicine Bow ranges; *Thomomys talpoides meritus* Hall (8) in the Sierra Madre Range; *Thomomys talpoides ocius* Merriam (9) in Sweetwater, eastern Uinta and Lincoln counties; and *Thomomys talpoides bridgeri* Merriam (10) in western Uinta and Lincoln counties. Long (1965) discussed the differences in pelage and skull characters between subspecies.

Reproduction: Northern pocket gophers breed in spring, from March to April and pregnant females have been taken in Wyoming from May in Sweetwater County to early July in the Black Hills. About four (3–10) young are born in a single litter each year. Young are kept in a maternal burrow and disperse by early June (Sweetwater County). Juveniles reach adult size in about 3 months and do not breed until the spring following their birth. Most pocket gophers live 18 months, but some may live up to 5 years.

Habits: Northern Pocket gophers are solitary. They spend their entire lives underground, emerging only briefly to cut forbs at the opening of their burrows and then pull these cuttings below. Burrow systems are elaborate and extensive and are marked by mounds of earth shoved out along a ramp so the mounds are not conical. All burrow entrances are kept plugged with soil. Excavated soil is shoved out an inclined lateral tunnel.

Pocket gophers do not hibernate. They are active all winter, eating food previously stored underground, and do not require drinking water. During the winter, these gophers build tunnels on the ground surface under snow. Casts of these dirt-lined tunnels or sections where these tunnels are filled with soil excavated from elsewhere remain after snowmelt as evidence of pocket gopher activity.

Food: Forbs and herbs make up most of the diet. These include small aspen, cacti, a wide variety of meadow forbs, and grasses. Pocket gophers feed underground in shallow tunnels where they chew on roots and occasionally pull plants below. Food is cached in deeper burrow chambers.

Remarks: Pocket gophers are preyed on by badgers and other predators capable of digging. These gophers are important in soil development adding organic matter, aerating soil and promoting water storage in soil during runoff in spring.

Wyoming Pocket Gopher
Thomomys clusius Thaeler

Description: The Wyoming pocket gopher is smaller and paler than the sympatric large, dark *Thomomys talpoides ocius.* The former has 46 chromosomes and the latter has 56 chromosomes. The hind foot of the Wyoming pocket gopher varies from 20–22 mm whereas the other pocket gophers in the geographic range of the Wyoming pocket gopher have hind feet that vary from 23–30 mm. This is the only species of mammal that occurs exclusively in Wyoming.

Size: Adults may attain the following dimensions: total length 161–184 mm; tail 50–70 mm; hind foot 20–22 mm; ear 5–6 mm; weight 44–72 grams. There is no significant difference in size between the sexes.

Range and Habitat: The Wyoming pocket gopher is limited to southeastern Sweetwater County and southwestern Carbon County. Populations in Carbon County are known only from Bridger's Pass but may occur elsewhere. This gopher is an upland species, preferring the drier ridge tops, often associated with gravelly loose soils and greasewood.

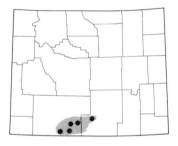

Reproduction: No studies have been made of reproduction of the Wyoming pocket gopher; it probably is similar to that of the northern pocket gopher.

Habits: Behavioral studies have not been made of the Wyoming pocket gopher. However, its burrows resemble those of the northern pocket gopher. Only one individual lives in each burrow system (C. Thaeler, pers. comm.), which suggests a solitary life style.

Food: No one has studied the diet of the Wyoming pocket gopher. The roots and shoots of forbs and grasses probably are eaten.

Remarks: Only 43 specimens are known of this species. Additional collection may increase the limits of its known range. This species may be abundant within its range.

Idaho Pocket Gopher
Thomomys idahoensis pygmaeus (Merriam)

Description: Idaho pocket gophers are extremely small with yellowish to dark brown fur. Other gophers in the same region include *Thomomys talpoides bridgeri,* which is much larger (hind foot 29–33 mm), and *Thomomys talpoides ocius,* which is larger (hind foot 23–30 mm), has small blackish patches around the ears, and has grayish cheeks and sides that contrast with the pale brown of the mid-dorsal fur. Idaho pocket gophers lack ear patches and contrasting cheeks, and are uniformly colored dorsally.

Size: Adults may attain the following dimensions: total length 167–203 mm; tail 50–70 mm; hind foot 21–22 mm; ear 5–6 mm; weight 46–63 grams. Females are slightly smaller than males.

Range and Habitat: The Idaho pocket gopher occurs from central Idaho through southern and western Montana, and in a separate area of southwestern Wyoming and adjacent Utah. This pocket gopher occurs in shallow, stony soils whereas the sympatric *Thomomys talpoides bridgeri* selects deeper soils with relatively few rocks 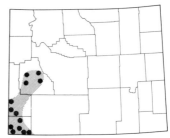 and stones. *Thomomys talpoides ocius* has been collected within 2 meters of the Idaho pocket gopher near Fort Bridger.

Reproduction: Studies of the reproduction of this gopher are lacking; presumably its reproductive biology resembles that of the northern pocket gopher.

Habits: Life history studies of this mammal are not available. Burrows systems appear to be solitarily occupied. In general, the natural history of the Idaho pocket gopher probably resembles that of the northern pocket gopher.

Food: Forbs and grasses are probably the main diet of this gopher.

Remarks: The area near Fort Bridger offers a remarkable opportunity to study three species of pocket gophers living almost side by side. Since different species of this mammal virtually never occupy the same geographic area, the situation is ripe for a comparative study of ecological coexistence and natural history.

An adult plains pocket gopher *(Geomys lutescens)*.

Plains Pocket Gopher
Geomys lutescens lutescens Merriam

Description: Distinctive parallel grooves on the front surface of its protruding incisor teeth separate this gopher from other pocket gophers in Wyoming. Like other pocket gophers, it is compact, has small eyes and small ears, and large, strong claws on the massive front feet. The tail is nearly naked, but elsewhere fur is a dense, glossy brown. A fur-lined pouch extends backward from the cheeks to the shoulders.

Size: Adults may attain the following dimensions: total length 255–355 mm; tail 55–105 mm; hind foot 27–43 mm; ear 4–9 mm; weight 170–300 grams. Females are about 20 percent smaller than males.

Range and Habitat: The plains pocket gopher occurs on the Great Plains of the central United States, and is found in the eastern one-fifth of Wyoming. It prefers deep sandy soils in treeless prairie.

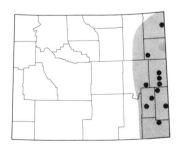

Reproduction: Plains pocket gophers enter breeding condition from February to April. Gestation is thought to be about 50 days and from one to six (usually four) young are born in a litter annually. Young are naked and poorly developed; in 5 weeks, eyes and cheek pouches open, and by 6 or 7 weeks they are weaned. When half grown, they disperse and begin to build a new tunnel system. Young do not breed until the late winter or spring following their birth.

Habits: Like other pocket gophers, this gopher rarely ventures above ground. It lives solitarily in elaborate, roughly linear burrow systems complete with separate chambers for resting, food storage, and defecation. These chambers are below the frost depth of the soil. Sloping tunnels lead to the surface where spoil piles of excavated dirt are shoved out into variously shaped loose heaps. Burrow entrances are kept closed.

Plains pocket gophers forage on roots and underground stems by burrowing shallow tunnels. Green food may be pulled under. Cheek pouches are used to move food to storage chambers. This gopher may be active at night above ground within a few meters of a burrow entrance. Plains pocket gophers do not hibernate and are active both day and night in their burrows. They can move forward or backward in their burrow equally well. When moving backward, the tail is used as a guiding tactile organ.

Food: Grasses, herbs, roots, and undergound parts of plants are eaten. This pocket gopher is often found near watercourses or where abundant green vegetation is available in friable soils, such as hayfields.

Remarks: Plains pocket gophers are prey for coyotes, badgers, and other predators capable of digging. Weasels and snakes, which are able to enter the burrow systems, also take these gophers. Plains pocket gophers are abundant within their range. Their activity enriches the soil, slows water runoff, and provides abandoned burrows for other animals.

An adult olive-backed pocket mouse *(Perognathus fasciatus)*. Photograph by R. E. Wrigley.

POCKET MICE AND KANGAROO RATS (FAMILY HETEROMYIDAE)
Olive-Backed Pocket Mouse
Perognathus fasciatus (Wied-Neuwied)

Description: Olive-backed pocket mice are small, light-colored mice with relatively large hind feet and external fur-lined pouches which open into the mouth at each cheek. Dorsal fur is olive brown with a brighter yellowish line (sometimes lined with black) along the sides. Underparts are white. The tail is less than one-half the total length.

Size: Adults may attain the following dimensions: total length 127–137 mm; tail 57–68 mm; hind foot 16–18 mm; ear 11–13 mm; weight 8–14 grams. Generally, sexes are similar in size, but in some localities females may be slightly larger than males.

Range and Habitat: Olive-backed pocket mice occur from south-central Canada to central Colorado. In Wyoming, this pocket mouse is found in a wide variety of dry habitats from gravelly soils below 1400 meters in the Black Hills, to sandy areas of short grass in eastern prairies to the sand dunes of Sweetwater County. Two sub-

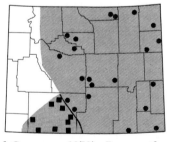

species occur in Wyoming (Williams and Genoways 1979): *Perognathus fasciatus fasciatus* Wied (circles) in the eastern and central part of the state; *Perognathus fasciatus callistus* Osgood (squares) in southwestern Wyoming.

Reproduction: Little is known of the reproduction of Wyoming's olive-backed pocket mouse. Breeding probably occurs in late winter or early spring, but some adults may not breed in a given year. Breeding males

127

are found as late as July. Gestation is probably about 1 month. From three to six (usually five) are born in a litter. Birth may occur from April to August. Females may have two litters a year. Young reach independence by September. We have kept these pocket mice in captivity for up to 3 years.

Habits: Olive-backed pocket mice are nocturnal and may be active all year. Food is cached in burrows and moved around in cheek pouches. Small seeds are gathered and swept into the mouth as the front feet rapidly sift sand. These pocket mice often forage under vegetation. They drink water by wetting the front feet (often wiping wet vegetation) and then licking the water off that fur. Olive-backed pocket mice kept in captivity and fed dry seeds without water must have the sand around their resting burrows kept wet. Like other pocket mice, they must have access to clean, fine sand, used by them to "bathe" and remove excess oil from their fur. Extensive burrows are excavated, and daytime resting chambers are lined with finely chewed, dry leaves of grass. Burrow entrances are kept plugged. During cold weather or when food is limited, pocket mice become "torpid" by curling into a ball in their nest, lowering their metabolic rate and sleeping. Social behavior is poorly known, but these pocket mice may occur at densities of less than 1 per hectare.

Food: Olive-backed pocket mice, like other pocket mice, are opportunistic seed-eaters. Virtually all small seeds found in their habitat are eaten.

Remarks: Nocturnal predators probably eat these pocket mice, but they can run faster than can be followed by the eye. Extensive trapping in Sweetwater County revealed these mice to be rare and restricted to sand dune habitats. In Goshen County, only two or three mice can be expected to be caught in 1000 trap nights. Olive-backed pocket mice are probably not abundant in Wyoming.

An adult plains pocket mouse *(Perognathus flavescens)*. Photograph by Herb Karcher.

Plains Pocket Mouse
Perognathus flavescens flavescens (Merriam)

Description: Plains pocket mice resemble olive-backed pocket mice in general characters, but have a relatively short tail, sandy light yellow or buff dorsal fur overlaid with a darker wash of black hair tips, and a small lighter patch of fur behind the ear. They are most likely confused with the silky pocket mouse, which is smaller and has larger ear patches.

Size: Adults may attain the following dimensions: total length 113–130 mm; tail 47–73 mm; hind foot 15–20 mm; ear 6–8 mm; weight 7–15 grams. Sexes are about the same size.

Range and Habitat: Plains pocket mice occur from Minnesota across the grassland states southwest to Texas and southern New Mexico. They occur in the sand dunes, sage grassland, yucca grassland and grama grass *(Bouteloua)* prairies of southeastern Wyoming. Only one subspecies of this wide ranging species occurs in Wyoming.

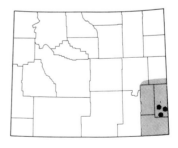

Reproduction: Probably this species produces one litter a year in spring; the young grow in maternal burrows. Observations on the time of breeding, number of young and their development are needed.

Habits: Plains pocket mice are nocturnal, active all year, and do not hibernate. At night, they forage for seeds in the soil and carry their finds back to a burrow in their cheek pouches. During the day, they rest in their cool burrows and may become torpid during cold weather. Burrow entrances are plugged when not in use. Seeds are cached in the burrow systems. Plains pocket mice usually rest on their back feet like kangaroos, freeing the front feet to sift sand and handle seeds. These pocket mice can leap rapidly away from disturbance.

Food: Plains pocket mice are granivorous. When different species of pocket mice live together in one area, they tend to forage in different microhabitats, which results in each taking slightly different sizes and kinds of seeds. Drinking water is not needed by these mice because their kidneys lose very little water; instead, they metabolize water from the carbohydrates they eat.

Remarks: Plains pocket mice are apparently rare throughout their range. In Wyoming, they are captured as rarely as once in 1000 traps set for a night.

An adult silky pocket mouse *(Perognathus flavus)*. Photograph by Thomas H. Kunz.

Silky Pocket Mouse
Perognathus flavus piperi (Goldman)

Description: The silky pocket mouse can be distinguished from the olive-backed pocket mouse by the tawny or sandy dorsal fur color. Hispid pocket mice are larger (hind foot 25–28 mm) than all other Wyoming pocket mice. Plains pocket mice have longer tails, shorter bodies, and a more distinct dorsal stripe down the tail than silky pocket mice. The light patch behind the ear of the silky pocket mouse is twice the length of its ear — this ear patch is much smaller in the plains pocket mouse. Like other pocket mice, silky pocket mice have fur-lined cheek pouches, grooved upper incisor teeth and pure white underparts.

Size: Adults may attain the following dimensions: total length 110–115 mm; tail 51–60 mm; hind foot 15–17 mm; ear 6–7 mm; weight 5–10 grams. Sexes are about the same size.

Range and Habitat: Silky pocket mice reach the northern limit of their distribution in east-central Wyoming. Their range extends south along the foothills and eastern prairies of the Rocky Mountains across New Mexico and west Texas. Silky pocket mice are ubiquitous over grasslands, deserts and juniper woodlands. These mice occur 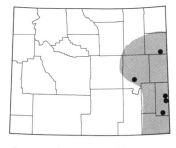 on a variety of soils, but are most abundant on loose and friable soils.

Reproduction: In New Mexico, female silky pocket mice carry embryos from March through October, implying some breeding may start in

February. The gestation period is about 28 days. Breeding is probably later than this in Wyoming, depending on the severity and length of winter. From two to six are born in a litter, and probably two litters are born when sufficient food is available. Adults may live up to 2 years.

Habits: Silky pocket mice are nocturnal and forage by sifting soil for small seeds. They live in burrow systems which are kept closed while occupied, and include various tunnels and side chambers. Food is cached in the burrow system. Burrows are often among the roots of cactus, bunchgrass or shrubs. Home ranges overlap considerably and vary from 0.2–0.6 hectares. Density varies enormously and can be as high as 370 per hectare, but is more often about 60 per hectare. Home ranges may shift with available resources, and may last only 3–4 months. Silky pocket mice are active all year, even on cold winter nights.

Food: Seeds of a variety of plants are eaten. These include Russian this-tle, pigweed, fescue grass, miners candle, cactus, and indian rice grass. Apparently silky pocket mice are able to eat a wide range of seeds and probably eat whatever is locally most abundant.

Remarks: Silky pocket mice are eaten by many nocturnal predators includ-ing foxes, coyotes, owls, and weasels.

Great Basin Pocket Mouse
Perognathus parvus clarus (Goldman)

Description: Great Basin pocket mice have relatively long tails and brownish sandy (buff) dorsal fur. Fur on the belly and underparts is white. Large light patches of fur occur behind the ears. If the ears are laid gently backwards, this light patch is still visible around the margin of the ear. This pocket mouse has a longer tail and hind foot than the sympatric olive-backed pocket mouse.

Size: Adults may attain the following dimensions: total length 148–198 mm; tail 77–97 mm; hind foot 19–27 mm; ear 6–10 mm; weight 16–30 grams. Females are slightly smaller than males.

Range and Habitat: Great Basin pocket mice occur throughout the Great Basin of central western states from eastern Washington to Nevada and Utah. They occur only in the southwestern corner of Wyoming. Habitats include the low basin shrub grasslands and less frequently in grassy openings in pine-juniper foothills.

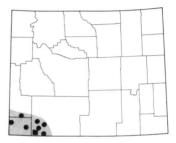

Reproduction: Great Basin pocket mice breed from May to August, but most young are born in May or June. Litter sizes vary from three to eight; usually four are born. If food is adequate, two litters may be produced. Very little else is known of the reproduction of this species.

Habits: Great Basin pocket mice are nocturnal and active all year. During cold spells or during food shortages, they can become torpid and reduce their metabolic rate. In daytime, these mice rest in burrows about 0.6–0.9 meters deep and keep the entrances plugged. Like other pocket mice, this species does not climb, but forages for seeds by sifting sand and then transports its seed harvest to nest caches using its cheek pouches. Although they seldom drink, their burrows are cool and moist. Great Basin pocket mice live solitarily with home ranges of from 0.05 to 0.23 hectares. Burrows are frequently found at the base of sagebrush plants. These pocket mice clean and groom their fur by bathing in dust.

Food: Great Basin pocket mice eat seeds of forbs and shrubs. Seeds of fescue and wheatgrass are important diet items. During the spring, some insects are consumed.

Remarks: Overgrazing of shrub grasslands, which virtually eliminates grass production and seed set, is probably harmful to the Great Basin pocket mouse. A wide variety of nocturnal vertebrate predators prey on this pocket mouse. Great Basin pocket mice are rare in Sweetwater County, but are abundant elsewhere. Of 36,700 trap nights throughout the county, only one individual (square) was captured (Belitsky 1981). Yet from 1900 to 1946, collectors did not report such rarity or difficulty in collecting specimens.

An adult hispid pocket mouse *(Perognathus hispidus).* Photograph by Robert J. Baker.

Hispid Pocket Mouse
Perognathus hispidus paradoxus (Merriam)

Description: Hispid pocket mice are the largest of the pocket mice in Wyoming, and are also unique in having coarse dorsal fur which is rough to the touch instead of the soft, silky fur of smaller kinds of Wyoming pocket mice. Dorsal fur is brownish gray or black. A creamy yellow line along the side of the body separates the darker dorsal fur and the white underparts. The tail is sharply bicolored — black above and white below, but lacks a terminal tuft of long hairs. Upper incisors are grooved. Large hind feet of the hispid pocket mouse have naked soles and its cheek pouches are fur-lined.

Size: Adults may attain the following dimensions: total length 200–223 mm; tail 90–113 mm; hind foot 25–28 mm; ear 12–13 mm; weight 40–60 grams. Males are larger than females.

Range and Habitat: Hispid pocket mice range from North Dakota south through the Great Plains of North America to central Mexico. They occupy habitats from the arid transition foothills of the Rocky Mountains to the mid-grass of eastern Kansas. Hispid pocket mice in Wyoming are found in a wide variety of habitats including 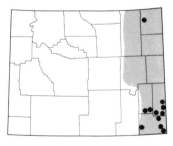 sand dunes, sage-grass, and prairies of buffalo grass and grama grass.

Reproduction: Reproduction in the hispid pocket mouse is poorly known. Evidently five or six young are born in a litter, and perhaps two litters are born each year. Young reach independence after about 1 month of maternal care.

Habits: Hispid pocket mice dig shallow burrows, usually at the base of a large shrub or rock outcrop. During the day, they rest in burows and keep the entrances plugged with soil. Nests are lined with dried plant fibers and seeds are cached in the burrow chambers. At night, these pocket mice forage on the ground, gathering seeds in their cheek pouches. Hispid pocket mice are active all year but may remain inactive during cold spells. Piles of litter and excavated soil often are seen around their burrow entrances.

Food: Elsewhere, a variety of seeds is taken (sage, sunflowers, cacti). Some green forbs and insects are eaten in the spring. Nothing is known about the diet of the hispid pocket mouse in Wyoming.

Remarks: Owls, snakes, foxes, coyotes, and other vertebrate predators active at night probably prey on hispid pocket mice. The word "hispid" means rough to the touch.

An adult Ord's kangaroo rat *(Dipodomys ordii)*. Photograph by Dick Randall.

Ord's Kangaroo Rat
Dipodomys ordii Woodhouse

Description: Ord's Kangaroo rat is unique among Wyoming mammals in having 1) a large body with short neck and a relatively large head, 2) a tail longer than the head and body length, 3) a tuft of hairs at the tip of the tail much longer than the hairs at the base of the tail, 4) hind feet much larger than front feet, and 5) thick hair on the soles of the hind feet. Like pocket mice, this rat has soft cinnamon-tan dorsal fur, white underparts, a fur-lined cheek pouch and five toes on each hind foot.

Size: Adults may attain the following dimensions: total length 249–280 mm; tail 138–163 mm; hind foot 40–45 mm; ear 12–15 mm; weight 45–100 grams. Males are slightly larger than females.

Range and Habitat: Ord's kangaroo rat is one of the more wide-ranging mammals of western North America, occurring from Washington and adjacent southern Canada south to central Mexico. In Wyoming, it occurs in the arid basins throughout the state. In Sweetwater County, it is relatively rare and restricted to open sand dunes,

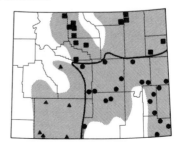

137

where it burrows at the base of sage, saltbush or greasewood plants which grow at the edge of the dunes. In Converse and Platte counties, kangaroo rats live in the foothills, grasslands and the shortgrass prairies.

Three subspecies of this rat occur in Wyoming. *Dipodomys ordii terrosus* Hoffmeister (squares) occurs in the Bighorn, Powder River, and Missouri River Basins. *Dipodomys ordii priscus* Hoffmeister (triangles) occurs in the central and southwestern lowlands. *Dipodomys ordii luteolus* Goldman (circles) occurs in the eastern and southeastern plains.

Reproduction: Breeding elsewhere has been observed in all months but December. Probably two litters are born each year in Wyoming—one in late winter or early spring and another in late summer. Litter sizes vary from one to six, and gestation is about 30 days. Young are born without hair and are helpless. Their eyes open in about 2 weeks, and by the age of 2 months they become independent of the female parent.

Habits: Kangaroo rats are nocturnal and are often seen at night along dirt roads. They forage solitarily in open areas by sifting sand with their front feet. Seeds are carried in their cheek pouches back to caches in the burrow system. Kangaroo rats can move about on their hind feet only, leaping and using their long tail as a counterbalance. During the day these rats sleep in their burrows. Burrow entrances are kept closed with loose sand and debris, and often are marked by a heap of excavated soil and seed husks. Distinctive tracks in the sand include long streaks made by dragging the tail. Home ranges vary from 2.3 to 3.3 hectares in New Mexico where densities of about 14 per hectare were observed. Kangaroo rats don't drink water in the wild. By staying in cool, humid burrows during the heat of the day, metabolizing water from food and minimizing water losses in urine and evaporation, they can live in extremely dry habitats.

Food: Many "weeds" in arid regions produce abundant seeds as a means to survive in patches where water is only briefly available. Kangaroo rats eat many of these abundant seeds. In addition, a wide variety of native plant seeds are consumed in proportion to their abundance and energy reward. During the spring some green plants, tubers, buds, and insects are eaten.

Remarks: Elsewhere, Ord's kangaroo rat can live with up to 11 other granivorous rodents. In Wyoming, it occurs with five other species having such life styles. In other areas, studies of its interactions with other species have been conducted to determine the importance of competition among these mice for food. Ants may significantly reduce the seeds available to these grain-eating rodents.

Many nocturnal animals prey on the kangaroo rat, although its extremely sensitive hearing alerts it to even the comparatively silent flight of owls. Snakes, foxes, and other nocturnal predators eat kangaroo rats.

An adult beaver *(Castor canadensis).* Photograph by Dick Randall.

BEAVERS (FAMILY CASTORIDAE)
Beaver
Castor canadensis

Description: Beavers are Wyoming's largest rodent. They are large, dark brown or red-brown mammals that have a large, flat tail covered with scales. Adaptations for swimming include webbing between the toes of the large hind feet, a nictitating membrane over the eye (a clear eyelid), ear and nose openings which close, and lips which seal closed behind prominent incisors. The massive lower incisors actually are rooted below and behind the molars! Front feet are relatively small and clawed. The extremely fine short hairs are dense and lead-gray in color; guard hairs extend above the fine underfur. Young beavers (kits) have black fur.

Size: Adult beavers may attain the following dimensions: total length 1000–12000 mm; tail 258–325 mm; hind foot 156–205 mm; ear 23–29 mm; weight 11–35 kilograms. Males and females are of similar size.

Range and Habitat: Beavers range throughout Canada and the United States except Nevada, southern California and Florida. They once occurred throughout Wyoming. However, they became locally extinct due to over-trapping in the mid to late 1800s. During the 1900s, the beaver was widely reintroduced in Wyoming. 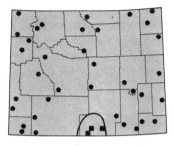 Inevitably, this probably reduced the differences between subspecies because one race, *Castor canadensis missouriensis,* was often introduced where it did not naturally occur. Nevertheless, two subspecies were still recognized by Long (1965); *Castor canadensis concisor* (squares) in the Sierra Madres and *Castor canadensis missouriensis* elsewhere in the state. Beavers can live wherever there is sufficient water and food.

Reproduction: Beavers breed once a year from January to February. Litters are born in May or June. Depending on food quality and abundance, there are from one to six (usually three or four) kits per litter. Kits are born fully furred, are weaned by 2 months, and become sexually mature in their second winter. They can live up to 20 years, but generally survive 8 to 10 years.

Habits: Beavers use their impressive incisors to cut trees, used to build dams across running water. Mud is packed into the interwoven branches and sometimes massive, long beaver dams flood large areas. Beavers either build large mound-like lodges with underwater entrances in their ponds or burrow into a stream bank to make a lodge. Lodges are lined with dry shavings. Beavers are generally nocturnal and are active all year. Trees are cut down by a distinctive chiseling around the base until they fall. Various branches are then chiseled off and dragged down into the water. Small trails sometimes are beaten down to the water's edge where these mammals are very active.

Beavers live in small colonies of four to eight related individuals. Adults are socially dominant over young, and males are more likely to disperse from the social unit. When disturbed, beavers will slap their tails on the surface and dive to deep water. Tail slapping warns other beavers of danger and they, too, dive. They can stay submerged at least 15 minutes, but most dives last 1 or 2 minutes.

Food: Beavers eat a wide variety of leaves and twigs, and the inner bark of most woody plants and many aquatic plants; aspen and willow are preferred. Small branches and twigs are cached for overwinter food; the former are often anchored on the pond bottom or stream edge where they can be retrieved under the ice during winter.

Remarks: Beavers attracted some of Wyoming's earliest European explorers. The "mountain men" of Jim Bridger's time and trappers after them exterminated beavers from many areas. Sweetwater County's isolated mountains (Pine, Little, Aspen, Steamboat) no doubt once supported beavers. Subsequent overgrazing eliminated the beaver's food (willows) and caused erosion which has gullied once wet meadows into greasewood-lined arroyos. Reintroduction of beavers into these and similarly abused watersheds would increase water tables, slow soil erosion and increase grazing capacity (Parker et al. 1985).

In other places, notably around irrigation structures, the beaver's efforts to dam flowing water are not appreciated. Coyotes and bobcats prey on beavers.

An adult plains harvest mouse *(Reithrodontomys montanus)*. Photograph by Herb Karcher.

NEW WORLD RATS AND MICE (FAMILY CRICETIDAE)
Plains Harvest Mouse
Reithrodontomys montanus albescens (Cary)

Description: Wyoming has two members of this genus. Both are small, delicate mice without cheek pouches, but they have a single groove on the outer surface of each upper incisor. Long hairs around the ears give them a rather grizzled look. The plains harvest mouse has a relatively short tail and a mid-dorsal black band through its pale brown or buffy gray fur. Ventral fur is yellow-gray to white, and the well-haired tail has a well-defined dorsal dark stripe.

Size: Adults may grow to the following dimensions: total length 105–143 mm; tail 48–55 mm; hind foot 14–20 mm; ear 12–13 mm; weight 10–13 grams.

Range and Habitat: Plains harvest mice occur in the grasslands of interior North America from northeastern Wyoming to central Mexico. These mice prefer grassland where little bare soil is exposed. They are most frequent in grama grasslands in eastern Wyoming, but also occupy sage grasslands, buffalo grass and mixed grasslands.

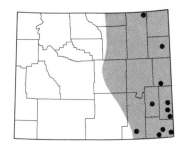

Plains harvest mice prefer well vegetated areas and may be locally abundant in weedy fields. Rocky outcrops may be used for shelter. Their distribution in eastern Wyoming is probably quite patchy.

Reproduction: Plains harvest mice breed in late winter. After a gestation period of 21 days, from three to seven young are born. Several litters may be produced each year. Young are born blind and naked, but by 2 weeks are weaned. By 3 to 4 weeks, they leave the nest. Young reach sexual maturity in 2 months. Adults usually live less than 1 year, but may survive many years in captivity.

Habits: Plains harvest mice are active all year and do not hibernate. During the day they rest in nests which are located in rock crevices, burrows or even dense thickets. At night, harvest mice gather food from home ranges of about 1 hectare. Nests are made from dried leaves and lined with finely chewed, dry plant fibers. Occasionally, a group of harvest mice will be found huddled together in one nest.

Food: The plains harvest mouse primarily eats seeds. However, a wide variety of green shoots, new grass leaves, fruits and berries are eaten. Food is cached in burrows or crevices for later use.

Remarks: Wyoming's two species of harvest mice are extremely difficult to tell apart. Plains harvest mice are relatively rare and bear a superficial resemblance to the deer mouse.

A wide variety of nocturnal predators eat the plains harvest mouse, including swift foxes, coyotes, weasels, and owls.

An adult western harvest mouse *(Reithrodontomys megalotis)*. Photograph by Thomas H. Kunz.

Western Harvest Mouse
Reithrodontomys megalotis dychei (J. A. Allen)

Description: Western harvest mice are somewhat larger than the very similar plains harvest mouse. They have conspicuous ears, a tail as long as the head and body, soft brown fur above without a distinct mid-dorsal strip, white underfur, and a nearly hairless tail that is blackish above and white underneath. All harvest mice have a single groove down the center of the outer face of each upper incisor.

Size: Adults may attain the following dimensions: total length 122–155 mm; tail 56–73 mm; hind foot 16–18 mm; ear 11–15 mm; weight 11–17 grams.

Range and Habitat: Western harvest mice occupy a large range including the upper midwestern states, the Great Plains, and all the western states except parts of the northern Rocky Mountains. In Wyoming, western harvest mice live in grassy areas and shrub-steppe in the eastern two-thirds of the state; forested areas are avoided.

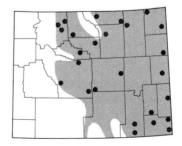

In eastern Wyoming, these mice prefer sage grasslands and yucca-grassland plant communities.

Reproduction: The western harvest mouse breeds throughout spring, summer and fall. Up to 14 litters a year are possible (in captivity), but probably three or four are common in the wild. Gestation takes 24 days, and from three to nine (usually five) are born in a litter. Young are born naked and helpless, by 20 days, are furry and weaned, and by 5 weeks reach adult size. Young can breed by the age of 2 months. Adults rarely live longer than 1 year.

Habits: Western harvest mice are active all year, but only at night. They build spherical nests, often in dense vegetation. Nests are about 10 cm in diameter and are woven of plant fibers. A small (1 cm) hole on the bottom leads to a single nest chamber, where these remarkably tolerant mice huddle together in cold weather. Their nest and huddling behavior can cut their energy consumption (metabolic rate) by more than 60 percent in cold weather.

Sometimes these small mammals use the runways of voles, which are built in dense vegetation. Home ranges elsewhere varied from 0.20 to 0.56 hectares. Densities vary from 2.5–123 per hectare.

Food: Western harvest mice eat a wide variety of seeds, insects, fruit, leaves, and basal parts of plants. They have such efficient kidneys that they can survive for long periods while drinking sea water! Many areas where surface water is extremely saline can thus be occupied by this mouse.

Remarks: Owls, hawks, weasels, skunks, badgers, snakes, and foxes prey on the western harvest mouse. Although this mouse is widespread, it is somewhat patchy in its distribution. Overgrazing and other practices which increase bare soil exposure will limit the distribution and abundance of these mice.

An adult deer mouse *(Peromyscus maniculatus).* Photograph by C. L. Scott.

Deer Mouse
Peromyscus maniculatus (Wagner)

Description: Deer mice are small, fastidious mammals with prominent ears, relatively short tails, soft dense fur and pointed snouts with long whiskers. They have tawny to dark brown or black dorsal fur which blends abruptly into the white ventral fur and white feet, and a finely furred tail that is white below and has a black dorsal surface whose borders are sharply defined. Incisors are smooth and hind feet are short (22 mm or less). These mice have relatively large black eyes.

Size: Adults may attain the following dimensions: total length 144–170 mm; tail 55–69 mm; hind foot 20–22 mm; ear 14–17 mm; weight 18–25 grams. Males and females are about the same size.

Range and Habitat: Deer mice occur all over temperate North America and into central Mexico except the south-eastern coastal states. There are three subspecies in Wyoming. *Peromyscus maniculatus nebrascensis* (Coues) was desribed from Deer Creek, Converse County, in 1877, and this subspecies (circles) occurs throughout most of

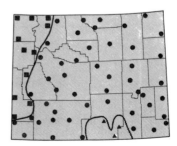

Wyoming. *Peromyscus maniculatus artemisiae* (Rhoads) occurs in the interior northwestern mountain areas of Wyoming (squares). *Peromyscus maniculatus rufinus* (Merriam) occurs in the Sierra Madre and Medicine Bow Mountains (triangles) (Armstrong 1972). Deer mice occur in virtually all Wyoming habitats and are usually the most abundant small mouse in any given area.

Reproduction: Deer mice can breed all year, but generally breeding is restricted to the period from late spring to fall. Gestation requires from 23 to 27 days, and litters of from one to nine are born into soft, lined nests often under logs or in rock crevices. Young are born with their eyes closed, naked and with folded ears. In a week, they are well furred, their teeth are present and their eyes are open. By a month, they are weaned and in another 2 weeks they leave the female. Young can breed by the age of 2 months. Adults rarely live longer than a year in the wild, but may live 7 years in captivity.

Habits: Deer mice are usually nocturnal and are active all year. During a winter day, many deer mice may huddle together in a nest. They remain active under the snow during the winter. Nests are woven from plant fibers, lined with extremely finely chewed fibers, and are kept clean. During spring and summer, females live separately with young, but male-female pairs are sometimes observed. Home ranges vary from 0.004–0.45 hectares. Densities vary from 5–40 per hectare and little year-to-year change in density occurs. Deer mice usually avoid wetlands (marshes, bogs). When white-footed mice are present, deer mice are excluded from woodlands. However, if no white-footed mice are present (most of Wyoming), deer mice occur throughout woodlands. Deer mice forage through the litter for food and drink water when it is available. Communication through scent and high frequency (ultrasonic) vocalization has been observed.

Food: Deer mice are about as general in their food habits as any mammal. Seeds, fruits, nuts, fungus, insects, buds, green shoots and carrion of other small mammals are all eaten. Females will cannibalize their young if food is scarce. Food is cached for later consumption.

Remarks: No Wyoming mammal has received more study than this mouse, and many aspects of its biology have been published (King 1968). Because it is so abundant, it is eaten by virtually all nocturnal predators. We even witnessed a trout eat a deer mouse as it swam across a stream!

An adult white-footed mouse *(Peromyscus leucopus).* Photograph by Thomas H. Kunz.

White-Footed Mouse
Peromyscus leucopus aridulus (Osgood)

Description: White-footed mice closely resemble deer mice, and because these two species may occur together, identification is often a matter for the expert. White-footed mice tend to have longer feet (22 mm or more), their tail's dark dorsal stripe merges more gradually into the white below, and their snout is longer. Generally, many characters must be considered together in distinguishing these two mammals. The mice themselves, however, recognize each other, and no interbreeding has ever been observed.

Size: Adults may attain the following dimensions: total lengths 140–190 mm; tail 60–110 mm; hind foot 21–24 mm; ear 14–19 mm; weight 18–25 grams. Males and females are about the same size.

Range and Habitat: White-footed mice occur in the eastern United States, generally east of the Rocky Mountains to Texas and eastern Mexico. Most of these mice occupy woodlands, extending west along the gallery forests of major rivers. Occasionally, adjacent open grasslands are inhabited. In the midwestern United States,

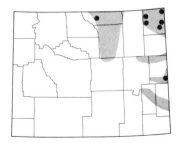

deer mice and white-footed mice live separately from each other in their preferred grassland and woodland (respectively). Habitat selection along the periphery of their range is more variable, where white-footed mice can be found in open areas.

Reproduction: White-footed mice breed from March through October and females may have two to four litters a year. Gestation requires from 23–28 days and young are born hairless and helpless. Their fur grows in within a few days and by 24–30 days the young are weaned. By 5 weeks, young leave the female and are capable of breeding by about 8 weeks of age. Adults generally live less than 2 years in the wild, but have lived 8 years in captivity.

Habits: White-footed mice are primarily active at night, and virtually never touch the ground, leaping and climbing through the understory shrubs and trees. Their tail is used as a counter-balance while climbing. White-footed mice forage on the bark of trees, often climbing through the top of the canopy. Large trees, both upright and fallen are main avenues and nests are often placed in hollow trees. Their nests are large affairs, made of plant fibers and lined with a downy layer of very finely chewed fiber. Adults drum or "buzz" with their feet, and call with very high frequency chirps. Deer mice and white-footed mice may use the same resources on habitat edges, and in these cases, white-footed mice exclude deer mice from woodlands. Adults usually have several nests, but most spend their lives within 30 meters of their natal nest. Densities may be as high as 25 per hectare.

Food: Green sprouts, insects, fruits, nuts and buds are eaten by white-footed mice.

Remarks: Owls, weasels, skunks, foxes and snakes all prey on white-footed mice. Riparian habitats along the creeks in eastern Wyoming are widely overgrazed so that the brushy understory has all but been removed. Thus, overgrazing may limit this species and it may have become rarer in Wyoming recently.

An adult canyon mouse *(Peromyscus crinitus)*. Photograph by Dick Randall.

Canyon Mouse
Peromyscus crinitus douttii (Goin)

Description: Of Wyoming's four species of *Peromyscus,* canyon mice are the habitat specialists in rock outcrops or cliffs. Canyon mice are delicate animals with long narrow, well-furred tails, finely-furred conspicuous ears, large eyes, and pointed snouts with long whiskers. They can be distinguished from *Peromyscus leucopus* and *P. maniculatus* by their longer tails (longer than head and body) and from *P. truei* by their smaller ears (about 21 mm).

151

Size: Adults may attain the following dimensions: total length 165–180 mm; tail 84–95 mm; hind foot 20–22 mm; ear 20–22 mm; weight 14–20 grams. Sexes are similar in size.

Range and Habitat: Canyon mice live in rock crevices in the arid Great Basin intermountain region of the western United States and northwestern Mexico. They are known from local areas in Sweetwater County where sandstone outcrops, sandy soils and limber pine or juniper trees occur (Long Canyon, Rock Springs, South Table Mountain). 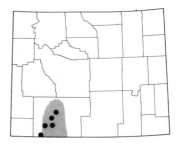 Isolated patches of this habitat occur in central and western Sweetwater County, and canyon mice probably occur in many of these (Belitsky 1981; pers. comm. 1983). Recently, extensive trapping in suitable habitats west of Flaming Gorge has failed to document any canyon mice in this former habitat.

Reproduction: Little is known of breeding by wild canyon mice. In captivity, breeding occurred all year. Probably canyon mice start to breed in early spring. The gestation period is between 24–25 days. Two or three litters of from one to five (usually four) are born each year. Young are weaned at 28 days and probably leave the nest by 4 to 6 weeks. Yong reach sexual maturity by 70 days of age. Adults probably rarely live longer than 1 year in the wild.

Habits: Studies of captive canyon mice shed some light on this interesting rock dweller. Nests are simple affairs, often loose accumulation of plant fiber. As nests are probably made in rock crevices, elaborate structures are not expected. Young are moved when necessary during nursing as they cling to the teats. Almost unique among *Peromyscus,* canyon mice bathe in dust or fine sand to remove excess oil from the fur. Females drive off males while raising young. Canyon mice can swim and are agile climbers. They dig their own burrows in loose sand, although they frequently use natural rock shelters.

Food: No studies have been made of the diet of this species in Wyoming.

Remarks: Probably the largest amount of habitat in Wyoming for this poorly studied mouse was destroyed when Flaming Gorge was flooded. Relict populations remain, and isolated rocky areas above riparian habitat offered by the various mountain tops in Sweetwater County are important as refugia for many small mammals, including this mouse.

Piñon Mouse
Peromyscus truei truei (Shufeldt)

Description: Walt Disney could have used the piñon mouse as a model for Mickey Mouse. This caricature embodies the distinctively large ears of the piñon mouse. In general, this mouse resembles the deer mouse. Wyoming piñon mice have tails slightly longer than the head and body with large naked ears. Dorsal fur is long, silky, and gray-brown, feet are white and the well-haired tail is sharply divided into dark above and white below. Piñon mice have white underfur.

Size: Adults may attain the following dimensions: total length 171–190 mm; tail 80–120 mm; hind foot 22–25 mm; ear 20–26 mm; weight 25–28 grams. Males and females are about the same size.

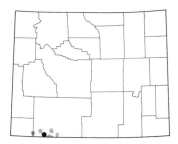

Range and Habitat: Piñon mice occur in the interior Great Basin of the southwestern United States and south into central Mexico. Open stands of piñon and juniper with various grasses in between are preferred habitat. Piñon mice also occur in shrubsteppe particularly where these shrubs are not dense. In Wyoming, they were collected in Flaming Gorge (near Linwood) which is now inundated. Intensive sampling of Sweetwater County (Belitsky 1981), revealed no recent records. Piñon mice probably persist on the rocky outcrops with scattered juniper above the Wyoming shores of Flaming Gorge Reservoir.

Reproduction: Piñon mice breed from spring to fall, producing from two to nine litters each year. Gestation requires from 25–27 days and a small litter of three or four young is usual. Young are nursed for up to 30 days. Nests are almost always constructed in hollow juniper trees, but may be found in rock crevices, and are made of shredded juniper bark and grass leaves. We kept a female in captivity for about 7 years. In the wild, fewer than 20 percent survive a year.

Habits: During the day, piñon mice sleep in their nests. At night, they climb trees and shrubs but also forage on the ground by digging and exploring crevices. These mice are probably not territorial. Home ranges vary from 0.13–0.47 hectares. Densities vary from 2–86 per hectare, but parts of any hectare may be avoided as unsuitable habitat.

Food: Seeds, mushrooms, leaves and a variety of insects are eaten. Piñon mice drink very little water (5 grams per day) and depend on juniper "berries" for food and water through the winter. When water is not available, they become torpid during the day.

Remarks: Quite rare in Wyoming, this mouse probably can still be found on the southern isolated mountains in Sweetwater County. It is abundant elsewhere in its range.

An adult northern grasshopper mouse *(Onychomys leucogaster)*. Photograph by Dick Randall.

Northern Grasshopper Mouse
Onychomys leucogaster (Wied)

Description: Grasshopper mice are small and stocky mice with furry, short thick, white tails. Their ears are furred and the dorsal fur is bicolored: brown-tipped with white bases. Ventral fur and feet are white. Grasshopper mice have large black eyes, a short, blunt nose and long whiskers.

Size: Adults may attain the following dimensions: total length 130–155 mm; tail 29–50 mm; hind foot 17–25 mm; ear 13–17 mm; weight 35–45 grams. Males and females are about the same size.

Range and Habitat: The Northern grasshopper mouse ranges across the Great Plains and the Great Basin from Canada to Mexico and from California to Iowa. In Wyoming, two subspecies are known. *Onychomys leucogaster arcticeps* Rhoades (squares) occurs in the eastern plains. *Onychomys leucogaster missouriensis* Au-

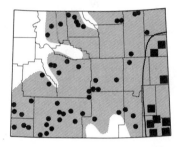

dubon and Bachman (circles) occurs over much of Wyoming. Grasshopper mice inhabit shrublands and semiarid grasslands and require silty or sandy soils.

Reproduction: Grasshopper mice breed in the spring and summer. Gestation requires from 32–47 days for nursing females and only 27–32 days for non-lactating females. Up to six (usually three or four) are born in a litter. From 2 to 10 litters may be produced each year. Young are born naked and helpless. By 2 weeks, they are furred, eyes are open and they are active. By 1 month of age, young are weaned. At 3 to 4 months, young reach sexual maturity.

Habits: Grasshopper mice are unique in this family of mice in regard to their carnivorous lifestyle. Most of their diet is insects, but they can kill other rodents up to three times their size. Males will kill and eat other grasshopper mice that stumble into their territory. Their long claws and sharp incisors reflect their predatory lifestyle. Nest burrows are shallow (15 cm) systems with one chamber and two entrances. Both sexes share the nest burrow and males help females feed the young. A variety of other shallow burrows and crevices provide escape cover, food caches and latrines. Grasshopper mice are impeccably groomed at all times. They roll through fine sand and silt in a distinctive sandbathing routine, scrubbing their faces and heads with their fore paws and nibbling their fur clean frequently. These mice communicate with scent posts and by distinctive, loud high-pitched chirps and squeaks. They maintain low densities and large territories (average 2.3 hectares) with predominately nonviolent encounters. Populations apparently are never dense. Grasshopper mice in other populations (Arizona) show erratic trends in abundance. Grasshopper mice are nocturnal and rarely hunt during the day. They do not climb but they can swim.

Food: During spring and summer, animal material (beetles, grasshoppers, spiders, larval moths, and small rodents) make up over 80 percent of the diet. This drops to about 60 percent in the winter when plant material (forbs, grass, seeds) is more frequently eaten.

Remarks: Grasshopper mice are rarely taken by vertebrate predators. Several studies have found that owls, hawks, swift foxes and coyotes infrequently eat these mice. Their habit of preying on grasshoppers is distinctive: they bite off the heads and feet and leave them in neat piles.

An adult bushy-tailed woodrat *(Neotoma cinerea)*. Photograph by Dick Randall.

Bushy-Tailed Woodrat
Neotoma cinerea (Ord)

Description: Bushy-tailed woodrats are large rodents, resembling a "giant" deer mouse with a bottle-brush tail. They have large ears, long whiskers, uniformly white hair on the underfur and feet. Upper parts are pale gray to cinnamon brown and the fur on the tail is dark above and white below. The tail is about as long as the head and body.

Size: Adults may grow to the following dimensions: total length 350–470 mm; tail 135–223 mm; hind foot 40–52 mm; ear 30–36 mm; weight

240–290 grams. In some populations in Wyoming, males are larger than females.

Range and Habitat: Bushy-tailed woodrats range along the west coast of North America from the Yukon to California and occur east across the Rocky Mountains to the Dakotas and northern New Mexico. Four subspecies of bushy-tailed woodrats occur throughout Wyoming. *Neotoma cinerea cinerea* (Ord) occurs in rocky out-

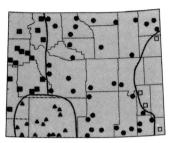

crops on the Yellowstone Plateau and into the Uinta mountains (solid squares). *Neotoma cinerea orolestes* Merriam (circles) occurs in rocky outcrops from 3500 meters in the Bighorn Mountains and Black Hills to similar habitat (rocks) in the lowest basins of northern Wyoming. *Neotoma cinerea rupicola* J. A. Allen (open squares) occurs in suitably rocky outcrops on the eastern dry prairies of Wyoming. *Neotoma cinerea arizonae* Finley (triangles) occurs sporadically in rock outcrops in isolated mixed conifer and sand dune habitats as well as the sage steppe of Sweetwater County.

Reproduction: Bushy-tailed woodrats breed in the warmer months. Gestation requires about 27–35 days and from two to five are usually born in a litter. Females may have two litters in a year. Young leave their nest area after 2 months and breed at 2 years of age. Males and females live together only briefly, generally living solitary lives. Adults usually live 3 to 4 years in the wild.

Habits: Vertical chimneys or cracks in a rock outcrop or shelves and attics in abandoned buildings are selected for nest sites. Nests are collections of just about any loose object in the vicinity that is small enough to be carried by these "pack rats." Bones, cactus fruits, sticks, bottles, cans, pine cones, bits of plastic, paper, and any other "treasure" it finds are heaped up in a pile about 0.5–1.0 meter tall. Nest piles are always well above ground. A high quality nest of fine, dry plant fibers is located in the center of the junk heap. Woodrats are active at night, year-round, and sleep in their "castles" during the day. Territories are defended but the size of Wyoming's woodrat territories are not known. In Sweetwater County, densities of about 0.80–4.6 per hectare were observed in suitable habitat (Belitsky 1981).

Food: Woodrats eat about 75 percent of available plants, but avoid sage *(Artemisia).* Foliage of most shrubs, seeds, bark, mushrooms, fruit and insects are all taken. Food is stored in crevices or the den for later use.

Remarks: Bushy-tailed woodrats often appear in the late afternoon. In many of our camps, we would suddenly realize that a woodrat was silently peering around a rock and observing us. At night, they occasionally pack off camp items. Their activities in old buildings at night are enough to drive one outside to get some quiet sleep.

An adult southern red-backed vole *(Clethrionomys gapperi)*. Photograph by Elmer C. Birney.

Southern Red-Backed Vole
Clethrionomys gapperi (Vigors)

Description: Red-backed voles are small, mouse-sized mammals. Their fur is distinctly red-brown on their shoulders and back, and gray below. Red-backed voles have short ears, white feet and relatively short, bicolored, well-haired tails. Both this vole and the heather vole have molars that are "rooted" with enamel that all but seals the base of the tooth. Other voles have "evergrowing" molars that retain large, open pulp cavities in the roots, and which grow continuously.

Size: Adults may attain the following dimensions: total length 125–172 mm; tail 30–50 mm; hind foot 16–20 mm; ear 12–16 mm; weight 18–42 grams. Males and females are of similar size and color.

Range and Habitat: Red-backed voles occur across Canada and extend south down the Rocky and Appalachian Mountains. In Wyoming, they occur in lodgepole pine, spruce-fir and mixed deciduous forests with an abundant litter of leaves, logs and windfall, often near marshy areas with willow communities along streams. Three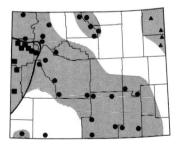
subspecies occur in Wyoming. *Clethrionomys gapperi idahoensis* (Merriam) (squares) occurs in the mountains of western Wyoming south of the Yellowstone Plateau. *Clethrionomys gapperi galei* (Merriam) (circles) occurs in the balance of Wyoming's mountains except the Black Hills.

There, *Clethrionomys gapperi brevicaudus* (Merriam) (triangles) occurs as an isolated, disjunct subspecies. Red-backed voles occur along major Wyoming rivers between the mountains (i.e., Sweetwater, Platte, Laramie). With the disappearance of beavers and the drying out and gullying of once perennial streams of the isolated mountains of Sweetwater County, only historic records exist despite recent intensive trapping (Belitsky 1981).

Reproduction: Red-backed voles have several litters from late winter to late fall. Gestation requires from 17–19 days. From two to eight are born in a litter, with larger litters at higher elevations. Young are nursed for up to 3 weeks, reach independence by about 1 month, and are sexually mature by 2 to 4 months. Red backed voles may live up to 20 months, but most live only 10–12 months.

Habits: Red-backed voles are active at night during summer, but increase their daytime activities in winter. After snow covers their habitat, these voles are active all day. They use runways in the litter layer of the forests or wet fields, which are kept open as tunnels under the snow in the winter. Males and females live apart and, although they are promiscuous, they do not form colonies. Males barely tolerate the young, and briefly live with the female when young are small. Densities vary from 2–48 per hectare and home ranges vary from 0.01–0.5 hectares. In woodlands, red-backed voles exclude meadow voles and deer mice (Grant 1976, Crowell and Pimm 1976). Red-backed voles build nests from 75–100 mm in diameter and made of dry grass and stems finely chewed and interwoven. These voles move about by hopping and climbing, and they readily swim. They can jump over barriers 15–20 cm in height. When handled, these shy, nervous mice sometimes chatter with their teeth, and if slightly stressed go into shock and may die. Red-backed voles select wet habitats probably because their drinking water requirements are twice that predicted by their body weight.

Food: Red-backed voles are omnivorous, eating leaves, nuts, seeds, berries, moss, lichens, ferns, fungi and arthropods. Food is sometimes stored in fall for later use. These voles lose weight in the winter and thus lower their food requirement.

Remarks: A wide variety of predators eat red-backed voles, including hawks, owls, falcons, snakes, coyotes, and foxes. During some years, these voles can become abundant in their habitat.

An adult heather vole *(Phenacomys intermedius)*. Photograph by Tom French.

Heather Vole
Phenacomys intermedius intermedius (Merriam)

Description: Heather voles are medium sized mice with short ears, small feet, grayish or tawny brown dorsal fur, a white tail and white underfur. These voles have rooted molars, but lack the red shoulders of the red-backed vole. Heather voles have grayer, fluffier fur than other sympatric voles. Unlike *Microtus*, heather voles are gentle and only rarely bite when handled. The lower molars of heather voles have deep notches on the inner sides so that the "midline" of the molars appears well off center (see Key, p. 287).

Size: Adults may attain the following dimensions: total length 115–145 mm; tail 22–33 mm; hind foot 14–19 mm; weight 25–40 grams. Males and females are about the same size.

Range and Habitat: Heather voles range from Alaska to the Atlantic across Canada and extend south along the Rocky Montains to New Mexico. In Wyoming, heather voles live in the cool forested ranges of the northwest (Yellowstone, Absarokas, Wind Rivers), the Uintas, and the Sierra Madre and Medicine Bow Mountains. A vari-

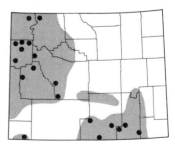

ety of habitats are preferred including grassy streamsides, spruce-fir forests, pure lodgepole pine forests, fell fields (boulders in alpine turf), alpine

meadows, sage-grass hillsides and brushy riparian areas. Although the
Black Hills and Bighorns apparently provide suitable habitat, heather
voles are not known from either area.

Reproduction: Heather voles breed from June to October, and gestation
takes about 30 days (Halfpenny and Southwick 1982). Two to six (usually
about five) are born in a litter. Young weigh only about 2 grams at birth.
Females usually have one litter each year, but some may have two litters.
Young reach independence at about two months of age, and sexual
maturity and breeding status in their first summer. Only a small percentage of the population reaches 18 months of age in the wild.

Habits: Heather voles are active year-round. Short (one meter) burrows
under roots, logs and rocks are shallow, and lead to summer nests 6–8
cm in diameter. During the winter, larger spherical nests of lichens and
grass are constructed under the snow at the base of a larger rock or stump.
Both sexes use the winter nests, but females drive other adults out of the
summer nests. During the summer, males have exclusive territories. Densities of 0.2–5.6/hectares have been reported for heather voles, but they
can be rare locally. Starting at dusk, heather voles wander around gathering food from the ground and low shrubs. This food is stored in various
crevices near the nest area and eaten during the day.

Food: Heather voles feed on seeds, beargrass, huckleberries, fungi, the
bark of willow and birch, and leaves or buds of a variety of shrubs.

Remarks: A variety of conflicting observations on the rarity of this vole
have been made. It is apparently rare in some places (Medicine Bow
Mountains), but it is widespread. The absence of heather voles from the
Bighorns and Black Hills is another indication of their isolation from
the "mainstream" Rocky Mountain fauna. Heather voles are listed as rare
in Utah.

Habitats of the heather vole (and many other small mammals) are
being destroyed by the widespread overgrazing of lands managed by the
federal government. So pervasive and politically driven is the overgrazing that the first objective study of the effect of this grazing was done
as a result of a lawsuit filed by environmentalists. The results found that
most federal land was, indeed, overstocked.

An adult meadow vole *(Microtus pennsylvanicus)*. Photograph by Karl H. Maslowski.

Meadow Vole
Microtus pennsylvanicus (Ord)

Description: Meadow voles are one of five small-eared voles in Wyoming. To distinguish the Wyoming voles, the middle upper molars must be inspected (see Key, p. 288). Meadow voles are medium-sized mice with small inconspicuous ears, dark gray fur above, dark feet, white underfur with a light brown wash, small eyes and a scantily-haired bicolored tail.

Size: Adults may attain the following dimensions: total length 160–185 mm; tail 45–60 mm; hind foot 20–22 mm; ear 11–14 mm; weight 30–65 grams. Males and females are about the same size.

Range and Habitat: Meadow voles occur throughout Canada, the northern and eastern United States and as isolated populations south through the Rocky Mountains to Mexico. Two subspecies of meadow voles live in Wyoming. *Microtus pennsylvanicus pullatus* S. Anderson (circles) occurs in western Wyoming and *Microtus penn*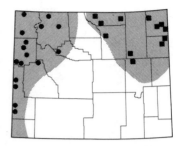
sylvanicus insperatus (J.A. Allen) (squares) occurs in the northeastern part of Wyoming. Meadow voles in Wyoming occupy moist grasslands, sedge meadows and riparian areas with dense stands of grass or cattails.

Reproduction: Meadow voles breed year-round. Copulation induces ovulation and gestation requires about 21 days. Summer litters are larger than those born at other seasons, varying from one to eleven (usually four to six). Pink, naked young are helpless at birth, but are weaned after 12–14 days, reach adult weight by 12 weeks, and can breed by 4 to 6 weeks. Mortality is high in young—90 per cent die within 30 days. Average adult life spans are 2–10 months, depending on population density.

Habits: Meadow voles are active all year and may be active at any time of day. More daytime activity is observed in areas with dense vegetative cover, under snow or on dark days. Meadow voles are active in runways that they form by trampling vegetation or by clipping. These runways are floors for tunnels under the snow, and are often lined with clipped vegetation. Nest areas and feeding areas are connected by these runways. Nests are woven with dry grasses and other plant fiber. Nests are above ground (at the base of stumps or shrubs) in the summer and underground in the winter. Meadow voles live solitarily and can drive off other species of small rodents from grassland. Populations cycle with a period of two to five years and dispersal behavior probably accounts for the cycles. Male home ranges include several females (90–200 square meters) and females excluded other females from smaller home ranges (30–90 square meters). Male home ranges overlap. Males congregate on territories of estrous females and compete for access to these receptive mates. Meadow voles can use the sun, like honeybees, to find their way home.

Food: Meadow voles eat most available herbaceous vegetation, including grasses and sedges. Like other *Microtus,* an unusually large caecum in the gut allows microorganisms to break down cellulose so that 90 percent digestive efficiency is achieved. Mean body weights and growth are reduced in the winter to reduce food requirements. Fat metabolism increases in the winter to keep meadow voles warm.

Remarks: Hawks, owls, snakes and a variety of other carnivores eat this vole.

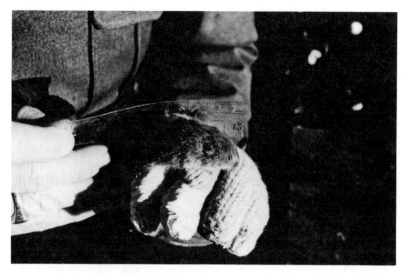

An adult montane vole *(Microtus montanus).* Photograph by C. Fudge.

Montane Vole
Microtus montanus (Peale)

Description: Montane voles are light brown above with white underparts, and have small, inconspicuous ears, small eyes and small feet. Their tail is bicolored and relatively short for Wyoming voles (see Key, p. 288). Further, their middle upper molar has only four enclosed triangles. Montane voles have long, sometimes grizzled fur.

Size: Adults may attain the following dimensions: total length 135–186 mm; tail 35–55 mm; hind foot 17–21 mm; ear 12–16 mm; weight 37–85 grams.

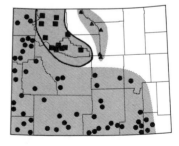

Range and Habitat: Montane voles have a widespread distribution in the Rocky Mountains from Canada to New Mexico. This distribution pattern resembles a drying pool of water with isolated pockets and fingers projecting from the main mass. Montane voles in Wyoming occupy grassy openings from boreal coniferous forests to juniper-sage communities, skirting the Bighorn Basin from Yellowstone southeast to the Medicine Bow Mountains. Three subspecies are known in Wyoming. *Microtus montanus nanus* (Merriam) (circles) occurs in the western and southern counties. *Microtus montanus codiensis* (S. Anderson)

(squares) ocurs from the east-facing slopes of the Absaroka Mountains to the western edge of the Bighorn Basin. *Microtus montanus zygomaticus* (S. Anderson) (triangles) lives in the Bighorn Mountains. Moist meadows and grasslands with friable soil from 1500 to 3000 meters in elevation support this vole. Isolated, small patches of aspen/mountain mahogany/ serviceberry and riparian meadow on the mountains of Sweetwater County also are inhabited by these voles.

Reproduction: Montane voles can breed all year, but most breeding occurs during the warmer months. Copulation stimulates ovulation and pregnancy lasts about 20 days. Young are born naked and helpless, but are independent of the nest by 2 or 3 weeks. In fact, females can mate as young as 21 days of age. From one to five litters of four to six can be produced by a female each year. The onset of breeding in the spring is stimulated by chemicals in the plant food. Adults generally do not survive 1 year in the wild.

Habits: Montane voles use runways and maintain them under the snow. They are active all year and may be active at any time of the day. Burrows are dug in soft soil and nests are made of dried grass. Females are territorial both with their own kind and with meadow voles. Males are not territorial in Montana. Home ranges vary from 7.3 square meters in winter to 76 square meters in summer. Montane voles can be excluded from areas chosen by meadow voles.

Remarks: Anderson (1954) and Long (1965) suggested that an isolated population of this vole persisted during colder glaciation in the relatively warm Bighorn Basin, and gave rise to *Microtus montanus codiensis.* This is one of several examples of distributional puzzles involving mammals surviving in isolated pockets of the Bighorn Basin.

Long-Tailed Vole
Microtus longicaudus longicaudus (Merriam)

Description: Long-tailed voles are medium-sized mice with small, inconspicuous ears, small eyes, small feet, gray-brown dorsal fur and dirty yellow-white underfur. Tails of these voles are 2.5–3.5 times as long as their hind foot. Upper middle molars have four closed triangles. These latter two features are unique to the long-tailed vole.

Size: Adults may attain the following dimensions: total length 175–220 mm; tail 55–90 mm; hind foot 20–25 mm; ear 13–17 mm; weight 40–55 grams.

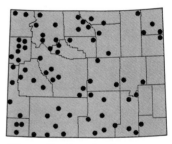

Range and Habitat: Long-tailed voles range along the west coast of North America from Alaska to California, and extend southeast from Montana to New Mexico. They occur throughout Wyoming except in the extreme southeastern part. Habitats of the long-tailed vole are variable, including grassland, alpine and wet meadows, and streamsides with deciduous trees in Teton County. In Sweetwater County, these rare habitats are occupied when available, but long-tailed voles also occur in big sage and juniper areas where dense grass is not present.

Reproduction: The warm months see a peak in breeding by long-tailed voles. In Wyoming, litters range from two to eight and several litters are born each year.

Habits: Long-tailed voles resemble other Wyoming voles in their herbivorous life among the grass stems. They are active at night, particularly in the summer, and remain active all year. They are less active runway-builders than other Wyoming *Microtus.* Long-tailed voles can dig, and they use shallow burrows for feeding and travel routes. Nests are built in the burrows and sometimes above ground (rock crevice, hollow log). Long-tailed voles vary in abundance up to 120 per hectare. Home ranges of males are larger (about 0.27 hectare) than those of females (0.19 hectare).

Food: Diet of the long-tailed voles includes grasses, sedges, bulbs and a wide variety of herbaceous vegetation.

Remarks: Although this vole is abundant, many aspects of its behavior and reproduction are poorly known. Overgrazing, which removes the litter layer in all habitats, may reduce vole populations. A wide variety of predators eat this vole including owls, kestrels, weasels, snakes, herons, skunks, and foxes.

An adult prairie vole *(Microtus ochrogaster)*. Photograph by Thomas H. Kunz.

Prairie Vole
Microtus ochrogaster (Wagner)

Description: Prairie voles are sturdily built, stocky, small mice with short legs and short tails. Their heads are relatively large and their eyes and ears are comparatively inconspicuous. Prairie voles are dark above (gray-brown) and they have a uniquely yellow-brown or buff belly. Their tails are dark above and lighter below.

Size: Adults may attain the following dimensions: total length 144–180 mm; tail 33–45 mm; hind foot 19–22 mm; ear 11–15 mm; weight 30–70 grams. Males and females are about the same size.

Range and Habitat: Two subspecies occur in Wyoming: *Microtus ochrogaster haydeni* (Baird) (circles), and *Microtus ochrogaster similis* Severinghaus (squares). Prairie voles followed the natural distribution of prairies in central North America from the central provinces in Canada along the eastern foothills of the Rocky 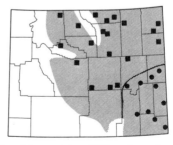 Mountains south to Texas. They occur in the drier prairies of Wyoming where shrubs are not co-dominants, but grasses were at least historically dominant.

171

Reproduction: Breeding occurs throughout the warmer months, generally from March or April to September. Copulation stimulates ovulation. Males and females form pairs and raise the young together. Gestation requires about 21 days and from four to six young are born in a litter. Females may have several litters during a year. Extremely warm or dry weather can limit breeding, but females can produce a litter about every 25–30 days. Young are weaned by 3 weeks and can breed by 30 days. However, if young remain with parents, sexual maturity and growth are suppressed. Prairie voles usually only live a few months, often breeding only once.

Habits: Prairie voles construct runways through vegetation by clipping grass or other plants in the way. They frequently dig burrows (about 4–5 cm across) at the base of a clump of grass. Runways weave between these burrow entrances. Nests are constructed either in the burrow or in depressions. Densities vary widely between habitats and over time. Densities of 60–100 per hectare occasionally "crash" to one or two per hectare. Prairie voles live in family groups and so have clumped spatial distributions in suitable habitats. These voles forage on a wide variety of plants occurring on the ground, but instead of climbing, stems of taller vegetation are clipped and discarded repeatedly until the more nutritious tips are lowered within reach. These voles are active at night year-round and may be active during the day. Home ranges vary from 0.3–0.6 hectare. Prairie voles might be territorial at some times of the year, but are known to be generally tolerant of others and live in large groups.

Food: Prairie voles feed on a small fraction of the available plant species and eat only certain parts of those at hand, depending on nutritional value and taste. They can increase their gut capacity, in response to cold temperatures or poor quality food, by lengthening their intestine (Gross et al. 1985). When green vegetation is not available, seeds, fruits, bark and tubers are eaten. Grass and seeds are stored in dry places for use in winter.

Remarks: Probably because they are so abundant, prairie voles are well studied. A variety of predators eat prairie voles including hawks, owls, foxes, coyotes, weasels and shrews.

An adult water vole *(Microtus richardsoni)*. Photograph by Daniel R. Ludwig.

Water Vole
Microtus richardsoni macropus (Merriam)

Description: Water voles are easily recognized by their dark brown or black pelage above and their large size. They are stocky mice with large heads and relatively inconspicuous eyes and ears. They are gray below with dark feet, the tail is dark above and gray below, and their fur is long, soft and dense.

Size: Adults may attain the following dimensions: total length 212–260 mm; tail 70–85 mm; hind foot 25–30 mm; ear 15–20 mm; weight 85–120 grams. Males are slightly larger than females.

Range and Habitat: Water voles live in the coastal ranges of Oregon and Washington and the northern Rocky Mountains of Canada, Idaho, Montana, western Wyoming to northern Utah. In the Absarokas, water voles are most abundant in subalpine and alpine meadow streams of low gradient bordered by overhanging banks.

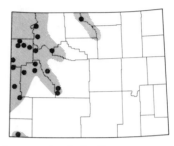

They occasionally occur in burrows in alpine grassland. In Oregon, water voles live along streams in Douglas fir forests with a shrubby understory dominated by vine maple, grasses, and sedges. Cut-over shrubby stages of this forest favored water voles. In the Owl Creek Mountains, water voles were living along a marshy creek at 2800-3000 meters with grass and sedge below aspen (Madson et al. 1980).

Reproduction: In Oregon, water voles were pregnant only in July and one had six embryos. By late August and September, young had left the nest. In Jackson Hole, water voles were pregnant from July to late August, and the mean litter size was six (range five to nine).

Habits: Water voles are rare and restricted to limited habitats. In Oregon, during a 6-year study when over 4500 other mice were caught, only 40 water voles were captured. In the Absarokas, only the streamsides of alpine meadows supported water voles. Behavioral studies are lacking, but even within a suitable habitat they are typically taken only in traps located next to the stream. In Oregon, individuals moved about 100 meters, but usually were recaptured in the same 0.2 hectare area. In the Absarokas, up to 23 per hectare were observed. In the Owl Creek Mountains, 9 per hectare were observed in late July and early August. In all three studies, most water voles were captured at one trap or only a few adjacent traps, suggesting they may live in groups. Water voles are good swimmers and dig burrows. Their runways near streams are littered with clippings, and are conspicuous. Nests are probably constructed in burrows which are dug into banks overhanging streams. Underwater entrances to the burrow system are constructed. A variety of small resting shelves along the edge of the stream are used.

Food: Diet of the water vole is poorly known, but probably includes a variety of grasses, sedges, seeds, inner bark of small, woody plants (willow), and nutritious herbs.

Remarks: Water voles were collected frequently in Wyoming through the 1940's. Since the 1960's, we are aware of only three specimens taken in a very small meadow area of the Grass Creek drainage. Improper grazing of federally managed lands is particularly harmful to this vole because the wet montane meadows are often overgrazed when cattle congregate around water sources.

An adult sagebrush vole *(Lemmiscus curtatus)*. Photograph by M. L. Johnson.

Sagebrush Vole
Lemmiscus curtatus levidensis Goldman

Description: Sagebrush voles are small, light gray mammals with long, soft, dense fur. Each hair is darker gray at the base and more ash gray at the tip. Dorsal fur is darker than the silvery gray ventral fur. Sagebrush voles sometimes have a tawny tinge to the ears and nose. The tail is very short and almost uniformly colored. Upper middle molars are rootless with four closed triangles. Unlike those of other voles, the soles of the feet are densely furred.

Size: Adults may attain the following dimensions: total length 110–140 mm; tail 16–25 mm; hind foot 11–18 mm; ear 9–16 mm; weight 17–35 grams. Males and females are about the same size.

Range and Habitat: Sagebrush voles live from the Great Basin of Nevada and Utah to the northern Great Plains of Montana and North Dakota. They live in most of Wyoming where sage, greasewood, or rabbitbrush are dense. Sage openings up to 3500 meters in elevation support these voles.

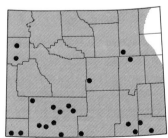

Reproduction: Sagebrush voles breed throughout the year, but appear to have a summer period of inactivity perhaps due to the dry season in sage areas. Gestation requires from 24–25 days. At least three litters (one to eight) can be produced by a female over a year. From two to thirteen are born in a litter (usually four to six). Young are born naked and blind but grow rapidly. If a nest is disturbed or if young detect weasel musk odors, they scatter from the nest and are later retrieved by their mothers. By 3 weeks they are weaned and start building their own nests. By 2 months, they begin to breed.

Habits: Sagebrush voles may be active 24 hours a day all year. If it is windy, they stay in their burrows more of the time. Burrows are shared colonial complexes with 10 or more entrances, may be as deep as 1 meter, and have many chambers. Sagebrush voles are extremely fastidious; droppings and urine are deposited outside the burrows and tunnels are paved with clippings of sage and grass. Above ground, vague runways can be seen through the typically sparse grass of dense sage areas. In winters, tunnels are kept open under the snow. Colonies of sagebrush voles periodically abandon a burrow system and build a new one in more favorable habitat. Females in captivity nurse young from other females in the colony. Breeding males can be aggressive, but no reports of territoriality are known. Home ranges are not known. Density in Sweetwater County ranged from 0.3–0.6 per hectare in suitable habitat patches.

Food: Sagebrush voles eat a wide variety of plants. They appear to be strictly herbivorous. Grass, seeds, tender shoots, flower buds, leaf buds and leaves from many plants are eaten. Sagebrush voles can survive on the water in their food alone if the food is sufficiently wet. Food is not cached.

Remarks: Sagebrush voles are not abundant in Wyoming, but new distribution records are constantly turning up. More work needs to be done to assess their status in Wyoming. Sagebrush voles are listed as rare in Montana. They are eaten by a wide variety of predators including burrowing owls, short-eared owls, rattlesnakes, bobcats, and long-tailed weasels. Jones et al. (1982) use the genus name *Lagurus.* Jones et al. (1984) use *Lemmiscus.*

An adult muskrat *(Ondatra zibethicus)*.

Muskrat
Ondatra zibethicus (Linnaeus)

Description: The muskrat is a large rodent with a tail that is as long as the head and body, and is laterally flattened like a rudder. Generally muskrats are dripping wet when seen and their fur appears black or dark brown. When dry, the fur varies from reddish brown to silvery gray. Muskrats have a large, blunt head on a stocky body. Molars are rooted, the large incisors grow continuously, and muskrats can close their lips behind the incisors to allow gnawing underwater.

Size: Adults may attain the following dimensions: total length 410–620 mm; tail 200–290 mm; hind foot 65–85 mm; ear 20–25 mm; weight 700–1,500 grams. Males and females are the same size.

Range and Habitat: Muskrats live throughout most of Alaska and Canada, and the contiguous United States, except the interior dry basins of the southwestern states, and occur throughout Wyoming. Two subspecies are known from the state. *Ondatra zibethicus osoyoosensis* (Lord) (circles) occurs in western Wyoming. *Ondatra*

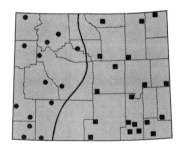

zibethicus cinnamominus (Hollister) (squares) occurs in eastern Wyoming. Muskrats occupy most aquatic habitats available including creeks, seeps, lakes, marshes and ponds.

Reproduction: In the cool climates of Wyoming, muskrats start breeding in April or May. Gestation requires from 25–30 days. In warmer climates, breeding starts sooner and more litters are produced. In Wyoming, two or three litters of six or seven young are common. Young are nursed for a month and reach independence at about 2 months. Most muskrats do not reach sexual maturity until their second spring. They usually survive 3 or 4 years.

Habits: Muskrats live a semi-aquatic life like that of a beaver, but unlike beavers, do not build dams. Their houses are of two types; a conical heap of mud and vegetation of up to a meter in height or a burrow into a bank. Nests are lined with fresh vegetation and are located in the center of the house or deep in the burrow. Muskrats have small home ranges of only 0.01 hectare and can be quite abundant (28–55 per hectare). They are generally active at night and during rainy days. Muskrats are territorial and have a dominance or pecking order; low ranking muskrats are driven from the best habitat. Males and females are barely tolerant of each other but the male will care for the young if the female dies. Muskrats swim about 1.5–5 kilometers per hour, and can dive for up to 20 minutes. Glands near their tail are used to deposit scent on their houses, trails and defecation sites. Populations of muskrats vary in density, perhaps following a 6 to 10 year cycle.

Food: Muskrats are primarily herbivorous. Roots and basal parts of locally available aquatic vegetation are eaten. Emergent vegetation (cattails) is important in their diet, but when crayfish, fish or molluscs are abundant, muskrats will eat them. The vegetation of the den is eaten in winter if necessary.

Remarks: Muskrats are an economic resource. Humans are the primary cause of mortality in muskrats and the harvest of their pelts continues to increase in value. Muskrats are only rarely eaten by foxes, feral dogs, mink, hawks, owls and raccoons.

An adult Norway rat *(Rattus norvegicus)*. Photograph courtesy of the Wisconsin Alumni Research Foundation.

OLD WORLD RATS AND MICE (FAMILY MURIDAE)
Norway Rat
Rattus norvegicus (Berkenhout)

Description: Norway rats are large rodents with a long round, naked tail. They have been introduced to Wyoming by humans. Their fur is short, coarse and grayish-brown above and pale gray below, and they have large, virtually naked ears and distinct rows of scales on the tail.

Size: Adults may attain the following dimensions: total length 300–450 mm; tail 125–190 mm; hind foot 35–45 mm; ear 22–24 mm; weight 250–450 grams. Males and females are the same size.

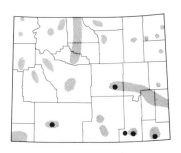

Range and Habitat: Norway rats occur throughout much of North America, Asia, and Europe. They were introduced to a variety of places by hitching rides on ships, wagons, trucks and trains. Norway rats typically occupy human dwellings and burrow in the basements. Norway rats can occur anywhere in Wyoming, but are more abundant near cities and towns.

Reproduction: The reproductive potential of Norway rats is staggering. These rats breed all year, and from six to eight litters of three to eight young can be produced annually. Gestation requires 21–23 days and young are independent by 3 weeks. Young start to breed by 2 months of age. Adults may live 2 or 3 years in the wild.

Habits: Norway rats function as global hitchiking companions of people and as vandals. These rats eat stored grain and food, and also forage in dumps. Norway rats are aggressive and will kill most native Wyoming rodents. They are agile climbers and good swimmers. These rodents dig burrows, often in rubble or at the base of buildings. Their nests are made of soft material, including grasses, leaves and paper. Home ranges are small — a single barn may be divided into several territories — and density can be quite high (up to 40–50 rats may live in a typical barn). Norway rats are most active at night but may be about at any time. They are active all year.

Food: Norway rats will eat anything which even closely resembles nutrition. Carrion, grain, alfalfa pellets, greasy paper, small mammals, green plants and any other available food is eaten.

Remarks: Norway rats are eaten by a variety of predators including coyotes, snakes, skunks, owls and hawks. Albino Norway rats are bred in laboratories for use in research. Norway rats are an economic problem causing much damage to human property. Warfarin, an anti-coagulant poison, was developed to control rats and is effective throughout the world. However, the ever-resilient Norway rat has developed several populations now resistant to Warfarin.

An adult house mouse *(Mus musculus)*. Photograph by Ernest P. Walker.

House Mouse
Mus musculus (Linnaeus)

Description: House mice are small rodents with a round, almost hairless tail covered with tiny scales. Their fur is gray to brown above and gray below. House mice have large, naked ears. Their upper incisors are smooth on the outer surface.

Size: Adults may attain the following dimensions: total length 130–200 mm; tail 63–102 mm; hind foot 16–21 mm; ear 11–18 mm; weight 18–25 grams. Sexes are the same size.

Range and Habitat: House mice originated in central Asia and have been repeatedly introduced throughout Wyoming by people. They occur throughout the world and because they disperse so well, subspecies cannot be identified with much certainty. House mice live in human habitations and occasionally establish breeding groups in adjacent fields.

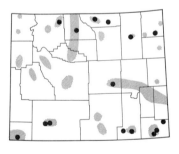

Reproduction: House mice rival most other rodents with regard to reproductive potential. They resemble annual weeds in their high output of young which receive minimal parental investment. After a gestation period of about 20 days, 2 to 12 naked, helpless young are born. In 3 weeks, young leave the female and she breeds again. Young begin to breed by about 4 weeks of age and the population breeds year-round. House mice usually die by 18–20 months in the wild, but can live up to 6 years.

Habits: House mice are active all year, usually at night. Their tiny tracks and droppings are indicative of nightly raids on stored food and household items. Nests are made of any soft material including paper, cloth, dried grass and the upholstery of abandoned furniture. House mice use runways and burrows abandoned by other rodents. This mouse is gregarious, and large mixed-sex groups often nest together.

Food: House mice eat anything edible. They will chew through paper and plastic wrappings, and often damage stored food.

Remarks: Laboratories throughout the world maintain inbred strains of house mice for use in medical and physiological studies. Thus, an extensive bibliography on the basic biology of the house mouse is known.

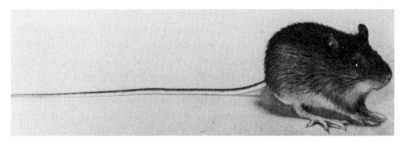

An adult meadow jumping mouse *(Zapus hudsonius)*. Photograph by Ernest P. Walker.

JUMPING MICE (FAMILY ZAPODIDAE)
Meadow Jumping Mouse
Zapus hudsonius (Zimmerman)

Description: Meadow jumping mice are long-tailed, medium-sized rodents with very long hind feet. Their round tails are sparsely haired, bicolored and longer than the head and body. Their ears are dark, edged with white. Meadow jumping mice have yellow-brown fur above with scattered long black-tipped hairs which produce a dark, mid-dorsal stripe. Their feet and ventral fur are white and their sides are yellow. They have small front feet, and lack cheek pouches. Young have softer, lighter colored fur than that of adults. Upper incisors have distinct grooves on the outer faces.

Size: Adults may attain the following dimensions: total length 180–220 mm; tail 115–136 mm; hind foot 28–31 mm; ear 11–16 mm; weight 12–22 grams. Sexes are about the same size.

Range and Habitat: Meadow jumping mice range across Alaska through Canada, the northern and eastern United States and across the Great Plains to the eastern foothills of the Rocky Mountains. In the plains states, these mice usually occupy marshy areas and moist streamside vegetation in open prairie. Two subspecies occur 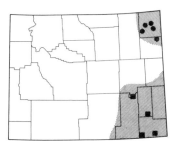 in Wyoming. *Zapus hudsonius campestris* Preble (circles) occurs in the Black hills. *Zapus hudsonius preblei* Krutzsch (squares) occurs in the eastern foothill marshes of the Laramie Range.

Reproduction: Female meadow jumping mice usually have two or three litters a summer. Gestation requires 17–20 days and from two to nine (usually four to six) are born in each litter. Young are born without hair and with their eyes closed. By 3 weeks, young are well haired, and by 4 weeks are weaned and become independent. Adult size is reached by

3 months of age. Most young breed in the summer following their birth. Meadow jumping mice usually survive up to 3 years.

Habits: Meadow jumping mice live solitarily and wander, shifting their nightly home ranges frequently. They are most active at night but are often seen during the day. These mice hibernate from October to May and their hibernation is profound and continuous. Hibernation burrows are usually in dry soil, often in naturally occurring mounds. During the summer, meadow jumping mice dig burrows as deep as 200 mm below the ground. Nests are probably in the burrows. When disturbed, these mice make two to four leaps of up to a meter each then they stop abruptly and try to avoid further disturbance by remaining motionless. They forage along the ground and clip tall herbs to reach the more nutritious terminal buds and leaves. Meadow jumping mice usually walk or take short (2–5 cm) hops. Home ranges shift up to a kilometer, probably in response to searches for wetter places during the summer dry periods. Males have larger home ranges (about 1 hectare) than females (about 0.6 hectare). Densities vary from year to year and range from 7.4–48 per hectare. Relatively dense vegetative cover is necessary for the maintenance of populations of meadow jumping mice. Other small mammals or the species of plants present apparently do not limit the distribution or abundance of these mice.

Food: Meadow jumping mice selectively eat buds, leaves, insects, grasses, fungi berries, and nuts. Food is not stored.

Remarks: Overgrazing of domestic animals, which consistently removes all dense vegetation along the eastern creeks of Wyoming, has no doubt contributed to the scarcity of these mice in Wyoming. They are listed as rare in the state.

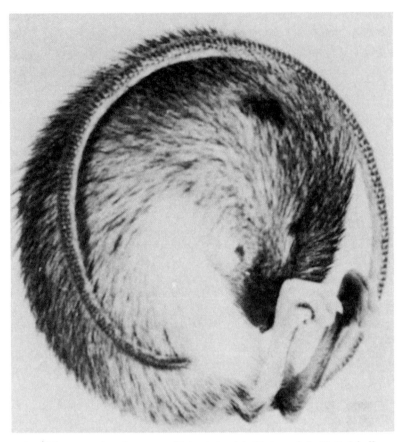

An adult western jumping mouse *(Zapus princeps)*. Photograph by V. B. Scheffer.

Western Jumping Mouse
Zapus princeps J.A. Allen

Description: Western jumping mice closely resemble meadow jumping mice, but have longer maxillary toothrows (3.7 mm or more) and are larger overall (total length more than 225 mm). For other general body characteristics, see the account for the meadow jumping mouse. These graceful mice are paler in color and the tail is less sharply bicolored than the meadow jumping mouse.

Size: Adults may attain the following dimensions: total length 210–250 mm; tail 125–150 mm; hind foot 27–33 mm; ear 12–16 mm; weight 18–25 grams. Sexes are about the same size.

Range and Habitat: Western jumping
mice occur throughout western North
America from Alaska to Arizona and
California. They also occur on the
Great Plains across Canada into the
Dakotas. In Wyoming, western jumping mice occur in suitable habitats in
the western parts of the state. They live
in wet, lush growth of streamsides,

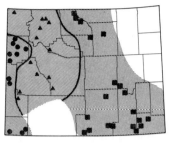

marshes and ponds. No obvious differences exist between the habitat
preferences of this mouse and the meadow jumping mouse. Western jumping mice occur in the mountains and along the rivers and streams descending from the high country. Their local distribution in Wyoming is
patchy, where three subspecies occur. *Zapus princeps utahensis* Hall
(circles) lives in the Teton, Salt River, Wyoming and Uinta mountains.
Zapus princeps idahoensis Davis occurs in the Absaroka, Wind River and
Owl Creek ranges (triangles). *Zapus princeps princeps* J.A. Allen occurs
in the Bighorn, Sierra Madre, Medicine Bow, and Laramie ranges
(squares).

Reproduction: Like the meadow jumping mouse, young depend on the
female for a relatively long time. As soon as spring thaw allows, males
and females emerge from hibernation. Within a week, they breed and
gestation requires about 18 days. Young number four to eight, and are
born helpless. They are nursed for a month and do not reach full independence for 2 or 3 months. In Wyoming, the mean life expectancy
of this small mammal is about 17 months (Brown 1970).

Habits: For the majority of the year, western jumping mice are deep in
hibernation. In Utah, this mouse is active only 90 days a year. A number
of studies have been done on hibernation in the western jumping mouse
(Cranford 1978). After raising young, these mice rapidly put on enough
fat to see them through the winter. Seeds are selectively eaten. Burrows
are dug in fine dry soils up to 0.5 m deep and spherical nests of finely
shredded, clean dry plant fibers are prepared. Mice enter these refuges
in September with body weights of up to 35 grams. Burrow entrances
are plugged with soil. By curling into a ball, loss of body heat is minimized. Many juvenile jumping mice die in hibernation or emerge too
early to face wet, freezing weather. Soil temperature warming in the spring
(8.5–9.0 °C) synchronizes emergence of the jumping mice. A critical
balance is struck between emerging too late to breed and emerging too
early and dying in the cold April winds. During the summer, these mice
live solitarily. Home range of males are about 0.30 hectare and 0.23 hectare for females. Home ranges are usually long and narrow (15–18 m wide).

Density is remarkably constant over several years and was about eight per hectare in eastern Wyoming. Densities of up to 40 per hectare are known.

Food: Western jumping mice eat a variety of seeds and invertebrates. Seeds are particularly important in late summer.

Remarks: Overgrazing by domestic animals of montane, streamside meadows reduces vegetative cover and wipes out annual grass seed production. This is harmful to jumping mice. These mice are widespread, but are not abundant anywhere.

An adult porcupine *(Erethizon dorsatum)*. Photograph by Dick Randall.

PORCUPINES (FAMILY ERETHIZONTIDAE)
Porcupine
Erethizon dorsatum (Linnaeus)

Description: Porcupines are large rodents with stout bodies, short feet, thick, muscular tails, quills, spines and fur. Quills may be 75 mm long and up to 30,000 grow in rows across the body. Not all quills are barbed. Feet have strong claws. There are no quills on the undersurface of the body.

Size: Adults may attain the following dimensions: total length 790–1030 mm; tail 145–300 mm; hind foot 75–91 mm; ear 25–42 mm; weight 3.5–18 kilograms. Males and females are the same size.

Range and Habitat: Porcupines occur throughout the northern parts of North America to the central Great Plains and south along the Rocky Mountains to northern Mexico. Two subspecies occur in Wyoming: *Erethizon dorsatum epixanthum* (Brandt) (circles) in western Wyoming, and *Erethizon dorsatum bruneri* (Swenk)

189

(squares) in eastern Wyoming. Porcupines tend to be confined to forests or vegetated riparian areas, but we have frequently encountered them in grassland or sage-grassland many miles from the nearest trees.

Reproduction: Porcupines breed very carefully and an elaborate courtship ritual is followed. A relatively long gestation period of 29–31 weeks follows breeding in the fall. Usually only a single, well-developed baby is born. Quills are soft at birth, but within a few hours young can climb and the quills become functional. Young are nursed for 2 or 3 weeks, and stay close to the mother for a few months. Sexual maturity is reached at two years of age. Free-living porcupines live as long as 10 years, and captive porcupines have lived 20 years.

Habits: Porcupines are slow moving, solitary rodents. They "talk to themselves" in a "voice" variously described as moans, mews, sobs, whines, hoots and wails. Porcupines do not hibernate and are active all year. They have good memories and make intelligent pets. Usually they are nocturnal. Porcupines live in dens in caves, hollow logs and trees. No nests are made and if such a shelter is not available, porcupines will often spend a winter in a tree. They tend to return to the same tree but are not territorial. Home ranges vary from 5 hectares in the winter to perhaps 14 hectares in the summer. Densities of 1 to 8 (usually 3–5) per square kilometer are normal. Porcupines actually cause minimal damage in a healthy forest stand unless their density is unusually high.

Food: Porcupines eat the inner bark of trees as well as evergreen needles. Buds, leaves, small twigs and herbs are eaten in the summer. They have a large caecum in the gut where bacteria digest cellulose and are in turn digested by the porcupine.

Remarks: Porcupines do not throw their quills, but the quills of a frightened porcupine are more easily detached. Porcupines may slap attackers with their tails. The fisher is specialized to kill porcupines. Natural populations of fishers can keep porcupine populations quite low (Powell 1979). Other causes of mortality are fire, automobiles, and falling out of trees.

An adult male coyote *(Canis latrans)*. Photograph by Dick Randall.

DOGS (FAMILY CANIDAE)
Coyote
Canis latrans Say

Description: The coyote is a medium-size to large doglike animal similar in appearance to the gray wolf. Coyote hair shows a banded appearance of blended color, gray mixed with a reddish tint. The pelage overall is grayish to brownish with occasional black. This mammal has long pointed ears, and the tail is well furred and similar in color to the rest of the body.

Size: Adults may attain the following dimensions: total length 1100–1225 mm; tail 330–400 mm; hind foot 180–195 mm; ear 100–125 mm; weight 10–20 kilograms. The largest coyote on record came from Wyoming and weighed 33.94 kilograms (Young 1951).

Range and Habitat: Coyotes occur throughout North America except the southeastern United States. They occur throughout Wyoming, where two subspecies are recognized: *Canis latrans latrans* Say (squares) and *Canis latrans lestes* Merriam (circles). Coyotes live in a wide variety of habitats including plains, deserts, and 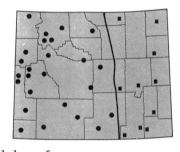 mountains with grass and shrubs, and dense forests.

Reproduction: Much is known about coyote reproductive biology largely because of the keen interest in coyote control. The monestrus females show one "heat" period annually, usually between January and March. Estrus lasts up to 10 days. Copulation terminates with the copulatory "tie" lasting up to 30 minutes. Males and females both show annual cyclic change in reproductive status. Courtship may begin 2 to 3 months prior to estrus. About 60–90 percent of adult females breed. Gestation is about 63 days. Litter size is affected by population density, but averages six (Bekoff 1977). Young are born helpless and blind, and weigh about 210–275 grams. Pups reach adult size in about 9 months.

Habits: Coyote ecology is better known than perhaps any other Wyoming carnivore. Several major studies, totaling over 10 years' work, were conducted in Jackson Hole (Camenzind 1974, Weaver 1977, Bekoff and Wells 1980). Coyotes tend to be most active at sunrise and sunset, but may be active at any hour. In winter, coyotes rest more than in summer. Dens are located in a wide variety of places, including old badger dens, brush covered slopes, rock ledges, dense timber, and in hollow logs. Home ranges, areas regularly used but not actively defended, vary seasonally, geographically, within populations, and by the type of social organization. They vary from 10–68 square kilometers. Coyotes form packs where food is relatively abundant but move as solitary animals in low-food areas. The basic social unit is the adult male, female, and their young. Coyotes are less social than wolves. Bekoff (1982) noted that it is "shocking" that so little is known about wild coyote predatory behavior on domestic livestock in view of the widespread assumption that they are extremely destructive.

Food: Coyotes eat almost anything edible, including voles, ground squirrels and carrion. In Jackson Hole, coyote stomachs containing ungulate carrion (dead elk, deer, moose, bison, pronghorns, bighorn sheep). Plants, frogs, lizards, and insects are eaten also.

Remarks: The coyote takes advantage of poorly devised and operated livestock programs, and because of its success in this regard, the coyote has obtained the reputation of being fierce and ruthless. Annually, large sums are spent trying to control coyotes. Little data support the contention that coyote predation limits game populations. Selective control targeted on specific problem coyotes seems much more appropriate than widespread use of Compound 1080, coyote-getters (cyanide), or the like. The coyote functions as a valuable ecological regulator, and should be appreciated because of this function and its remarkably versatile behavior.

Adult gray wolves *(Canis lupus)*. Photograph by Dick Randall.

Gray Wolf
Canis lupus Linnaeus

Description: The gray wolf is the largest member of the dog family. It has relatively larger legs than a German shepherd, larger feet, and a narrower chest. Its face can be identified by the wide tufts of hair that project down and outward from below the ears. A wolf's tail is straight, whereas a domestic dog's tail generally curls upward posteriorly. Adult wolves, except for the dark forms, have white fur around the mouth. Coloration is highly variable. The "gray" wolf may vary in color from pure white to coal black. The usual color is not gray but a cream mixed with brown or light tan.

Size: Adults may attain the following dimensions: total length 1300–1835 mm; tail 300–450 mm; hind foot 250–275 mm; weight, males 20–80 kilograms, females 18–55 kilograms; male shoulder height is about 700–800 mm. The feet are more than 35 mm in diameter.

Range and Habitat: Gray wolves once occurred throughout much of North America. They formerly occurred throughout Wyoming (Long 1965), but were nearly exterminated by the 1940's (Weaver 1978). There were three subspecies represented then: *Canis lupus irremotus* Goldman (solid circles); *Canis lupus nubilus* Say (solid squares); and *Canis lupus youngi*

Goldman (triangles). Today, there are intermittent reports of wolf-like canids, quite possibly wolves, in Yellowstone National Park and adjacent Park and Teton counties. The gray wolf exists in varied habitats, including grasslands, sagebrush steppes, coniferous and mixed forests, usually co-associated with ungulates such as elk, 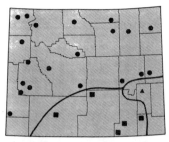 deer, moose. Reasons for wolf decline include loss of habitat throughout much of Wyoming, drastic reduction of bison and other prairie ungulate herds, and intensive and long-lasting control by humans. Otto Franc, a rancher on the upper Greybull River, noted in his diary that wolves only became a problem to his livestock once the bison were gone. By 1894, livestock depredations were common and poison baits were used to eliminate wolves. Ernest Thompson Seton noted that bounties were paid on 4,281 wolves from eastern Wyoming in 1897–1898. In the 11-year period ending in 1908, bounties were paid on 10,819 Wyoming wolves (see Long 1965).

Reproduction: Breeding data have been summarized by Mech (1974). Wolves reach sexual maturity in their second year, but may not breed until 3 years old. They show signs of mate preference and probably mate for life. Females become receptive anytime between January and April. An estrus of 5 to 7 days is followed by copulation in the typical canid fashion with a tie up to 30 minutes in length. Gestation is 63 days and about six young (range one to 11) are born blind and helpless usually in a den. Pups emerge from the den in the third week. Socialization into the pack follows. By 10 months, pups are adult size and participate in hunts.

Habits: Gray wolves do not make use of regular shelter. Dens, usually on slopes or other high ground near water, are used only for birth and care of young. These mammals use rendezvous sites varying from about 0.4–1.0 km long, where the pups remain while adults hunt. In fall, pups join in hunting. Winter movements are surprisingly rapid and lengthy. Reports include seven wolves moving 65 km in 20 hours. One wolf per 26 square kilometers is a high density, and densities are usually lower (Pimlott 1967). Pack home ranges of 3100 square kilometers are more common (Mech 1970). Wolves are very social and nearly always live in packs. Pack members, ranging up to 36 animals, are loosely associated with one another. Pack cohesion is based on strong bonds of affection. The social structure within a pack is centered on a dominance hierarchy of both males and females. Wolves communicate by scents, sounds, and contact, as well as by posturing themselves to signify aggression or submission.

Food: The gray wolf is a carnivore and feeds typically on large prey such as elk, deer, and moose in present times, but mammals smaller than beaver may comprise up to about 20 percent of its total intake. Wolves also eat domestic animals. Wolves can consume up to 9 kilograms at a single feeding and food is digested rapidly. It is estimated that an average healthy wolf needs 1.8 kilograms of meat per day. Wolves can go several days without food. They spend nearly all their waking time either hunting or eating. Predation by wolves can serve to: (1) cull injured animals, (2) control or partially control prey population sizes, or (3) stimulate productivity in prey herds.

Remarks: Wolves may reach 16 years of age, although 10 years is considered old. Wolf attacks on humans are very rare. There is strong evidence that the North American wolf is harmless to humans. The wolf receives full protection under the 1973 Endangered Species Act. A proposal to restore the wolf, a native animal, to Yellowstone National Park, has been recommended (U.S. Fish and Wildlife Service, 1985).

An adult red fox *(Vulpes vulpes)*. Photograph by Ken Stiebben, courtesy of the Kansas Fish and Game Commission.

Red Fox
Vulpes vulpes (Linnaeus)

Description: The red fox is a small dog-like animal with long, pointed ears and an elongated, pointed snout. The large bushy tail is white-tipped and distinguishes this species from swift and gray foxes. The pelage is dense and the upper body is reddish yellow and darkest near the shoulders and back. Black stockings are present on the long legs. There are several color phases, especially in cold regions: black, silver, cross (dark cross on shoulders), bastard (bluish gray), and Samson (no guard hairs).

Size: Adults may attain the following dimensions: total length 827–1015 mm; tail 291–461 mm; hind foot 124–182 mm; ear 65–102 mm; weight 3–7 kilograms.

Range and Habitat: Red foxes live throughout North America from Alaska to Mexico except in the higher western mountain ranges. They are found throughout Wyoming. Two subspecies are recognized in the state: *Vulpes vulpes macroura* Baird (circles) and *Vulpes vulpes regalis* Merriam (squares). Red foxes prefer a mixture

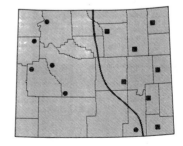

of streamside communities, rolling farmlands, brush, pastures, and open areas. They use areas diverse in habitats with many communities intermixed (Ables 1974).

Reproduction: Female red foxes are monestrus. Breeding takes place from December to March. Gestation is 51–54 days. Estrus lasts 1 to 6 days and females may breed at 10 months of age. About 10 percent of all adult females may not breed. Uterine blood vessels and placental scars are conspicuous following parturition. Average litter size was 5.5 based on placental scar counts and 6.4 based on embryo counts. Newborn pups range from 71–119 grams and are full grown in about 6 months. Red foxes may move the pups between dens up to three times before they are 6 weeks old. By late September the young disperse.

Habits: Red fox home ranges vary greatly, but may be up to 5 square kilometers. Along stream sides, home ranges are narrow and long. Red foxes may use abandoned dens of marmots or badgers or may dig their own. They have been reported to live in the same den with marmots. Cover type, distance to water, and human disturbances determine den sites. Communal dens used by several red foxes are known. Mange is sometimes present as well as rabies and distemper. This mammal produces a series of short, sharp yaps to long howls and screeches.

Food: Red fox foods are well known. They often store food in caches by digging a small hole, placing the food item in it, and covering it over. Caches are more common in areas where food is seasonally scarce. From stomach and scat analysis, mice (in summer) and rabbits (in winter) are often the most common food eaten. Insect and plant matter are heavily used in summer also.

Remarks: Maximum red fox longevity is 4 to 5 years. There have been few management programs aimed specifically at foxes, especially habitat manipulation (Pils and Martin 1978). Bounties appear to be of little value in regulating fox numbers.

An adult swift fox *(Vulpes velox)*. Photograph by Ken Stiebben, courtesy of the Kansas Fish and Game Commission.

Swift Fox
Vulpes velox velox (Say)

Description: Swift foxes are identified by their small size and black-tipped tails. Their fur is orange-yellow above with frosty or black tips. Side and belly fur is white or light yellow.

Size: Adults may grow to the following dimensions: total length 735–880 mm; tail 240–350 mm; hind foot 114–135 mm; ear 56–78 mm; weight (males) 2.2–2.9 kilograms; (females) 1.8–2.3 kilograms. Males are slightly larger than females.

Range and Habitat: Swift foxes occur throughout the northern Great Plains from the foothills of the Rocky Mountains across the prairies of the Dakotas, Nebraska, Oklahoma and west Texas. Extensive trapping in recent years has revealed no evidence of breeding populations of these foxes in western or central Wyoming. From 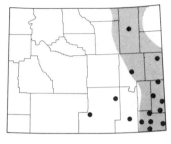 1858 to 1898 swift foxes occurred in Carbon County, but are apparently extinct there now.

Swift foxes were once common in shortgrass and mid-grass prairies, but now occur only on the remnants of shortgrass prairie. In Laramie county, they are locally abundant (one pair per 5–8 square kilometers) in the wetter shortgrass prairies often inter-mixed with winter wheat fields. Foxes followed with radio collars revealed that up to 10 dens were used by a breeding female. Dens are dug on rolling ridge tops which command wide views. Old corrals and building foundations, junk piles and virtually all parts of the prairie were visited by the foxes. Dens sometimes are dug and occupied near roads.

Reproduction: In Laramie County, male and female swift foxes occasionally share dens from early March through July. The gestation period is not known, but is probably about 50 days. From three to six young are born in a litter. In Laramie County, young emerged from the burrows by the first of June and were 80 percent of adult size by late June. Both adults stayed with the litter through early July. Only one litter is born each year. In Laramie County, swift foxes use many dens and some foxes move their litter frequently and at the slightest disturbance. The hunting areas of a pair of foxes partially overlap during gestation and pup growth in Laramie County. Swift foxes may live up to 12 years.

Habits: Swift foxes are active at night during which they can cover 8–10 square kilometers. In Laramie County, these foxes move 3–4 kilometers per hour in an erratic pattern. Snow tracks reveal they encountered sleeping horned larks and chased jack rabbits. Swift fox eyes reflect gold into a headlight. They are often killed by cars as they feed on road-killed carrion, and are notoriously easy to trap.

Adults and puppies sun themselves in the cool mornings, then remain in their burrows until dusk. Dens are concentrated in areas of suitable soil and some are used alternately by either red foxes or swift foxes during a given year. Swift foxes support an amazing density of fleas.

Food: Scats collected in Laramie County revealed a seasonal change in diet. During winter, horned larks, jack rabbits, and deer mice are frequently eaten. When ground squirrels emerge from hibernation in spring, they are taken. During the summer and fall, beetles, small mammals, and grasshoppers form almost all the diet. Pups may be provisioned with vertebrate prey while adults continue to eat mostly insects. Elsewhere, swift foxes are known to take a wide variety of prey (Kilgore 1969, Egoscue 1979).

Remarks: Swift foxes are rare in Wyoming, probably due to habitat alteration, predator poisoning programs, and over-trapping. These foxes are useful to humans and often den near buildings. Coyote traps often inadvertently kill swift foxes. Swift foxes are listed as endangered in Nebraska, uncommon in North Dakota, of concern in Montana, and abundant in Colorado.

An adult gray fox *(Urocyon cinereoargenteus)*. Photograph by Ken Stiebben, courtesy of the Kansas Fish and Game Commission.

Gray Fox
Urocyon cinereoargenteus ocythous Bangs

Description: The gray fox is grizzled in appearance on its back and sides because of its long guard hairs of black-white and gray. A cinnamon color is present on the neck, sides, and limbs. The tail is black-tipped and a crest of dark hairs is present. Portions of the ears, throat, chest, belly, and hind legs are cinnamon-rufous.

Size: Adults may attain the following dimensions: total length 800–1125 mm; tail 275–443 mm; hind foot 100–150 mm; weight 3–7 kilograms. Males are slightly larger than females.

Range and Habitat: Gray foxes range from the California coast to Panama and throughout the eastern United States. They are found only in the eastern part of Wyoming. The northern Great Plains subspecies extends from the Dakotas to its western limit in Wyoming. It is associated with deciduous forests, stream courses, and 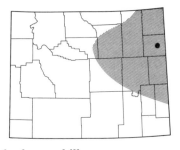 shrublands and brushy woodlands in broken or hilly country.

Reproduction: The gray fox breeds from January to April and is thought to be monogamous. Gestation is 53 days. Most young males as well as older males show spermatozoa in October and November. Average litter size is four. For the first month after birth, the pups remain at the den.

Habits: Gray foxes den in woodpiles, hollow trees, brushpiles, or rocky outcrops. One den was found in a tree 7.6 meters above the ground (Grinnell et al. 1937). Home ranges are often about 100–200 hectares. Juvenile foxes may disperse up to 84 km (Sheldon 1953). Studies elsewhere show that about 45 percent of new born foxes died in their first 7 months, and that population numbers peak following a wet, warm winter. Gray foxes are largely nocturnal or crepuscular. Social organization is probably based around a family unit of an adult male and female, and possibly juveniles. Family units maintain separate home ranges. Urine and feces are thought to play a role in communication.

Food: Gray foxes eat a wide variety of animal and plant materials. Animal food includes rabbits, squirrels, mice and rats, weasels, pocket gophers, songbirds, crows, ducks, bird eggs, turtles, muskrats, house cats and dogs, and insects. These foxes eat wheat, corn, grass, sedges, nuts, elderberries, apples, grapes, pears, and many grains also.

Remarks: Gray foxes are well known for their tree climbing ability and have been observed to climb vertical, branchless tree trunks to at least 18 meters by grasping with their forefeet and pushing with their hindfeet. Beyond a crude idea of gray fox distribution in Wyoming, little else is known of their biology in the state, and this animal is considered rare (Clark and Weaver 1981).

An adult black bear *(Ursus americanus)*. Photograph by Dick Randall.

BEARS (FAMILY URSIDAE)
Black Bear
Ursus americanus cinnamomum Audubon and Bachman

Description: The black bear is one of two bear species in Wyoming, and can be distinguished from the grizzly bear by a lack of long hairs on its shoulders and by its foot prints which seldom leave claw marks. Black bears show a variety of colors, including cinnamon, black, brown, and beige, with black most prevalent. This bear may occasionally have white patches on its chest and neck.

Size: Adults may attain the following dimensions: total length 1000–2000 mm; tail 85–130 mm; hind foot 185–290 mm; ear 130–150 mm; weight 40–70 kilograms. A very large bear may weigh 300 kilograms.

Range and Habitat: Black bears are no longer common in many places; historically they ranged from Alaska throughout Canada to central Mexico and across the United States except interior Nevada and western Arizona. They occur in the western two-thirds of Wyoming and the mountains of the northeast and south central part of the

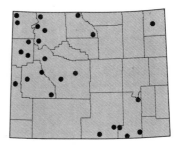

state. Black bears are most abundant in the mountains, but are very adaptable. They prefer roadless areas with thick understory vegetation.

Reproduction: Breeding occurs in summer, peaking in June and July. Females become sexually mature at 3 to 5 years of age. Gestation is 210–220 days. Black bears have delayed implantation. After the egg is fertilized, there is some development to the blastocyst stage. The blastocyst floats free in the uterus until late November-December, when it implants in the wall. Cubs are born in winter dens in January-February, hairless, eyes closed, and helpless. At birth, they are about 200 mm in length. Litter size averages two. Cubs stay with their mothers through the second winter and disperse the following spring.

Habits: In their dens, black bears enter a deep sleep but do not truly hibernate. The body temperature and metabolism do not decrease very much. Transition into and out of denning may last up to a month. Black bears are most active at dusk and dawn, and generally avoid man, except for those individuals which become habituated as a result of unburied trash dumps and garbage cans in camping areas. Bears claw trees; such trees are called "mark trees." The function of this is unknown. Black bears are usually solitary animals except for female and cub groups. Bear home ranges vary from 5–200 square kilometers based on individual requirements and the availability of resources in the region. They may move up to 160 kilometers. Characteristics of most bear populations are unknown largely because bears are very difficult to study.

Food: The black bear diet is mainly grasses, forbs, buds, berries, and roots, and only a small part is animal matter—insects, beetles, carrion. Black bears feed on other animals such as elk calves only when the opportunity presents itself, and are not generally active predators. The preferred foods are high in carbohydrates and low in fats and proteins.

Remarks: The former Yellowstone National Park roadside black bear population, now much smaller, has ceased depending on human hand-outs and has returned to the wild today, unlike its relatives a decade or two ago.

An adult grizzly bear *(Ursus arctos)*.

Grizzly Bear
Ursus arctos horribilis Ord

Description: Grizzly bears can be distinguished from black bears by: (1) a large skull with the second molar longer than 30 mm; (2) a prominent shoulder hump; (3) front feet with an indentation in the pad just behind the outer toe and a relatively straight edge along the front of the pad; and (4) claws of adolescents and adults typically longer than 5 cm. The pelage varies individually from black-brown to buff to nearly white. Long hairs on top of the shoulders have gray or white tips — giving the "grizzled" appearance. Lower parts of the legs are usually darker and pelage on the back may change slightly from summer to fall (Wright 1909).

Size: Adults may attain the following dimensions: total length 1700–2300 mm; tail 60–150 mm; hind foot 225–290 mm; ear 80–140 mm; weight 140–540 kilograms.

Range and Habitat: The grizzly bear formerly ranged throughout western North America. Today it occurs only in and around Yellowstone National Park and a few other areas in Montana, Idaho and Washington. The reasons for population decline are loss of wilderness habitat and over-hunting by humans. Grizzly bear habitat is

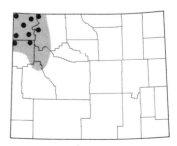

varied: non-forested valley and plateau grasslands and herblands with Idaho fescue and hairgrass, subalpine and alpine grasslands, stream bottoms, wet meadows, burns, ridgetops, avalanche chutes, and ungulate ranges (March-May). Forested areas used include those with wet to medium conditions, herbs, and fruiting shrub understory among spruce and subalpine firs.

Reproduction: In the Yellowstone ecosystem (Craighead et al. 1974), mating occurs from mid-May to mid-July (*ca.* 45 days). Grizzly bear copulation is vigorous and lengthy (up to 1 hour). Bears are polygamous. Estrus may last up to 27 days. Females produce their first litter at 5.5 years, and may then produce a new litter every 3 or more years. Delayed implantation occurs as in black bears. Two-cub litters are most common. Litters of one, three or four cubs are less common. Cubs are born in the winter den and may stay with their mothers 1 to 2 years.

Habits: Denning allows bears to escape periods of food shortage and inclement weather. Bear physiology in hibernation is different from most other true hibernators, and they do not become torpid. Bears enter dens in October and November and emerge between late March and early May. Factors governing denning behavior are not well understood.

Grizzly bears use over 2 million hectares in the Greater Yellowstone ecosystem. Many bears in the Yellowstone region use well-defined seasonal ranges separated in many cases by long migratory corridors. Home ranges vary by age and sex of the bear. The life range of one male probably exceeded 2,600 square kilometers. Ranges of 55–324 square kilometers are common. Overnight movements up to 24 km are known. Extensive grizzly bear movements are believed to be directly related to the absence of defined territories and a socially linear hierarchy, which allows bears the freedom to travel in addition to the ability to exploit resources over wide areas.

Food: Grizzly bears are omnivorous and feed on a wide variety of foods. John Muir noted, "Almost everything is food [to the grizzly bear] except granite." As much as 50–60 percent of the diet may be animal matter such as ants, moths, gophers, ground squirrels, elk, or bison. They prefer high protein animal food, but also eat large amounts of vegetable matter. Grizzlies will also eat at garbage dumps. In general, grasses ("survival rations") and forbs are heavily utilized in spring and summer, berries in summer, and pine nuts in fall.

Remarks: The grizzly bear receives full protection under the 1973 Endangered Species Act and is classed as a "trophy game" animal under Wyoming Game and Fish Department regulations with a current moratorium on legal hunting. Because of heavy illegal killing of grizzly bears, the National Audubon Society recently offered a $10,000 reward for information leading to the conviction of grizzly bear poachers.

Nearly all grizzly bear attacks on humans, which are very rare occurrences, are caused by: (1) humans approaching bears too closely, especially females with cubs or individuals defending food; or (2) permitting bears to become habituated to humans at dump sites, hunting camps, or other food sources (see Hoak et al. 1984). Special care by backcountry users and solid commitment by state and federal management agencies will be needed to prevent the grizzly's extinction from Wyoming in coming years.

An adult ringtail *(Bassariscus astutus)*. Photograph by Lloyd Ingles.

·Raccoons and Allies (Family Procyonidae)
Ringtail
Bassariscus astutus fulvescens (Gray)

Description: Ringtails are more slender and smaller than raccoons. They have large ears, large eyes, a pointed face, and a bushy tail nearly as long as the body. Guard hairs on ringtails are black-tipped over tan on the back and yellowish-white on the belly. The tail has six to nine black and white bands and a black tip. The eyes are prominently ringed with white and there are white spots just in front of the ears.

Size: Adults may attain the following dimensions: total length 630–810 mm; tail 305–438 mm; hind foot 55–77 mm; ear 45–54 mm; weight 0.7–1.1 kilograms.

Range and Habitat: Ringtails range throughout Mexico, Texas, and the Great Basin of the southwestern United States. They are rare in Wyoming, occurring only in the lower Green River Basin and along the North Platte River south of Seminoe Reservoir. One unconfirmed report exists from east of Centennial. They live in

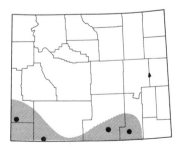

210

a wide variety of habitats, including dense riparian, mountain evergreen forests, oak lowlands, pinyon-juniper, deserts, and chaparral communities often with rocky outcrops. Ringtails are seldom more than 0.8 km from water. Their occurrence in Wyoming represents their northernmost range in the Rockies.

Reproduction: Little is known about courtship and copulation. Gestation is about 56 days. Ringtails give birth from April to July. Young are about 25–30 grams at birth, and are fuzzy and blind. Eyes open 22 to 34 days after birth. They begin to walk at 35 to 42 days and climb at 48 days. Both parents bring food to young. By late fall, young are independent of the parents.

Habits: Ringtails are usually nocturnal, but may be active at dusk and dawn. Daytime resting sites as well as dens for rearing young are most often in rock crevices or burrows dug by other animals. Monthly home ranges averaged 136 hectares (range 49–233 ha) in Utah (Trapp 1978). Ringtails are excellent climbers.

Foods: Ringtails are omnivorous. Principal foods are insects, crickets, beetles, ants, lizards, pocket gophers, squirrels, cottontails, birds, and fruits of hackberry, prickly pear, persimmons, and juniper.

Remarks: The ringtail should receive full protection. Hides are not considered valuable. Virtually nothing is known about this rare mammal in Wyoming.

An adult raccoon *(Procyon lotor)*. Photograph by Dick Randall.

Raccoon
Procyon lotor hirtus Nelson and Goldman

Description: The raccoon has a characteristic black-brown face mask sharply set off by adjacent areas of white. The five to seven conspicuous rings on the tail and the "bandit's" mask identify this medium-sized mammal. The pelage is grizzled in appearance and may be grayish to blackish, sometimes with a reddish tinge. The hands are adapted for grasping.

Size: Adults may attain the following dimensions: total length 600–1050 mm; tail 200–400 mm; hind foot 80–140 mm; ear 40–65 mm; weight 3.6–9.0 kilograms.

Range and Habitat: Raccoons occur from Mexico to central Canada and across the United States except in the Great Basin. Although Long (1965) reported raccoons only in the eastern one-half of the state, they have expanded their range in the last 20 years to include all of Wyoming except for mountainous areas in the northwest.

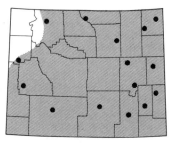

Raccoons are found almost anywhere water is available. In the Red Desert, they are restricted to streams and rivers and in mountainous areas are seldom found above 2000 meters. Raccoons are common in urban areas.

Reproduction: Raccoons may breed from early spring to late summer. In Wyoming, both females and males probably do not breed until their second year. Some bonding between mated pairs may occur. First mating begins just after the start of spring activity. Copulation may last up to an hour. Gestation is 63 to 65 days, with extremes of 54 and 70 days. A minimal nest is built in a den just prior to birth and one to nine young are produced. Equal numbers of males and females are born. Eyes open at 18 to 24 days after birth. The face mask and tail are evidenced only by sparse hairs on pigmented skin at birth. Young can walk by 30 days, and follow their mother on foraging excursions after they are 8 to 12 weeks old. Mother raccoons sit up to nurse and may hold one or more young in their forearms. Young are weaned by 16 weeks.

Habits: A family of raccoons may stay together throughout their first winter. As October and November snows and cold weather become frequent, an entire raccoon family may begin sleeping together in a winter den—hollow tree, rock crevice, old badger or fox den. Raccoons undergo variable periods of winter dormancy, which is not a deep torpor nor true hibernation. They can be easily aroused from their sleep, which may last about four months. By fall, 20–30 percent of a raccoon's body weight is fat and must suffice for the overwinter sleep.

Raccoons are most often active from sunset to sunrise, but are most active just before midnight. Home ranges of 40–150 hectares are common and are usually associated with waterways. Raccoons show little ability to home if they have been moved to a new area.

Food: This species is best known for its food washing behavior. Raccoons have an unspecialized gut. They are generalized, opportunistic feeders.

Plants are generally more important food items than animal matter. Literally hundreds of different plants and animals are eaten by these mammals. Aquatic animals and insects are more often eaten than animals like mice or small birds.

Remarks: A factor in the dramatic range extension of raccoons in Wyoming is no doubt due to the animal's generalized food habits.

An adult female marten *(Martes americana)*. Photograph by Roger A. Powell.

WEASELS (FAMILY MUSTELIDAE)
Marten
Martes americana (Turton)

Description: The marten is a house cat-sized weasel, but it is longer and more slender, has a bushy tail and a sharply pointed face. Pelage is usually golden brown with darker legs and tail and a distinctive orange or yellow patch of irregular shape and size on the throat and upper chest.

Size: Adults may attain the following dimensions: total length 465–659 mm; tail 135–160 mm; hind foot 91–94 mm; ear 42–50 mm; weight 400–1400 grams. Males are about 15 percent larger than females.

Range and Habitat: Martens occur from Alaska, across Canada to the northeastern United States and south along the major mountain ranges in the western United States. They inhabit the mountains of the south-central, western, and northern parts of Wyoming. Two subspecies are recognized in the state: *Martes americana*

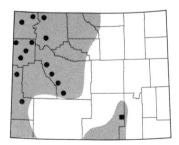

origenes (Rhoades) (squares) in the Sierra Madres and Medicine Bow Mountains, and *Martes americana vulpina* (Rafinesque) (circles) in the western and northwestern mountains.

Martens prefer mature spruce-fir forests, but also occupy lodgepole pine, Dougas fir, and cottonwood river bottom communities (Clark 1984a). Use of habitat is related to food availability, especially in winter. Dens are key habitat components, both those at considerable height from the ground in hollow trees and lined with grass, leaves, and mosses, and those on or under the ground.

Reproduction: Martens generally breed at 15 months of age. During estrus, the female squats and urinates frequently and rubs her abdominal glands on logs, sticks, and rocks. Courtship may last 15 days, and there is much playing and wrestling. Copulation occurs on the ground and may last up to 90 minutes. Several matings may occur in a single day. The polygamous marten mates in mid to late sumer. Gestation is 220 to 276 days. They have delayed implantation and the period of active pregnancy is about 27 days. Litter sizes average three (range one to five). Young are born from mid-March to late April. They weigh about 28 grams at birth, but grow rapidly and by 90 days of age are nearly adult size. Sex ratios at birth are 50:50.

Habits: Home range size for male martens in Jackson Hole was 2.3 square kilometers and for females 1.1 square kilometers (Clark et al. 1984a). The largest home range was 8.1 square kilometers. Martens are easily trapped, and a live capture and release study in Grand Teton National Park resulted in 39 different martens caught a total of nearly 400 times or about 13 captures per marten.

Marten live to be 15 years old. They are solitary except during the breeding season. Martens communicate by vocalizations as well as scents. Belan et al. (1978) described them as emitting huffs, growls, screams, and a chuckle.

Martens are curious and are active year round. They may den during heavy rains or extremely low temperatures (Clark and Campbell 1977). Although they are often considered to be arboreal, most of their time is spent on the forest floor. They can swim, even underwater.

Food: The foods of martens fall into four general categories: small mammals, birds, insects, and fruits and berries. Throughout marten range in North America, there is a uniformity in food habits. Mice, especially red-backed voles, are the staple food. Other voles, deer mice, chipmunks, flying squirrels, pine squirrels, and snowshoe hares are eaten. Martens have been recorded as eating over 100 different kinds of foods.

Remarks: The marten played a key role in the fur trade and was second only to beavers in pelts trapped and dollars earned. About 100 martens are trapped annually in Wyoming, almost all in Teton County.

An adult female fisher *(Martes pennanti)*. Photograph by Roger A. Powell.

Fisher
Martes pennanti columbiana Goldman

Description: Fishers are medium-sized, stocky, weasel-like mammals. The head is "V" shaped with some narrowing in the muzzle. They have long bodies, short legs, dark fur, small rounded ears, and a long bushy tail.

Size: Adults may attain the following dimensions: total length 990–1033 mm; tail 340–422 mm; hind foot 89–115 mm; ear 40–60 mm; weight 2–5.5 kilograms.

Range and Habitat: Only a few fishers have been reported in Wyoming, mostly from the northwest, but one report came from the eastern side of the Bighorns. They generally occur throughout northern coniferous forests in North America, and prefer forests with continuous closed canopy.

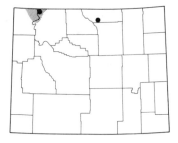

Reproduction: Breeding occurs from March through May, but the fertilized egg does not implant until 10 to 11 months later. Details of courtship are unknown. Copulation may last up to seven hours. Birth occurs in February through May. Litters average three (range one to six). Kits have a coat of fine hair at 3 days and are weaned at about 10 weeks. Young reach adult size in 3 to 4 months. Both sexes reach sexual maturity at 1 or 2 years.

Habits: Fishers are solitary except during breeding and maternal care of young. They may be active anytime of the day or night. An animal followed by trappers moved 90 km in three days, 45 km in two days, and 10–11 km in a few hours. Resting sites are usually temporarily used, such as logs and stumps, hollow trees, brush piles, ground holes, rock falls, and snow dens. Fishers are much less arboreal than often thought. Home ranges are from 15–35 square kilometers. Fishers of the same sex overlap slightly, but opposite sexes overlap considerably.

Food: Fishers are generalized predators of small to medium-sized birds, mammals, and also eat carrion (Powell 1981). Snowshoe hares, red squirrels, flying squirrels, mice, voles, shrews, and porcupines are the major food. Deer carcasses are the major carrion source. Fishers require from 2000 to 6600 calories each day; this is equivalent to one snowshoe hare every 2.5 to 8 days or one porcupine every 10 to 35 days.

Remarks: Fishers are active at $-20\,°C$. They are considered very rare in Wyoming.

An adult ermine *(Mustela erminea)*. Photograph by L. E. Bingaman.

Ermine
Mustela erminea muricus (Bangs)

Description: Ermines are small to medium-sized weasels. The tail is distinctly black-tipped and is 30 to 45 percent of the head and body length. The tail is slightly longer than the hind feet. In summer, the back is light brown and the belly white. In winter, the ermine is all white except for the black-tipped tail.

Size: Adults may attain the following dimensions: total length 190–340 mm; tail 55–62 mm; hind foot 26–30 mm; ear 13–16 mm; weight 75–200 grams.

Range and Habitat: Ermines occur from Alaska south to northern New Mexico in the western United States. They also live throughout Canada and northern and eastern United States, and cocur throughout Wyoming in various habitats, although they are most often found near coniferous forests.

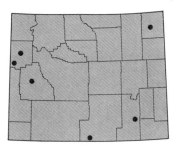

Reproduction: Ermines have delayed implantation. Males become sexually mature at one year and females at three to four months. They breed in July and August. Gestation is about 270 days and active pregnancy is 21 to 28 days after implantation. A single litter of six to nine young is produced.

Habits: The ermine alternates activity periods and rest periods within each 24 hour interval. It appears more active diurnally in summer and nocturnally more active in winter. In Idaho, ermines followed 10 to 15 day circuits and did not utilize a central den. In deep snow, all weasels burrow under the snow to hunt. They may hunt in pocket gopher tunnels. The ermine holds the record for weasels for greatest travel distance of 35 km (airline) in 7 months. Home ranges vary from 7 to 34 hectares. Densities may reach 8 per square kilometer. Males and females show exclusive territorial use at all seasons.

Food: Small mammals are the predominant prey item. In other states, 36 percent of all food was voles, 16 percent shrews, 11 percent deer mice, 9 percent rabbits, 4 percent rats, and 4 percent chipmunks. Song birds, beetles, grasshoppers, and frogs are also eaten.

Remarks: Longevity is probably 1 to 2 years in the wild. Ermine skins were prized by Indians who used them for headdresses and ceremonial purposes.

An adult male least weasel *(Mustela nivalis).* Photograph by Roger A. Powell.

Least Weasel
Mustela nivalis campestris Jackson

Description: The least weasel is Wyoming's smallest carnivore. It can be distinguished from other weasels by its small size, number of tail vertebrae, and lack of a black tip on the tail. This species turns white in winter like the two other weasel species in the state.

Size: Adults may attain the following dimensions: total length 166–216 mm; tail 26–44 mm; hind foot 20–28 mm; ear 9–15 mm; weight 32–63 grams. Males are about 30 percent larger than females.

Range and Habitat: Least weasels oc-cur from Alaska across Canada and southward in the United States to Kansas and the Appalachian Mountains. Only a single specimen has been collected in Wyoming (Stromberg et al. 1981), and it was found about 19 km west of Sheridan. Habitat along the eastern side of the Bighorn Mountain

ranges in elevation from 1280–1580 meters, and consists of rolling gentle ridges dominated by sagebrush and grasses that are divided by riparian habitats of willows and cottonwoods.

Reproduction: Males and females are sexually mature at 3 to 4 months. They do not have delayed implantation. Young become self-sufficient and reach adult size in 28 to 35 days. Two or three litters may be produced annually and breeding may take place at anytime. Gestation is 34 to 37 days. Four or five young (range one to ten) are born.

Habits: All weasels are active year round and do not hibernate. They have a high metabolic rate because of their elongated body shape, which indicates a higher surface to volume ratio than other mammal shapes. Summer pelage is brown and in winter white. Movement is related to hunting. Males use a home range of 7 to 15 ha, females 1 to 4 hectares. Least weasels are solitary except during breeding and care of young. Dominance relationships are established, and animals tend to avoid one another.

Food: Least weasels utilize small mammals, voles, mice, and shrews, mainly, as well as birds and insects. They are voracious predators and highly successful in prey capture and killing behavior. They hunt using a "random search" straetgy.

Remarks: Least weasels do not suck blood as popularly believed, nor do they subsist on the blood of their prey. The population near Sheridan may be relict and separated by great distances from other least weasels known in Kansas, Nebraska and South Dakota.

An adult long-tailed weasel *(Mustela frenata)*. Photograph by K. Maslowski and W. Goodpaster.

Long-Tailed Weasel
Mustela frenata Lichtenstein

Description: This weasel is larger than the ermine, up to 45 cm long, and has a much longer black tip on the tail. The tail is more than 44 percent of the head and body length. It can be further distinguished from the ermine by its rusty orange belly in summer. Upper parts are brown in summer. In winter, its color changes entirely to white except for the black-tipped tail.

Size: Adults may attain the following dimensions: total length 300–450 mm; tail 110–175 mm; hind foot 39–54 mm; ear 12–27 mm; weight 130–316 grams. Males are up to 15 g heavier than females.

Range and Habitat: Long-tailed weasels occur from British Columbia to South America. They are found in most parts of the United States. They live throughout Wyoming in a variety of habitats, including open fields, willows, desert shrubs, and grasslands.

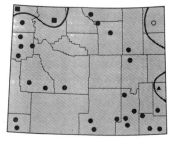

Four subspecies are present in the state: *Mustela frenata alleni* (Merriam) (open circle) in the Black Hills; *Mustela frenata longicauda* Bonaparte (triangles) in the high plains of Goshen County; *Mustela frenata nevaden-*

sis Hall (solid circles) in the central portions of the state; and *Mustela frenata oribasus* (Bangs) (squares) in northern Yellowstone and the Big Horn Basin.

Reproduction: Long-tailed weasels breed in July and August and have delayed implantation. Males are sexually mature at 1 year and females at 3 to 4 months. Gestation is about 270 days, with active pregnancy only 21–28 days. A single litter of six to nine young is produced. Young weigh about 3 grams at birth and are about 56 mm long. They are flesh colored with long, white hair and are capable of high-pitched vocalizations. By the end of the first week, they weigh up to 9 grams. By the second week, sexual disparity in size is evident. In the fifth week, fights over food occur and young weasels consume nearly their own body weight daily. Weaning also starts then and pelage approaches adult summer coloration.

Habits: Long-tailed weasels may be active at any time of the day or night. However, peak activity coincides with that of prey—dawn and dusk usually. In laboratory studies, long-tailed weasels prefer the brightest illumination available probably because of visual needs for greater color, contrast, pattern, and intensity discrimination. Darkness restricted running behavior.

Hunting activities and locating mates are the two main reasons for movement. Weasels traveled an average of 214 m per night for males and 105 m for females (Glover 1942). Weasels in open timber travel greater distances per trip than weasels in brushland and dense timber. In Idaho, weasels used circuits not associated with one or more centrally located dens. They followed circuits taking 7 to 12 days and use the same general route each time. Long-tailed weasels have the largest home range of the three species at 12–16 hectares. Population densities of 6 to 7 per square kilometer are common. Numbers may fluctuate dramatically over several consecutive years. Weasels tend to be solitary except during mating and rearing of young.

Food: Long-tailed weasels use a wide variety of foods. Small mammals—shrews, mice, rats, squirrels, and rabbits—are the major food items. Birds up to grouse size are readily taken along with eggs and chicks. Insects, carrion, and almost anything edible may be consumed.

Remarks: The weasel is sometimes trapped as a fur resource. Average price per pelt is 60 cents. Considering this low economic return compared to the ecological role weasels play as a community regulator, especially on small mammal populations, trapping should be eliminated.

An adult black-footed ferret *(Mustela nigripes)*. Photograph by Tim W. Clark.

Black-Footed Ferret
Mustela nigripes (Audubon and Bachman)

Description: This rare mink-sized mammal is the only ferret native to North America. Its upper parts are buff and underparts and face somewhat whitish. The black feet, black raccoon-like face mask, and black tip on an otherwise whitish tail identify this animal. It does not molt to white in winter. The ferret should not be confused with domestic European ferrets which can be purchased in pet stores.

Size: Adults may attain the following dimensions: total length 480–567 mm; tail 114–127 mm; hind foot 60–73 mm; ear 29–31 mm; weight 530–1300 grams.

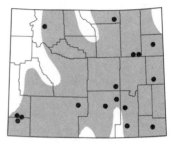

Range and Habitat: Black-footed ferrets once ranged from south central Canada through the grasslands of North America to New Mexico and Texas (Anderson et al. 1986). Historically, they occupied all the nonmountainous areas in Wyoming. Today, they are known from only a single location in the Big Horn Basin. A summary of a 5-year search for ferrets in Wyoming up to 1977 was given by Clark (1978).

Ferrets nearly always occur at prairie dog colonies. Both historic and recent literature documents the close association of ferrets and prairie dogs (Hillman and Clark 1980). Characteristics of prairie dog colonies in ferret-occupied areas in South Dakota showed colonies averaged about 19 hectares and were 1.5 km apart. In Wyoming they averaged 322 hectares and were 0.6 km apart (Hillman et al. 1979, Clark et al. 1982). Thirty-seven white-tailed prairie dog colonies are used by the Wyoming ferrets (Forrest et al. 1985; Clark et al. 1986a).

Reproduction: Black-footed ferrets breed from mid-March through early April (Clark et al. 1986b). Age at first breeding is unknown. Gestation is probably about 42 to 45 days and young remain in the nest about another 40 days before coming above ground. Nests are in prairie dog burrows. At first appearance above ground, young ferrets are nearly adult size. Litter sizes in Wyoming averaged 3.3 and in South Dakota 3.5. Female-young groups stay together throughout July and early August and then begin to separate as young become independent.

Habits: Black-footed ferrets are extremely rare. Even when they are known to occupy an area, they are seldom seen. They tend to be nocturnal, but in summer females and young may be seen nearly every night and sometimes after sunrise till noon (Henderson et al. 1969). Because ferrets hunt in prairie dog burrows and seek shelter there, they may be active above ground for only very short periods. In winter, they may remain below ground for a week or longer (Richardson et al. *in press*).

The easiest way to locate ferrets is in winter, when tracks and the unique ferret diggings are most easily located (Clark et al. 1984 a,b). These diggings are thought to be related to prey acquisition and may require a ferret 2 to 3 hours to produce. Stringers of subsoil are thrown out on the ground from prairie dog burrow openings. Most diggings have a trough down the center, and some are multi-lobed. Diggings averaged 1.17 m long, 42 cm wide, and 11 cm deep. Early mornings with light snow cover from December through February are the best times to find these distinctive signs, because white-tailed prairie dogs are hibernating or black-tailed prairie dogs have not emerged and starting digging.

Food: These ferrets eat prairie dogs almost exclusively (90 percent), but they also eat deer mice, pocket gophers, pocket mice, birds, and ground squirrels.

Remarks: The black-footed ferret was formerly much more abundant than it is today. Its decline is the result of destruction of prairie dog colonies through shooting, poisoning, and agriculture. Its historic range in Wyoming is shown in the accompanying map. This species receives full protection under the 1973 Endangered Species Act. A few additional relict populations probably still exist. Recovery of this endangered species would be greatly facilitated by the finding of additional populations. Only one Wyoming population is known from near Meeteetse, and it was largely destroyed by canine distemper in 1985. Seventeen ferrets from that population are in captivity, and concentrated recovery efforts are underway (Clark 1985, 1986).

An adult mink *(Mustela vison)*. Photograph by W. D. Zehr.

Mink
Mustela vison Schreber

Description: Mink are weasel-like mammals, usually a uniform brown except for an occasional white patch on the chest or throat. The fur is extremely fine and soft.

Size: Adults may attain the following dimensions: total length 460–700 mm; tail 150–230 mm; hind foot 60–80 mm; ear 22–27 mm; weight 0.9–1.6 kilograms.

Range and Habitat: Mink live from Alaska throughout much of Canada and the United States except parts of the Southwest. They occur throughout Wyoming in suitable habitat, are semi-aquatic, and always live near open water. Habitat use is related to food supply. Mink hunt in and under the water, and in the plant communities adjacent to streams, rivers, ponds, and lakes.

Two subspecies are recognized in Wyoming: *Mustela vison energumenos* (Bangs) (circles) is found in the western one-half of the state and *Mustela vison letifera* Hollister (squares) occurs in the eastern one-half of the state.

Reproduction: Because the mink is a valuable fur animal, its biology is relatively well known. Mink emerged as a fur resource in the 1920's, and most data come from mink farms. Mink become sexually mature at 10 months of age and may breed annually for 7 or more years. Breeding occurs in late February to early April. As the breeding season approaches, males and females increase their activity and travel widely. Mating is quite vigorous and copulation may be prolonged. Females are receptive at 7 to 10 day intervals throughout the breeding season. Ovulation occurs 33 to 72 hours after coition. Pregnancy averages 51 days (range 40 to 75). Young are born 28 to 30 days following implantation, usually in late April to mid-May. Litters average four (range one to nine). Neonatal mink weigh 8 to 10 grams. They grow rapidly and are 40 percent of their adult body weight and 60 percent of their body length by 7 weeks of age. The kits are playful until the litter breaks up in early fall.

Habits: Mink are primarily nocturnal at all seasons. They may be inactive during periods of snow and low temperatures. Home ranges are often linear along streams and rivers. One study showed an average home range length to be 1,630 meters. Mink do not suffer much mortality from predation other than humans. Densities range from 0.3 to 8 per square kilometer.

Food: Foods consist of mice and rats, rabbits, muskrats, frogs, fish, crayfish, birds, invertebrates, and snakes, in order of descending importance. Mink are well adapted for both terrestrial and aquatic hunting.

Remarks: Mink are very susceptible to residues from environmental pollution, including mercury and halogenated hydrocarbons (PCB's, DDT, DDE, dieldrin, and others).

An adult wolverine *(Gulo gulo)*.

Wolverine
Gulo gulo luscus (Linnaeus)

Description: Wolverines are the largest member of the weasel family and more closely related to martens than to other weasels. They appear to have a clumsy manner, because of their heavy body and lumbering gait, but this is misleading. Their back is usually arched and the head and tail are carried lower. The head is broad and rounded. The jaws are almost doglike, eyes are wide-set and small, and ears are short and rounded. Long guard hairs give this carnivore a shaggy appearance. It is blackish brown with a pale brown or reddish stripe extending from behind the shoulders to the rump on each side. Its legs are stocky and powerful with sharply curved claws about 2 to 3 cm long.

Size: Adults may attain the following dimensions: total length 650–1050 mm; tail 170–260 mm; hind foot 177–198 mm; ear 50–85 mm; weight 14–27 kilograms. Height at shoulders is 355–432 mm.

Range and Habitat: Wolverines formerly ranged from Alaska, throughout Canada, the northwestern United States, the West Coast, interior Rocky Mountains, and the Dakotas. They occur in extreme western and northwestern Wyoming. About 90 wolverine reports have been published since 1872. Long (1965) listed 10 reports, 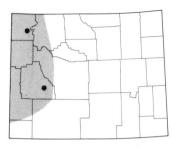 Houston (1978) listed 27 for Yellowstone National Park, and Hoak et al. (1982) listed another 50 reports. Wolverines occur throughout major mountain ranges, and recent reports are further south than previously reported.

Reproduction: Yearling males may be sexually mature; female wolverines attain maturity at 12 to 15 months. Breeding occurs in summer and birth takes place from early January to late April. Total gestation is about 250 days; active gestation is only about 30 to 40 days. Litter sizes average 3.5 (range one to six). Females have four mammae. Young are about 85 grams at birth, and adult size is reached by the first winter.

Habits: Wolverines are primarily nocturnal, but may be active at any time. They do not hibernate. They can travel at least 65 km without stopping. Wide ranging males are the first to colonize new areas. Wolverines tend to be solitary and probably territorial. Territories of males may be 2,000 square kilometers and females 450. Social behavior is not well known.

Food: Foods include mule deer and elk, moose, rabbits and hares, porcupines, beaver, squirrels, chipmunks, marmots, mice, birds, gophers, and berries in summer. Wolverines can capture large animals when snows are deep enough to hinder such prey. Forepaw blows and head bites are used to kill prey. Carrion is an important food source in late winter and spring.

Remarks: The 1973 ban on poison for predator control on federal lands has probably benefited the wolverine and resulted in the apparent range extension to the south.

An adult badger *(Taxidea taxus)*. Photograph by J. Knox Jones, Jr.

Badger
Taxidea taxus (Schreber)

Description: Badgers are stout, short-legged, flat-bodied, and adapted for digging. The tail is short and bushy. The back color is grayish, tinged with brown, and grizzled with black. The snout and top of the head are black with a white stripe running down the face.

Size: Adults may attain the following dimensions: total length 600–730 mm; tail 105–135 mm; hind foot 95–128 mm; ear 50–60 mm; weight 6.4–11.5 kilograms.

Range and Habitat: Badgers occur throughout the central and western United States and central Mexico. They occur throughout Wyoming in habitats with relatively deep soils because they burrow for prey in these areas. Badgers are found from desert areas to tundra (in summer), but are most common in grassland and sage-brush areas.

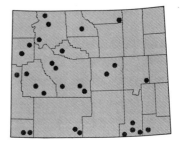

232

Reproduction: Badgers mate in summer and autumn. Females 4 or 5 months of age may be impregnated by males over 1 year old. Implantation of fertilized eggs is delayed until December through February. Birth occurs in March and early April. One to seven young are produced.

Habits: Badgers are usually nocturnal, but may be active at all hours. They tend to stay underground in daylight. Young are mostly diurnal. Badgers do not hibernate, but simply reduce their time above ground in periods of cold weather and low prey availability. Stays in burrows of 12 days during cold weather are common, and periods of inactivity up to 38 days have been reported (Messick 1981). Dens are key habitat features for badgers. They serve as resting sites daily and for raising young.

Home ranges of badgers vary considerably, but generally range from 150 to 1,700 hectares. Badgers may be as dense as 2 to 4 per square kilometer, but they are generally solitary. Little is known of their social behavior.

Food: Badgers are adapted for capturing fossorial prey in their burrows. Ground squirrels, prairie dogs, rabbits, hares, chipmunks, marmots, squirrels, gophers, mice and rats, coyotes, and skunks are all eaten.

Remarks: Badgers are generally not appreciated for their exceptional value to humans as a predator on injurious rodents.

An adult eastern spotted skunk *(Spilogale putorius)*. Photograph courtesy of the New York Zoological Society.

Eastern Spotted Skunk
Spilogale putorius interrupta (Rafinesque)

Description: This little skunk has small white spots in front of each ear and one on the forehead. Six white stripes on the back are joined to the ear spots. The lower pair of white stripes begins on the back of the forelegs. It has a solid black tail except for some white near the tip.

Size: Adults may attain the following dimensions: total length 426–567 mm; tail 140–235 mm; hind foot 33–70 mm; ear 25–26 mm; weight 425–661 grams.

Range and Habitat: Eastern spotted skunks occur throughout the eastern one-fourth of Wyoming. They generally live near streams and rivers, but are found also near human habitation around fence rows, barns, and brush piles. Eastern spotted skunks occur in the Great Plains and southeastern regions of the United States.

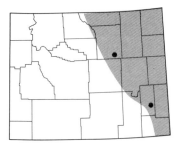

Reproduction: Both males and females may become sexually active at 5 months of age. Females come into heat in late March and within 30 days nearly all are bred. Fertilized eggs may not implant for 14 days. Gestation is 50–65 days and kits are born in May or June. Young are pinkish with a fine coat of hair and the alternating black and white colors are evident. After a month, their eyes and ears open. Solid foods are eaten within 36 days. At 14 to 16 weeks, the young disperse.

Habits: This species is more nocturnal than the commonly observed striped skunk and is seldom seen in daylight. When hunting, it stays close to cover. One or more dens may be used and usually are found in the burrows of other animals, under buildings, brush piles, or rock crevices. During cold temperatures, these skunks greatly reduce their activity. During the breeding season, they may range over 10 square kilometers. Densities may reach 5 per square kilometers.

Food: Eastern spotted skunks eat a wide variety of plant and animal matter. Fruits, berries, corn, carrion, nuts, voles, mice, birds, and birds' eggs are taken.

Remarks: Spotted skunks seen during daylight should be avoided because they may be rabid. They live 6 years in captivity, but probably only 1 or 2 years in the wild.

Western Spotted Skunk
Spilogale gracilis gracilis Merriam

Description: This small house cat-sized skunk has black upper parts and four to six white stripes which are frequently broken into spots or short segments. White markings are more extensive than on the eastern spotted skunk. The black and white stripes on the upper back are nearly equal in width. The white are on the face is large, extending from the nose pad to behind the eyes. The tail is white on its underside for half its length.

Size: Adults may attain the following dimensions: total length 415–575 mm; tail 135–241 mm; hind foot 32–73 mm; ear 25–26 mm; weight 420–650 grams. Males are about 7 percent larger than females.

Range and Habitat: Western spotted skunks occur in the interior western United States. They live in the western three-fourths of Wyoming and prefer dry grass and shrub lands.

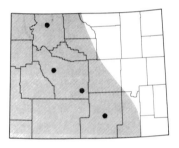

Reproduction: Spotted skunks have delayed implantation and an active pregnancy of 28 to 31 days. Females come into heat in September, and most are bred by the second week in October. Three to six young are born in the spring. By fall, young females may breed and all young are independent.

Habits: Spotted skunks may den in any hole, rock pile, or fallen log, but they often use burrows of other animals. Almost nothing is known of their activity patterns, home ranges, population density, or social behavior.

Food: Western spotted skunks eat beetles, crickets, grubs, grasshoppers, worms, carrion, rodents, young rabbits, bird eggs, frogs, crayfish, lizards, and some fruit.

Remarks: Like other skunks, the spotted skunk's principal means of defense is by spraying a musk. It can spray about 8 to 10 cc of musk. The anal fluid is a watery milky white. The active ingredient is mercaptan, a sulfide. The spotted skunk usually stamps or pats its front feet rapidly or raises to its front feet in a handstand, and only uses the musk as a last resort.

The musk odor can be neutralized by washing clothing several times in detergent with household ammonia added to the wash. Dogs can be cleaned first by saturating them with tomato juice and then bathing them.

The single most useful deodorizer is neutroleum-alphos. About 15 cc of this water soluble chemical can be used in baths for dogs and humans. Skunks do not like water and can be induced to leave tight hiding places by spraying them with a garden hose.

An adult striped skunk *(Mephitis mephitis).* Photograph by Larry Miller.

Striped Skunk
Mephitis mephitis hudsonica Richardson

Description: Striped skunks are about the size of domestic cats. Pelage is usually black except for a white stripe on the nose and forehead, and a round white patch on the pate that extends to the rump as two white stripes of various widths. The tail is bushy, long, and may contain some white hairs.

Size: Adults may attain the following dimensions: total length 520–770 mm; tail 170–400 mm; hind foot 55–85 mm; ear 25–35 mm; weight 1.8–4.5 kilograms.

Range and Habitat: Striped skunks occur throughout North America and Wyoming. Habitats supporting the most striped skunks are characterized by mixed woodlands, brushy areas, and open fields with broken wooded ravines and rocky outcrops.

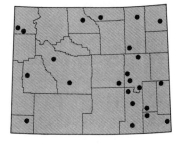

Reproduction: Breeding takes place in February or March. After females attain estrus, they remain receptive until ovulation. Ovulation occurs about 42 hours after copulation. Gestation ranges from 59 to 77 days with earlier dates of mating resulting in the longer gestation. Birth occurs in May or early June, and the average litter size is six (range two to ten). Females possess 12 mammae. Young are about 34 grams at birth. Even though young skunks are pink, the faint white and black areas are distinguishable just before birth. Their eyes open at 22 days. Young breed the following spring at 10 months of age.

Habits: Striped skunks become inactive during winter and live off stored body fats. They may remain in dens singly or communally for as long as 118 days. During winter inactivity, they undergo a mild reduction in body temperature. At other seasons, skunks are active throughout the night. Each skunk uses about 1.5 to 5.0 square kilometers as a territory. As many as 80 percent of all skunks do not live to be a year old. Owls, badgers, and foxes prey on them.

Food: Skunks are opportunistic feeders but are primarily insectivorous. They will eat animal or plant matter as the occasion arises. Grasshoppers, beetles, crickets, butterfly larvae, deer mice, voles, bird eggs, berries, and fruits are consumed.

Remarks: Striped skunks can swim, and their top running speed is 16.5 kilometers per hour. Skunks can hit a target with their musk at about

6 meters, but greatest accuracy is at less than 3 meters. Before spraying, skunks usually face a threat, arch their backs, elevate their tails, erect tail hairs, stamp the ground with their front feet, and shuffle backwards. When spraying, the skunk everts the anus to expose the scent gland papillae. The generic name *Mephitis* is Latin for "bad odor."

An adult river otter *(Lutra canadensis)*. Photograph by Dick Randall.

River Otter
Lutra canadensis pacifica Rhoads

Description: River otters are large, semi-aquatic mustelids with short legs, a long tapering tail, and a rather blunt, small, and somewhat flattened head. They have dense, relatively short fur. Pelage color ranges from a pale chestnut to dark chocolate brown on the back to silver gray on the belly.

Size: Adults may attain the following dimensions: total length 915–1346 mm; tail 352–510 mm; hind foot 110–139 mm; ear 12–24 mm; weight 5–13.7 kilograms.

Range and Habitat: River otters once lived from Alaska throughout much of Canada and the United States. Currently, they are most common in northern Wyoming, but may occur in most major river drainages throughout the state in low numbers. They are most abundant in Yellowstone National Park and in the Snake River

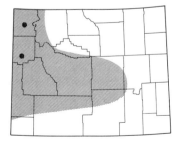

and its tributaries. Little is known about the range of water quality the otter will tolerate, but streams and rivers that it inhabits must have adequate food supplies.

Reproduction: Otters mate in late winter and early spring, with about a 3-month breeding period. Copulation occurs in the water or on land. Otter pregnancy rates are 50 to 100 percent. They may breed yearly or every other year. Gestation is long because of delayed implantation, but the active period of pregnancy is about 50 days. Birth occurs from November through May, peaking in March and April. Litter sizes range from one to six, but two to four young are normally produced. Females seek out natal dens for birthing.

Young are born as the females stand upright on all four feet. Birth may require 3 to 8 hours. Newborns weigh about 130 grams, are about 270 mm long, and are blind, helpless, and fully furred—miniature replicas of adult otters. Otter milk is high in fat and protein content, and low in carbohydrates. The eyes of the young open at 21 to 35 days, and by 25 to 42 days they participate in play. About day 48 they may enter the water, and after 59 to 70 days they venture from the den by themselves. At 63 to 76 days they begin eating solid food, and weaning occurs at 90 to 100 days of age.

Habits: Otters are active anytime of day or night, but peak activity is at dusk and dawn. They are active year round. These mammals do not excavate dens, but instead use dens dug by other animals (especially beaver) or natural shelters.

Home range sizes and movement patterns of otters are generally unknown, and densities are poorly understood. Estimates of one river otter per 1 square kilometer of water, one otter per 2.5 km of lake shore, and one otter per 5 km of stream have been reported.

Females are devoted parents and teach their young to swim and hunt. They aggressively protect their young from danger, and this accounts for reported attacks on humans. Little is known of their social structure. They are generally solitary.

Food: River otter food habits have been well studied. Nearly all the diet is fish, with a small fraction of amphibians, insects, birds, and mammals. Otters require 700–1000 grams of food per day.

Remarks: Otters are highly intelligent and curious animals, and are well known for their keen ability to play.

An adult mountain lion *(Felis concolor)*.

CATS (FAMILY FELIDAE)
Mountain Lion
Felis concolor Linnaeus

Description: Mountain lions are generally a uniform slate gray to rufous brown dorsally. The upper lip and underside of the body are whitish. Kittens are spotted with black-brown and have a dark-ringed tail. These big cats are easily recognized by their size and long tails.

Size: Adults may attain the following dimensions: total length 2000–2500 mm; tail 650–800 mm; hind foot 225–300 mm; ear 52–110 mm; weight 34–91 kilograms.

Range and Habitat: The mountain lion occurs throughout Wyoming where two subspecies are recognized: *Felis concolor hippolestes* Merriam (squares) and *Felis concolor missoulensis* Goldman (circles). This mammal has the largest north-south range of any carnivore in the western hemisphere; it occurs from Alaska through-

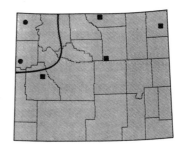

243

out Canada and the United States to South America, preferring dense cover and rocky rugged terrain (Hornocker 1976). A major habitat requirement is the presence of deer. In Wyoming, mountain lions are probably most abundant in the foothills and low mountains on the eastern side of the Big Horn Basin.

Reproduction: The estrus cycle of mountain lions is about 23 days, and ovulation is induced by copulation. Estrus lasts 8 to 11 days. Males may accompany a female until she is receptive. Males fight each other at this time, and mating, which then takes place with the dominant male, lasts less than 1 minute. Breeding generally takes place when lions are 2.5 years old. Mature mountain lions can breed throughout the year, although peak litter production is in summer. Gestation is 82–98 days and one to six kittens are produced.

Habits: Simple dens are used for parturition, and may be in caves, rock crevices, dense shrubs, or under logs. Mountain lion home ranges vary from about 40 to 80 square kilometers for adult males. Mountain lions have a "land tenure" system rather than a true territory (Seidensticker et al. 1973)—boundaries are maintained by active avoidance by two adjacent mountain lions as opposed to active defense. Transient mountain lions are tolerated by residents.

Mountain lions scrape pine needles, leaves, or dirt into piles with their hind feet. Feces and urine may be deposited on these piles. Scrapes apparently function as signals to other mountain lions and as home range boundaries. Mountain lions also claw tree trunks, but this probably serves only to sharpen their claws.

Food: Mule deer are the principal food of mountain lions in Wyoming, although some white-tailed deer, elk, and a variety of small mammals may also be eaten. Results of studies on mountain lion food habits throughout western North America show that three major foods make up 86–100 percent of the diet: mule deer, porcupine, and grass. Predation follows a pattern of search, approach, pursuit, capture, and ingestion. Mountain lions follow the seasonal altitudinal migration pattern of mule deer. Mountain lions also sometimes prey on domestic livestock.

Remarks: Little scientific information exists on mountain lions compared to other big game species, largely because of long-held popular feelings and historical official policies encouraging reduction or elimination of their populations (Russell 1978). The future of the mountain lion in Wyoming and elsewhere depends on habitat maintenance, research data, additional management, and public appreciation for their valuable ecological role.

An adult lynx *(Felis lynx)*. Photograph by L. E. Bingaman.

Lynx
Felis lynx canadensis (Kerr)

Description: Lynx are medium-sized, short-bodied cats with long legs and an overall stocky build. They have large, well-furred paws, prominently tufted ears, a flared facial ruff, and a blunt, short tail. Upper parts are usually grizzled brownish-gray mixed with buff or pale brown. The top of the head is brownish, and the tail is black-tipped.

Size: Adults may attain the following dimensions: total length 670–820 mm; tail 10–15 mm; hind foot ca 20–35 mm; ear 6–10 mm; weight 9–12 kilograms.

Range and Habitat: Lynx once occurred throughout Alaska, Canada, and the northern half of the United States. They are found in high mountains in the western three-fourths of Wyoming, usually in extensive tracts of dense coniferous forests with an occasional bog, thicket, or rocky outcrop. Lynx are often found in areas where deep snow accumulates in the winter.

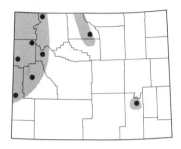

Reproduction: The lynx is thought to ovulate following copulation. Depending on food, lynx generally reach sexual maturity by 22–23 months of age. Mating probably occurs in March and early April. Gestation is about 9 weeks, and young are born in late May and early June in litters of three to four kittens.

Habits: Lynx tend to be solitary animals, associating only for reproduction and rearing of young. Young may stay with their mothers over their first winter. Home ranges may overlap, but mutual avoidance serves to separate individuals. Home ranges in other states are about 10–243 square kilometers.

Food: The lynx depends on the snowshoe hare as its primary food. Other foods such as mice, grouse, and squirrels are also eaten.

Remarks: Lynx have never been studied in Wyoming because of their scarcity. We agree with Long (1965) that this beautiful cat should receive continued protection.

An adult bobcat *(Felis rufus).* Photograph by Dick Randall.

Bobcat
Felis rufus pallescens Merriam

Description: The bobcat is two to three times larger than a domestic cat, more muscular, and its hind legs are proportionately longer than its front legs. The ears are prominent and pointed, with a tuft of black hair at the tip. The tail tip has a series of indistinct dark bands on the upper surface, while the underside is white.

Size: Adults may attain the following dimensions: total length 813–1010 mm; tail 100–165 mm; hind foot 165–195 mm; ear 67–80 mm; weight 9–12 kilograms.

Range and Habitat: Bobcats are distributed throughout the United States, southern Canada, and northern and central Mexico. They occur throughout Wyoming in broken, brushy country and in mountains, and are often found in rocky areas with cliffs. It is believed that prey abundance, availability of resting sites, cover type, 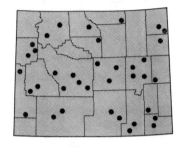 and an undisturbed existence are key habitat factors for this carnivore.

Reproduction: Females may breed the first or second year of life. Mating occurs between mid-January and July. The polyestrous female bobcat is sexually receptive on a cycle of about 44 days. Gestation is 50–70 days. Births occur from mid-April to early September with an average litter size of 2.8 cubs. Females produce a single litter annually. Birth weights are near 300 grams. Males reach maximum weights after about 500 days, and females after about 700 days.

Habits: Adult female and male bobcats may actively defend a territory, with transient bobcats excluded from these territories. Transients are primarily dispersing juveniles. Home range sizes vary from 1–200 square kilometers, depending on sex, age, population density. Male and female home ranges may overlap, but home ranges for animals of the same sex do not. Bobcats may move 5–12 km per day, with a rate of movement estimated at 0.3 to 0.7 km per hr, and are most active at dawn and dusk.

Food: Bobcats kill and eat mammals and birds usually between 0.7 and 5.5 kg in size. This includes rabbits and hares, marmots, porcupines, beavers, ungulates, squirrels, voles and mice, and pocket gophers. Bobcats are opportunistic and also eat fish, amphibians, reptiles, and insects. They occasionally prey on livestock.

Remarks: Bobcats can generally coexist with people in areas where human density and distribution are relatively low. Overtrapping can severely reduce population sizes. Even though the state of Wyoming manages the bobcat, pelts exported out of the country are monitored by the federal government under provisions of the Convention on International Trade in Endangered Species of Wild Flora and Fauna.

Adult elk *(Cervus elaphus)*.

DEER (FAMILY CERVIDAE)
Elk
Cervus elaphus nelsoni (V. Bailey)

Description: This large deer has relatively long, coarse fur, which is light tan with a dark mane and a straw-colored rump patch. The tail is short and inconspicuous. Calves are born with cream-colored spots on a russet coat. The elk is a "six-point" deer, indicating the most frequently occurring number of tines on mature bulls. Yearling bulls may have a spike, and cows lack antlers. Antlers are shed each winter and regrown in the spring.

Size: Adults may attain the following dimensions: total length 108–234 cm; tail 8–14 cm; hind foot 43–69 cm; ear 13–22 cm; weight 118–497 kilograms.

Range and Habitat: Elk once ranged from northern Canada southward along the California coastline, and throughout much of the United States. They occur throughout Wyoming from deserts to timbered areas, and occupy habitats dominated by shrubs and grasses to high mountain meadows of grasses and forbs. They use dense coniferous forests for shelter.

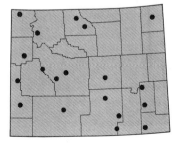

249

Reproduction: The ovarian cycle of elk is initiated by decreasing day length in the fall. Four estrus periods probably occur during rut. A single calf is usually born each year the following May or early June. Yearling cows sometimes breed, and the adult cow pregnancy rate is usually over 90 percent. Fertility drops off after 8 years. Yearling males may also be fertile, but bulls of 3 years or older do most of the breeding.

Rutting groups in fall often consist of 2 to 26 elk, including an adult bull associated with cows, calves, and occasionally a yearling bull harem. Fighting by bulls for possession of a harem can be intense and may result in death. Rutting behavior of bulls involves bugling, thrashing, digging, rubbing antlers, wallowing, sparring, and a series of other aggressive displays (Struhsaker 1967).

Habits: Elk have been well studied in Yellowstone National Park and in Teton County, especially those elk associated with the National Elk Refuge (Craighead et al. 1972, Craighead 1973, Houston 1974). Some elk make extensive seasonal migrations between winter and summer ranges (up to 88 km), whereas other elk are essentially nonmigratory. Calving areas are sometimes on the limits of winter range in sagebrush and timbered areas. The interspersion of cover and open areas seems to be critical. Cows and calves appear to lag behind bulls in moving back to summer range.

Elk may live to be 20 years old, but the average life expectancy is much lower, and there are great differences in life spans. Sex ratios are equal at birth, but favor females as time passes. Adult sex ratios may be 31 males to 100 females on the National Elk Refuge. Calf survival is highly variable between years, depending on the nutritional condition of the female, weather, and predators. Hunting is by far the largest mortality factor, although in some cases disease is important.

Elk are gregarious, but group size depends on age, sex, time of year, and vegetation type. Large elk groups may congregate in the most open meadow habitats.

Elk management has undergone dramatic alterations in the last few decades, and strict enforcement of game laws has increased elk numbers. Winter range of elk in many cases is now protected. Competitive relations with livestock for forage are better understood, and management is better designed for elk. Elk numbers can be drastically reduced by timber harvests, excessive or poorly timed logging, or energy developments.

Food: The elk diet is variable and depends on local availability of food plants. Elk eat the same plants consumed by other members of the deer family as well as cattle. About 159 forbs, 59 grasses, and 95 shrub species are known to be eaten. Grasses and forbs make up the major winter foods while the spring diet is largely grasses. As summer approaches, forbs are consumed. Shrubs are eaten anytime, especially on winter range low in grasses.

Remarks: Elk have always occupied mountain meadows and it is a misconception to think they were only a "plains" animal before being forced into mountainous areas by European settlers. Elk are one of the most popular game animals in western North Amreica. They are adaptable, but sensitive to human disturbances. Clearly, their habitat must be protected from intrusions.

Adult mule deer *(Odocoileus hemionus)*. Photograph by Dick Randall.

Mule Deer
Odocoileus hemionus hemionus (Rafinesque)

Description: Mule deer are variable in size and can be distinguished from white-tailed deer by a white belly, throat and chin, a short tail tipped in black, large ears, and antlers (males only) with Y-shaped forks. Antlers are shed during winter and in spring new growth begins. The overall color is reddish-brown in summer and grayish-brown in winter.

Size: Adults may attain the following dimensions: total length 116–280 cm; tail 10–23 cm; hind foot 32–89 cm; ear 12–25 cm; weight 50–520 kilograms.

Range and Habitat: Mule deer occur throughout western North America and Wyoming in a wide variety of habitats from deserts, riparian areas, broken grasslands, shrublands, foothills, forests, to tundra.

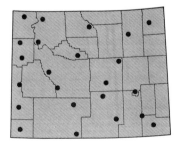

Reproduction: Sexual maturity is usually reached at 18 months of age in both sexes. Age at first breeding is influenced by nutritional condition. Breeding is in fall and early winter, and births occur the following June after a gestation of 203 days (range 183–218 days). Estrus cycle in females is 22 to 28 days, and the estrus period in which the doe is receptive to the buck is only 24 to 36 hours. Twins are common. Mule deer may live in captivity to 22 years (does) and 16 years (bucks). In the wild, 10–12 years is a long life span.

Mule deer are polygamous and the males move about extensively, seeking and pursuing does in estrous. Mature bucks are very aggressive towards each other at this time. Buck rutting behavior includes snorting, urine marking, thrashing and rubbing antlers in vegetation, sparring, and antler fighting.

Habits: Mule deer use small seasonal home ranges where ideal travel distances to food, water, and cover are short. Extensive movements are associated with winter, spring migration and rut. Migration is triggered largely by snow depth and movements of over 160 km are known. Seasonal areas used by adults may be traditional. Home ranges in wintering areas may be 40–100 hectares. In nonmigratory areas, home ranges of 3 to 33 square kilometers are known.

Population size is determined by a variety of factors, the foremost of which is habitat availability. Wyoming Game and Fish Department (1978) produced an informative bulletin describing deer life histories of 60 different herd units. Mule deer densities in open prairie are usually low, less than two deer per square kilometer. In broken hilly country, densities of up to five per square kilometer are known. In foothills and mountains, densities of up to seven per square kilometer are reported. Most deer populations constantly fluctuate from year to year. Severe weather, deep snows, and hunting are major factors limiting deer survival. The role of diseases and parasites is not well understood.

Generally, mule deer are neither solitary nor highly gregarious animals. They generally occur as small groups or individuals. On winter range when they are forced together, groups may number in the hundreds. Some groups, led by adult does, are identifiable throughout the winter, and persist into the prefawning period. But overall, a high degree of association is seen only between a doe and her fawns. Mackie (1976) and his students noted that individually marked deer on winter ranges do not continuously associate with one another. Mule deer attempt to detect danger at a distance and do not necessarily hide from predators. They use their large ears, excellent vision, and open habitats to out-maneuver any enemies.

Food: Mule deer have a four-chambered stomach and their diet is totally herbivorous. They commonly visit salt and other mineral "licks," especially in spring. Foods are extremely varied. Over 750 species of plants including

200 shrubs and trees, 480 forbs, 84 grasses, sedges, and other vegetation are eaten by Rocky Mountain mule deer throughout their range. Mule deer will select plant parts from nutritionally superior soil sites. They use a wide variety of habitat types, and the kinds and amounts of different plants eaten varies by age, sex, season, and condition of the deer.

Remarks: Based on annual hunter harvests (more than 60,000 deer annually), mule deer are the most frequently taken big game animal in Wyoming.

An adult male white-tailed deer *(Odocoileus virginianus).* Photograph by E. P. Haddon.

White-Tailed Deer
Odocoileus virginianus (Zimmermann)

Description: White-tailed deer are distinguished by their long bushy white tails, long legs, conspicuous ears, and antlers (in the males) that have a single-curving main beam bearing unforked tines. The tail is carried erect like a waving flag when deer are fleeing. Overall color is brown to reddish brown. Adults have a distinctive white band across the nose and a less obvious white eye-ring. Fawns are spotted.

Size: Adults may attain the following dimensions: total length 1340–2150 mm; tail 152–360 mm; hind foot 480–538 mm; ear 140–230 mm; weight 40–215 kilograms.

Range and Habitat: White-tailed deer live from northwestern Canada across the United States and south to South America. They occur throughout Wyoming except in dry lowland areas and dense coniferous forests, and oc- cupy most major water courses in the state, but are most abundant in the Black Hills. Dense deciduous riparian 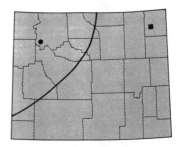 communities are favored habitat. Two subspecies are recognized: *Odocoileus virginianus dacotensis* Goldman and Kellogg (squares) and *Odocoileus virginianus ochrourus* V. Bailey (circles).

Reproduction: Females may breed during their first year, but males usually breed at 16 months of age. Females in good condition often bear twins. White-tailed deer are fall breeders. Estrus usually lasts about 24 hours, and if the doe does not breed, estrus will recur in about 28 days. Gesta- tion is 201 days. Bucks become very aggressive during rut. Sex ratio at birth is slightly in favor of males.

During rut, bucks have high testosterone levels, antlers are polished by mock fights with vegetation, and males seek estrus females by smell. Several bucks may follow a single doe, but the dominant buck is most likely to mate.

Habits: After breeding, bucks lose their antlers and tend to be gregarious again. White-tailed deer may "yard-up" during severe weather, when they concentrate in areas such as river bottoms or south-facing hillslopes. In many areas, they are migratory.

On ranges with deep snow where white-tailed deer are restricted to trails, older does are dominant and lead movements to food areas. Older deer secure first access to the food and in severe winters they may even drive their own young away. White-tailed deer cannot be driven from poor or depleted winter food areas to areas of more abundant food, but, like mule deer, they will eat artificial food such as alfalfa when it is brought to their winter range. The basic social unit is a doe and her fawns of the previous year or two. Adults and young will often play.

Food: White-tailed deer are extremely adaptable animals and this is reflected in their food habits. They are both browsers and grazers. They have a four-part stomach and depend on very specific rumen bacteria and protozoa for digestion. In the Black Hills, bearberry, cottonwoods and aspen, snowberry, willows, serviceberry, ponderosa pine, and Douglas fir are eaten. Martin *et al.* (1951) listed hundreds of plants which white-tailed deer use, including cultivated crops. About 3600 calories per day of good quality, air-dried feed are needed for a 23–27 kilogram deer. A very big buck may require 9900 calories per day.

An adult male moose *(Alces alces).* Photograph by Tim W. Clark.

Moose
Alces alces shirasi Nelson

Description: Moose are the largest members of the deer family. They are heavy and deep bodied with long legs, a short tail, long ears, a "bell" of long hairs hanging from the throat, and a long head and muzzle. The coat is generally black with lighter underparts. Calves are reddish-brown.

Size: Adults may attain the following dimensions: total length *ca* 2500 mm; tail *ca* 60 mm; hind foot *ca* 760 mm; ear *ca* 250 mm; weight 400–500 kilograms.

Range and Habitat: In North America, moose occur from Alaska to the northeastern United States and south along the Rocky Mountains to Colorado. Wyoming moose are found from high spruce-fir zone down to willow and riparian communities. Houston (1968) found that moose in Jackson Hole strongly preferred the 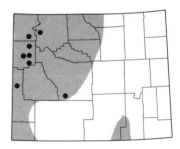 willow vegetation-type, followed by upland forests.

Moose range is determined by winter availability of food plants, and snow depth and hardness. Their long legs and tolerance of deep snows allow moose to survive winters in habitats that are inhospitable to other species. Snows up to 50 cm do not affect them, whereas 60–70 cm impedes their movements, and 90–100 cm are critically limiting. Snow hardness is also important to moose distribution and determines both the force needed to move through snow and whether the snow can support a moose. Moose can withstand cold temperatures, but areas with extended periods above 27 °C, no shade in summer, and no access to water do not support them.

Reproduction: Breeding occurs from September to late October. Cow receptivity lasts 7 to 12 days, but true estrus lasts less than 24 hours. Cows are seasonally polyestrous, with the period between heats about 20–22 days. Females usually breed at from 4 to 12 years of age (range 1.5–18). Usually a single calf is produced, but twins are not uncommon (4.5% in Wyoming), and triplets are rare. Nutrition largely controls twinning rates. The percentage of cows pregnant is about 90 percent in Wyoming (Houston 1968). Gestation is about 226 to 246 days (Peterson 1955). Calves are born in late May and early June. Cows nearing parturition seek seclusion and become intolerant of their calf yearling, driving it away. Cows generally lie down to give birth. Labor takes about 15 minutes. Cows eat the afterbirth. Calves weigh 11 to 16 kg and are able to stand on the first day. Cows lick their calves, helping to establish and maintain maternal bonds. Calves grow about 1 kg per day for the first 5 months.

Habits: Moose tend to be solitary. Movement between winter and summer home ranges is generally short in Wyoming (less than 35 km). Home ranges vary from 2 to 20 square kilometers. Individuals use the same home ranges seasonally. Besides regular seasonal movements, moose may also show nomadic movements resulting in occasional dispersal. Bull rut consists of a sequence of behaviors, the "build up," "mock battle," "displaced feeding," and "fighting" or "yielding" (Altmann 1959). Cows generally fight by striking opponents with their front feet. Moose are most active at dusk and dawn. In Canada they make an average of five to six beds per day.

Food: Moose in Jackson Hole eat at least eight species of willows, antelope bitterbrush, Douglas fir, subalpine fir, white-barked pine, cottonwoods, sedges, rushes, and blue spruce (Houston 1968).

Remarks: Historical records show that moose were very rare in northwestern Wyoming in the mid-1800's, and were absent from Jackson Hole until the early 1900's. Today, large populations occur in northwestern

Wyoming. There are at least 750 moose wintering in Jackson Hole now. Successional changes in vegetation and fire suppression by humans have favored moose.

Adult pronghorns *(Antilocapra americana)*. Photograph courtesy of the American Museum of Natural History.

PRONGHORN (FAMILY ANTILOCAPRIDAE)
Pronghorn
Antilocapra americana americana (Ord)

Description: Pronghorns are robust with relatively long legs and feet. The head and eyes are large; eyes are black with heavy black eyelashes. Pronghorns are a contrasting white underneath and rusty brown to tan above, with black and dark brown markings on the head and neck, and a large white rump. The horns are blackish with anterior prongs, and superior hooks project from ridges just above the eyes. Horns on females usually do not have prongs, or these are rudimentary.

Size: Adults may attain the following dimensions: total length 1245–1475 mm; tail 97–178 mm; hind foot 390–430 mm; ear 142–149 mm; weight 40–70 kilograms. Height at shoulders is 860–875 mm.

Range and Habitat: Pronghorns occurred throughout western North America from Canada to northern Mexico. They range throughout Wyoming except for timbered mountains and alpine tundra areas. Their habitat consists of the open high plains, desert shrub grasslands, and mountain basins. At least 50 percent vegetative cover is required.

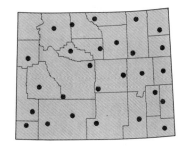

Reproduction: Pronghorns are polygamous. Females become sexually mature at 16 months. Breeding occurs from mid-September to early October. Gestation in captivity is about 252 days. Single kids are uncommon; twins are the rule. Fawns, born while the doe is lying down, weigh about 3.5 kg.

Habits: Pronghorns are active both day and night with peaks just after sunrise and before sunset. A typical daily cycle includes feeding, bedding, ruminating, and — in dry areas — travels to and from water. Home ranges vary from 165 to 2300 hectares. Large males are often territorial. Spring daily movements are about 1 km/day, while the longest seasonal daily movements in the fall are 3–10 km/day. Migration in spring and fall may involve distances of 18 to 160 km.

Pronghorns are social and form herds that contain all age and sex classes, and may reach a thousand or more animals. Densities range from 0.6 to 3.3 pronghorns per 100 hectares. Thirty-one separate behavior patterns, along with a variety of vocalizations, have been described for them. Pronghorns may run up to 86 kph.

Food: Pronghorns use a wide variety of foods. Shrubby plants are essential the entire year and are most critical in winter. Winter, spring, and summer use of forbs is high. Grasses are eaten least. Browse makes up 62 percent of the diet on an annual basis, forbs 44 percent, grasses 7 percent, and other items 10 percent. Pronghorns do not compete with cattle, but do compete in varying degrees with sheep. Forage requirements on pronghorn habitat are strong forb component (25–35 percent by composition), high quality winter browse above snow level (10–20 percent by composition), and a mixture of native grasses.

Remarks: Pronghorn populations were estimated at 45 million before European settlement. By 1924, about 14,000 were left. Since then, their numbers have increased. Wyoming has the largest population of pronghorns in North America.

An adult bison *(Bison bison)*. Photograph by Dick Randall.

Bovids (Family Bovidae)
Bison
Bison bison (Linnaeus)

Description: Bison have an unmistakeable appearance with their massive head and high shoulder hump. The snout and neck are short. The front half of the animal looks huge compared to the rear half. The medium length tail is tufted. Short, round, black horns rise just above the medium-sized ears. Bulls are larger and more massive than cows. The coat is blackish-brown. Bison are the largest territorial mammal native to North America.

Size: Adults may attain the following dimensions: total length 1980–3800 mm; tail 430–815 mm; hind foot 460–660 mm; ear 110–150 mm; weight 410–910 kilograms.

Range and Habitat: Historically, the bison occurred from northwestern Canada to Florida over most of the United States. Bison once lived throughout Wyoming in the millions. Today, they occur in the wild only in Yellowstone and Grand Teton National Parks.

In Wyoming, two subspecies are recognized: *Bison bison athabascae*

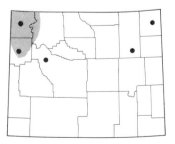

Rhodes and *Bison bison bison* (Linnaeus), but their historic distribution is not well documented.

Bison occupy grasslands and meadow communities as well as (in former times) shrub-grass and desert grassland communities.

Reproduction: Bison generally breed between July and October. Females are polyestrous with about a 21-day cycle. Yellowstone bison first conceive at a greater age than bison elsewhere — 50 percent of 3.5 year olds were pregnant, and 92 percent of those 4.5 or over were pregnant. Males can become sexually active as yearlings, but do so more often as 2-year-olds. In Hayden Valley at Yellowstone males of 8 years or older were the most sexually active. Rut for bison is a period of intense activity. Herd sizes increase and bulls become active in sexual investigation, tending cows, mounting (either fertile or incomplete), and loud bellowing. Gestation is about 270 to 285 days, which is similar to domestic cattle. Just prior to parturition, cows become restless and excitable and may wander away from the herd. Bison usually give birth while lying down. The afterbirth is eaten. Suckling is the first directed calf behavior and begins anywhere from 12 to 95 minutes after birth. Later, calves may be protected not only by their mothers but by other herd members too. A single calf is produced and twins are rare in the calving season from April to June. Sex ratio at birth shows about 56 percent males. Calves make up about 19 percent of mixed bison herds in the spring. Bison may live to be as old as 41 years.

Habits: Bison are known for their wallowing behavior. This activity is practiced by both sexes and all age classes. Wallows are usually dry areas but occasionally muddy. This behavior functions in grooming, sensory stimulation, alleviating skin irritations, and in reproductive behavior.

Bison are dominant over elk, deer, moose, bighorn sheep, and livestock. They are largely indifferent to wolves until attacked. Winter-killed bison may be an important food source to grizzly bears each spring. We have observed coyotes hunting ("mousing") in bison foraging pits in the snow in Yellowstone.

Bison herds range from 19 to 480 animals in Yellowstone (average 175). These big mammals show a large degree of herd fidelity, and disturbances increase herd cohesiveness (McHigh 1972). Bison may undertake annual migrations. In Yellowstone, cows show a strong affinity to winter range (Meagher 1973). A stampede is a rapid, disorderly movement of a large number of bison. The stimuli for a stampede vary and include sudden running of one individual towards the herd after being alarmed by another bison.

Food: Bison are nonselective grazers: they vary their diet by selecting microhabitats. In Yellowstone, the habitat is characterized by meadows interspersed with lodgepole pine forests. Meadows are composed of sedges and grasses. Sedges are the main bison food at all seasons and grasses are second. Sedges make up 37 percent of their diet in the fall and 56 percent in the winter, while grasses make up 30 percent of their diet in the fall and 46 percent in the spring. Some forbs (6 percent) and browse (2 percent) are consumed, mostly in summer.

Remarks: Today, there are about 65,000 bison in North America, up from an estimated 1,100 in 1904. An estimate of bison numbers before European settlers arrived was 60,000,000. A small wild bison herd was present in the Red Desert of Wyoming until the mid-1960's and was allowed to go extinct through ineffective management. Today, Wyoming has about 3,300 bison.

Adult mountain goats *(Oreamnos americanus)*. Photograph by Dick Randall.

Mountain Goat
Oreamnos americanus missoulae J. A. Allen

Description: The mountain goat is only about 1–1.2 meters tall, has a stocky build and a slight hump on the withers. It has short legs and well developed dew claws. Horns, which are present in both sexes, are conical, unbranched and moderate in size. Mountain goats are predominantly white or yellowish white except for eyelids, horns, hoofs, and nose — all of which are black (Wigal and Coggins 1982).

Size: Adults may attain the following dimensions: total length 1245–1787 mm; tail 84–203 mm; hind foot 300–368 mm; ear 10–21 mm; weight 46–136 kilograms. Males are about 20 percent larger than females.

Range and Habitat: Mountain goats once lived along the West Coast of North America from Alaska to Washington and in the northern Rocky Mountains to central Idaho. They are not native to Wyoming (Long 1965), but introduced populations exist in the northern Absaroka Mountains and in the Teton Mountains. The total state

population is thought to be about 100 animals. Mountain goat habitat is typically high, rocky mountains.

Reproduction: The breeding season is from mid-November through early December. The females' first heat is at 2.5 years of age. Parturition occurs from mid-May through mid-June after a gestation of about 180 days. A single kid is born, but twins are not uncommon. Mountain goats are polygamous and males seek out females during rut.

Kids can negotiate rough terrain when only a few hours old. Females are protective of young. Nursing occurs at frequent intervals. Kids may eat forage and ruminate within a few days of birth. Mountain goats have low rates of increase and generally have stable populations.

Habits: Mountain goats generally remain at or above timberline and within reach of rocky outcrops for escape cover. They forage on high windblown slopes. They need watering areas, which they can usually obtain from springs, streams, or snow banks.

Goats seldom fight and resolve conflicts by threat displays. During summer and fall females remain with nursery bands consisting of an adult female, a kid or a yearling, and rarely a two-year-old. Adult males may join these bands for short periods. Adult nannies are dominant.

Daily activity generally consists of feeding and bedding. Feeding starts at dawn and goats work their way up from low to high elevations as the day progresses. Daily summer movements may take a goat a few hundred meters to 0.5 km. Seasonally, goats migrate each spring and fall between winter and summer ranges. Wintering areas are usually on rocky south-facing slopes with patches of plant cover. Fall migrations are influenced by snow depth and distance, since 5 to 24 km may separate seasonal ranges.

Food: Mountain goats have been described as "snip" feeders and rarely graze intensely on a particular plant or site. A variety of plant species are used. Montana studies show that 72 percent of the summer diet is sedges, grasses, or rushes, 26 percent forbs, and 2 percent evergreen shrubs. In winter, 74 percent is sedges, grasses or rushes, 12 percent coniferous trees, and 14 percent other items.

Remarks: Three major management tools for mountain goats are population control via hunting, protection of habitat, and prevention of overhunting. Coyote predation is insignificant. In British Columbia, dollars generated from nature photography are significant. No competition exists between mountain goats and livestock.

An adult male bighorn sheep *(Ovis canadensis)*.

Bighorn Sheep
Ovis canadensis canadensis Shaw

Description: Bighorn sheep are medium-sized bovids. Their most distinguishing feature is the massive curled horns of older males. Their hoofs have tough, leathery pads capable of gripping rocky surfaces. Bighorn sheep are whitish to gray-whitish.

Size: Adults may attain the following dimensions: total length 1490–1953 mm; tail 80–127 kmm; hind foot 394–482 mm; ear 11–23 mm; weight 75–168 kilograms.

Range and Habitat: Bighorn sheep once ranged in western North America from Canada to northern Mexico. Today, they occur in the mountains of northwestern Wyoming. They have been introduced to several mountain ranges in the eastern and southern parts of the state.

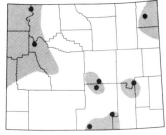

Currently, only one subspecies is present, but historically there were two. *Ovis canadensis auduboni* Merriam, Audubon's bighorn, which was found on the Black Hills and other areas in eastern Wyoming, is now extinct as a result of overhunting and diseases introduced from domestic sheep.

Bighorn sheep are well adapted to life in high mountain terrain. Historically, they descended in winter to lower areas including foothill sagebrush country. They frequently mingled with deer and pronghorns on the prairies.

Reproduction: There are few data on the reproductive anatomy and physiology of bighorn sheep. Young rams may court a ewe even when she is not in estrus. Ewes become aggressive in estrus and seek out the largest bighorn ram. Ewes in estrus may leave their band. A ram's position in the dominance hierarchy determines if he will breed; dominant rams do most of the courting and breeding. Fights become severe during rut. Sheep are polygamous and rams freely move among bands seeking estrous females. Ram bands of up to eight males may roam together at this time. A ram checks a ewe's status by sniffing her vulva and tasting her urine. The male may attempt to drive off other males. A brief chase may follow and terminate with copulation. Ewes usually attain sexual maturity as yearlings or 2-year-olds. Rams reach sexual maturity between 18 and 36 months of age. Bighorn sheep may live to be 15 years old. Bighorn sheep can and do interbreed with domestic sheep.

Habits: Bighorn sheep are active almost exclusively in the daytime. The daily activity pattern consists of alternative periods of feeding and bedding with little overall movement. In winter, less time is spent eating. While resting, sheep chew their cud and occasionally rise to defecate or stretch.

Bighorn sheep are not territorial, but use specific seasonal home ranges connected by migration routes. Winter home ranges are smaller. In summer, sheep in Yellowstone usually travel 3 to 5 km daily.

The band is the basic unit of sheep social organization. Sexes are usually segregated into separate bands, but they may be aggregated on limited winter range. One or more bands constitute a herd. Ewe and kid bands vary from 2 to 15 sheep. Ram bands number 2 to 15. Dominance contests are typical in ram bands, especially the first time two rams meet. The two rams stand about 10 to 12 meters apart and then run at each other, rising on their hind legs just before butting heads (Geist 1971). Rams may attain a top speed of 54 kph. Eventually, one of them is shown to be subordinate. Lambs often play with each other and their mothers.

Food: Bighorn sheep have a relatively large rumen that accommodates the coarse forage in their diets. Microbes in the rumen digest 90 percent of the cellulose and 69 percent of the organic matter eaten. Selection of food items depends on plant succulence, nutrient content, and availability. Succulents and snow provide nearly all the water they need. Blue bunch wheatgrass is the most nutritious forage eaten by bighorn sheep. A variety of other grasses, forbs, and browse species are eaten.

Remarks: Bighorn sheep numbers in North America have been reduced drastically since pre-settlement times when they were estimated at 1 to 1.5 million. Today, there are about 20,000 in the Rocky Mountains. Bighorn sheep suffer from a pneumonia disease complex caused by at least seven species of round worms. Infestation of lungworm approaches 100 percent in some herds, and this, along with heavy livestock competition and overhunting, has reduced bighorn sheep numbers. The Whiskey Basin sheep herd near Dubois is one of the largest remaining herds in Wyoming.

GLOSSARY

Many of the following terms used in mammalogy were employed in the text of this book (modified from Bee et al. 1981).

Altricial. Young usually born naked, blind, and unable to care for themselves at birth (see precocial).

Alveolus. Socket in jaw that holds a tooth.

Angular process. Lower projection on posterior, ventral end of mandible; below articular process.

Annulation. Growth ring in cementum of some teeth used for aging; also, scaly ring on tail.

Antlers. Bony growths from frontal bones of skull. They are shed annually and renewed shortly thereafter.

Antorbital process. Anterior growth of supraorbital process in rabbits.

Apposable. Ability to touch the thumb to the tips of each finger on the same hand.

Articular process. Extension on vertebra connecting with the preceding or subsequent vertebra; also, projection on posterior end of mandible that hinges with skull.

Aspection. The seasonal aspect of an environment, and its regular pattern of change through the year.

Auditory bulla. Bony capsule enclosing the middle and inner ear (see tympanic bulla).

Axial skeleton. The skull, vertebrae, sternum and ribs.

Baculum. Penis bone (os penis) found in some mamals, and sometimes useful in identification.

Basioccipital. First ventral skull bone (single) anterior to foramen magnum.

Basilar length. Skull measurement from the lower lip of the foramen magnum to the posterior border of alveolus of the first incisor.

Basisphenoid. Single ventral skull bone immediately anterior to basioccipital.

Bifid. Divided into two approximately equal units; with regards teeth, two lobes on the crown.

Biome. A major biotic community characterized by certain types of dominant plants and animals; for example, eastern deciduous forest biome.

Blastocyst. A ball of cells formed by repeated divisions of the fertilized egg in the early embryonic development of mammals.

Brachyodont. Low-crowned teeth that cease to grow when fully erupted.

Braincase. Part of skull that covers the brain.

Buccal. Parts of tooth nearest the cheek; see also lingual.

Calcaneum. The "heel bone" of mammals.

Calcar. The cartilagenous spur connected to the calcaneum in bats, which helps to support the uropatagium.

Cancellous. Having a latticelike structure, spongelike.

Canine. Tooth on each side of jaw posterior to incisors.

Carnassial. The last upper premolar and lower first molar teeth of carnivores, used for cutting flesh.

Cementum. A spongy bone-like material. In most teeth it covers dentin in region of roots, and anchors tooth in socket.

Cheek pouch. An infolding of the skin of the cheek to form a pouch; may be external and fur-lined as in pocket gophers and pocket mice, or internal and not lined with fur, as in certain squirrels.

Cheek teeth. Premolar and molar teeth.

Cingulum. Ridge around the base of a tooth crown.

Climax. A biotic community that has reached an equilibrium with its environment, and whose constituent species are capable of maintaining themselves within the community.

Community. Any association of living organisms living in the same area and linked by biotic interactions.

Condylobasal length. Measurement of a skull from the posterior surface of the occipital condyles to the anterior end of the premaxillary bone.

Coronoid process. The uppermost projection at the posterior end of the lower jaw; above the articular process.

Cranial breadth. The widest part of the cranium.

Cranium. The bones enclosing the brain and sense organs of the head.

Crepuscular. Active in dim light before sunrise and after sunset.

Crown (of tooth). The part of the tooth farthest from the root, at least part of which comes into contact with a tooth in the opposite jaw (see occlusal surface).

Cursorial. Specialized for running.

Cusp. Projection on the crown of mammalian tooth.

Deciduous. Shed or lost during development, as in antlers or milk teeth.

Delayed implantation. Inhibition of embryo (blastocyst stage) from implantation in uterine wall.

Dental formula. Letters and numbers indicating the kind and numbers of teeth in mammals.

Dentary. Bone that forms mandible in mammals.

Dentine. Hard material forming the major portion of a tooth; in most teeth surrounds the pulp cavity and contacts the enamel on the crown of tooth and the cementum at base of roots: sometimes exposed on surface of crown.

Dew claw. Vestigial digit on the foot, especially of ungulates.

Diastema. Space between teeth, usually between incisor and first cheek tooth.

Dichotomous. Dividing into branches of equal size.

Digit. Finger or toe.

Digitigrade. Mammals which walk on their toes with the heel and wrist bones elevated above the ground surface.

Dominant (animal or plant). A species found in a community that because of abundance, size, and/or importance of its interactions helps to define the characteristics of that community.

Dorsal. Of, on, or near the back.

Ear from notch measurement. Distance from notch at base of ear to uppermost edge of fleshy part of ear.

Ear ossicles. Three bones in the air-filled middle ear that transmit vibrations to the inner ear.

Ecosystem. The biotic community, together with those features of its abiotic environment that interact with the community and sustain the life processes of its member species.

Ecotone. A transition zone between two distinct communities, such as a forest-grassland ecotone.

Edaphic. Pertaining to soil.

Enamel. Hardest part of tooth: calcium salts in form of apatite crystals; most frequently on crown of tooth.

Epiphyses. Terminal secondary centers of ossification.

Estivation (also aestivation). Inactivity during hot periods of summer or drought.

Estrous (also oestrous). Period when female is receptive to mating (copulation).

Exoccipital bone. One of a pair of bones on the sides of the foramen magnum bearing occipital condyles.

External auditory meatus. Canal leading to the tympanic membrane of the ear.

Femur. Thigh bone, between knee and pelvic girdle.

Fenestrated. Window-like perforations in a structure.

Fibula. Smaller of two bones between the knee and ankle of the hind leg.

Foramen magnum. Large posterior opening of skull where spinal cord leaves the brain.

Foramina. Openings or holes in bone for the passage of nerves and blood vessels (singular—foramen).

Fossa. A pit or depression on the surface of bone.

Fossorial. Digging or burrowing habits.

Frontal bone. Large bone covering anterior surface of brain.

Frontal sinus. Vacuities in the frontal bone opening into the nasal cavity.

Gestation. The period of embryonic development in a mammal from fertilization to birth (parturition), during most of which the embryo is in the uterus.

Glenoid fossa. Cup-shaped cavity on side of pectoral girdle that receives the head of the humerus forming a shoulder joint.

Greatest length of skull measurement. Length from anteriormost point on incisors, premaxillary bone, or nasal bone to posteriormost point on braincase.

Guard hairs. Outer protective hairs in pelage in mammals.

Hectare. An area 100 meters square.

Hibernation. Period of inactivity or dormancy in mammals during winter when body temperature and metabolism decrease.

Hind foot measurement. Length from end of claw to heel.

Home range. The area in which an individual mammal spends most or all of its time, and in which all activities can be conducted; need not be defended, and may thus overlap with the home range of an adjacent individual.

Horn. Permanent (non-deciduous) structure of keratin growing over bony core.

Humerus. Bone of upper forelimb, between elbow and shoulder.

Hyoid. Cartilage or bones supporting the base of the tongue.

Hypsodont. Teeth with high crowns and short roots.

Incisive foramen. One of the paired foramina in the anterior part of bony palate.

Inferior. Lower in space, placed lower down.

Influent (animal or plant). A species found in a community that may not be particularly abundant or large, but whose interactions with other species are essential in maintaining the character of the community.

Infraorbital canal. Opening through the maxillary bone from orbit to face, varying in size especially in rodents, according to the specialization of the masseter, a jaw muscle.

Inguinal. Region of the groin.

Interorbital. Region of skull between bony sockets of eyes.

Interorbital breadth. Least width between the orbits.

Interparietal. Single bone in posterior roof of skull, surrounded by two parietal and one supraoccipital bones.

Interptergoid. Between ptergoid bones.

Jugal. Bone in the zygomatic arch between the maxillary and squamosal bones.

Keel. Thin flap of flesh, often almost transparent, extending away from uropatagium from calcar.

Keratin. A horny, acellular, protein substance produced by skin cells, and which composes nails, claws, hooves, and horns.

Lamboidal crest. Ridge where the occipital bone joins the parietal and squamosal bones.

Lacrimal. Small bone at inner corner of orbit whose ducts drain tear glands.

Lateral. Pertaining to or next to the tongue; parts of tooth nearest the tongue (see buccal).

Longitudinal. Of, or in length.

Lophodont. Dentition in which cusps fuse to form transverse ridges.

Mamma. Mammary gland producing milk, characteristic of all mammals (plural—mammae).

Mandible. Lower jaw bone of mammals.

Marsupium. An external pouch formed by a fold of skin on the abdomen which encloses the mammae in many marsupials such as the opossum; serves to protect the poorly developed young during early postnatal growth.

Masseter. Muscle of the mandible in certain vertebrates.

Mastoid. A bone surrounded by the squamosal, exoccipital, and tympanic bones.

Mastoid breadth. Greatest distance across mastoid bones.

Mastoid process. Projection extending from the mastoid bone.

Maxillary bone (maxilla). Part of upper jaw that supports the canines, premolars, and molars.

Maxillary tooth row length. Length of teeth in maxilla (upper jaw) parallel to axis of skull, from canine to last molar.

Metatarsal. Bones of foot bewteen toes and heel.

Metacarpal. Bones of hand between fingers and wrist.

Meatus. A hole or opening.

Milk teeth. Deciduous teeth (incisors, canines, premolars) in juvenile mammals which are replaced by permanent teeth.

Molar. The most posterior set of teeth, often specialized for grinding and crushing.

Molariform. Teeth that have the appearance of molar teeth, such as modified premolars, as well as molars proper.

Molt. Process of periodic replacing of old worn hair with new hair.

Musk gland. Specialized scent-producing glands used for defense or recognition.

Muzzle. The projecting jaws and nose of the mammalian facial region.

Nail. Flattened, modified claw.

Nares. Opening to the nasal cavity.

Nasal. Bone on dorsal surface of rostrum bordered laterally by premaxillary and maxillary.

Natal. Pertaining to birth.

Neonate. Newborn young.

Occipital bone. Bone surrounding foramen magnum, and bearing occipital condyles.

Occipital condyles. Articulating surfaces of both sides of foramen magnum that support skull on vertebral column.

Occlusal surface. Contact surfaces of upper and lower teeth.

Omnivorous. Feeding on all sorts of plant and animal material.

Orbit. Bony socket of the eye.

Orbitosphenoid. Small bone forming a part of the lower median wall of the orbit.

Os penis. The baculum, or penis bone.

Palate. The bony roof of the mouth comprised of the premaxillary, maxillary and palatine bones.

Palatal breadth. Length across, width of the palatine bone.

Palatal length. Length from posterior border of palatine bones to the anterior end of the premaxillary bones.

Palatine foramen. Opening through the bony roof of the mouth.

Palmate. Branched.

Parietal. Paired bones of the braincase behind the frontal bone and anterior to the occipital bone.

Paraoccipital process. Projection on occipital bone.

Parturition. Process of giving birth to young.

Pectoral girdle. Bones to which forelimbs are attached.

Pelage. The hair of mammals.

Pelvic girdle. Bones to which the hind limbs are attached.

Pinna. The external ear.

Phalanx. One of the bones in the fingers or toes (plural—phalanges).

Placental scar. A pigmented area produced on the uterine wall from a previous attachment of the placenta.

Plantar. Sole of the foot.

Plantar tubercules. Protuberances on the sole of the foot.

Plantigrade. Walking on the soles of the feet with heel touching the ground.

Postauricular. Behind the ear.

Posterior. Later part, hind part of body.

Postglenoid. Behind the glenoid bone.

Postorbital process. Projection of the frontal bone on upper posterior orbital margin.

Postpartum. Pertains to events that follow after parturition, such as postpartum estrus.

Precocial. Young born with hair, eyes open, and able to move about immediately after birth.

Prehensile. Capable of grasping, as in a prehensile tail.

Presphenoid. A single bone in front of the basisphenoid.

Premaxillary bone (premaxilla). Bone that supports the upper incisors.

Premolars. Cheek teeth in front of molars; may be variously modified.

Prism. A shape whose ends are polygonal.

Pterygoid. Paired bones behind the palatine bones forming basal portion of skull.

Pubic symphysis. Midventral joint between the two halves of the pelvic girdle.

Quills. Spines of a porcupine.

Radius. The medial of two bones in the lower forelimb.

Retractile. The ability of certain mammals to raise their claws above a flat surface (i.e., cats).

Riparian. Adjacent to water, especially streams or rivers, as in riparian (bottomland) forest.

Rostrum. The portion of the skull in front of the orbits.

Rudimentary. Imperfectly developed and incapable of normal function, small.

Sagittal crest. Longitudinal ridge of bone along top of skull, including parietal and frontal bones.

Saltatorial. Adapted for leaping.

Scansorial. Specialized for climbing with sharp, curved claws.

Scent marking. The behavior of depositing odors on objects in the environment.

Scrotum. Pouch of skin in the pelvic region of males containing testicles.

Septum. Bony partition.

Seral. A biotic community that has not yet reached an equilibrium with its environment, and whose constituent species may be succeeded by others, a process called ecological succession (see also climax).

Squamosal. Bone on the posterior side of skull below the parietals, supporting the base of the zygomatic arch.

Superior. Having greater elevation, higher, upper.

Supraoccipital. Bone above the foramen magnum.

Supraorbital process. Process of the frontal bone above the orbit, prominent in rabbits.

Suture. Interlocking edges of bones forming an immovable joint.

Temporal ridge. Raised edge on parietal bone for attachment of temporal muscle.

Territory. Specific area established and defended from intrusion by another member of the same species; usually established for breeding or feeding purposes.

Tibia. Larger of two bones bewteen knee and ankle in hind limbs; the shin bone.

Tine. Prong of an antler.

Total length. Length from tip of nose to end of fleshy part of tail when mammal is laid on its back on a flat surface.

Tragus. A small flap in front of the external opening of the ear in bats.

Trifid. Divided into three approximately equal units; with regards teeth, three lobes on crown.

Tympanic bulla. Bony capsule enclosing the middle and inner ear (see auditory bullae).

Underfur. Fine, dense inner coat of hair.

Ungulate. Collective term applied to hoofed mammals (orders Perissodactyla and Artiodactyla).

Ulna. Outermost of two bones in forearm.

Unicuspids. Conical teeth in a shrew between the large anterior incisor and premolars (includes posterior incisors, canine, and anterior premolars).

Uropatagium. Skin between the hind legs and tail of bats; interfemoral membrane.

Venter. The belly, underside.

Ventral. Of, near, on, or toward the underside.

Vibrissae. Long tactile whiskers on side of muzzle behind nasal opening.

Vomer. Thin, flat bone forming part of nasal septum separating the nasal passages.

Weaning. The process by which nourishment of the developing juvenile mammal is shifted from maternal milk to foods of the sort eaten by the adult.

Zygoma, zygomatic arch. A slender bridge of bone extending along the side of the skull.

Zygomatic breadth. Greatest distance across zygomatic arches.

Zygomatic plate. The base of the zygomatic arm of the maxilla.

TECHNICAL KEYS TO WYOMING MAMMALS

ORDER INSECTIVORA—Shrews and Moles

1   Feet adapted for digging; eyes and ears not evident externally; tail less than
     3/4 as long as hind foot .... TALPIDAE
1 ' Feet not adapted for digging; eyes and ears tiny but evident; tail more than
     3/4 as long as hind foot .... SORICIDAE

FAMILY TALPIDAE—Moles

     .... *Scalopus aquaticus*

FAMILY SORICIDAE—Shrews

1   Pelage flecked with silvery white hairs on dark, grayish background, hind
     foot fringed with stiff hairs, tail scaley and scantily haired, total more than
     130 mm .... *Sorex palustris navigator*
1 ' Not as in 1, tail haired, total length less than 130 mm 2
2   Third and fifth unicuspid teeth tiny (Fig. 5), total length 62–106 mm, tail
     21–39 mm, hind foot 8–12 mm .... *Sorex hoyi montanus*
2 ' Not as in 2, third unicuspid visible, usually at least 1/2 size of first .. 3
3   Third unicuspid larger than fourth (or about equal) (Fig. 5) 4
3 ' Third unicuspid smaller than fourth (Fig. 5) 7
4   Whitish underparts, crowded unicuspid row, no medial tines on first up-
     per incisor (Fig. 6) .... *Sorex merriami*
4 ' Brownish underparts, uncrowded unicuspid row, medial tines present on
     first upper incisor (Fig. 6) 5
5   Condylobasal length less than 14.2 mm, maxillary breadth less than 4.2
     mm in northwestern mountains (Fig. 7) .... *Sorex preblei*
5 ' Not as in 5 6
6   Pigmentation on lower teeth continuous, teeth massive, from northeastern
     Wyoming (Fig. 8) .... *Sorex haydenii*
6 ' Pigmentation on lower teeth discontinuous, separate cusp pigmentaion on
     I_1 (Fig. 8) .... *Sorex cinereus cinereus*
7   Tail equal to or less than 40 mm, hind foot less than 11 mm, greatest length
     of skull usually less than 15.2 mm .... *Sorex nanus*
7 ' Tail usually more than 40 mm, hind foot more than 11 mm, braincase con-
     vex when viewed laterally 8
8   Tail 41 mm or less, total length 108 mm or less, medial tines on first upper
     incisors approximately *at* upper edge of pigment (Fig. 6) *Sorex vagrans*
8 ' Tail often more than 41 mm, total length often more than 108 mm,
     medial tines on first upper incisors well below pigmented line (Fig.
     6) .... *Sorex monticolus obscurus*

Figure 5. Differences in upper tooth rows in Wyoming shrews: Pigmy shrew (left); Masked, Merriam's, and Preble's shrews (center); vagrant, dwarf and dusky shrews (right). The first unicuspid is actually the third point because the first tooth has two cusps. Anterior is to the left; teeth are counted starting with the most anterior tooth. Drawing from Diersing (1980).

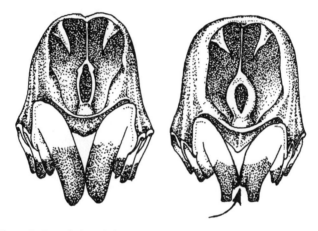

Figure 6. Frontal view of shrew teeth to show medial tines (arrow) in relation to pigmentation line.

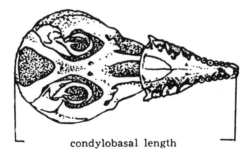

condylobasal length

Figure 7. Ventral view of Preble's shrew skull showing condylobasal length measurement. (Drawing from Hoffmann and Pattie 1968).

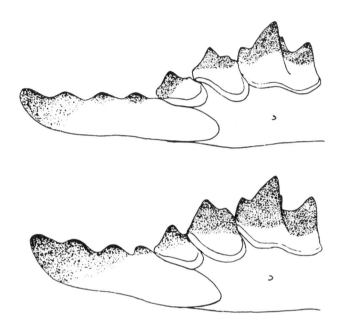

Figure 8. Typical pigmentation patterns of the lower anterior toothrow in the masked shrew (above) and Hayden's shrew (below). Note also the differences in the incisors and other teeth, which are more massive in Hayden's shrew. Drawing from Van Zyll de Jong (1980).

ORDER CHIROPTERA—Bats

FAMILIES VESPERITILIONIDAE AND MOLOSSIDAE—Common Bats and Free-tailed Bats

1   About half the tail projecting from the interfemoral membrane (uropatagium) .... *Tadarida brasiliensis*
1 ' Tail enclosed in uropatagium with no more than a few millimeters projecting free (Fig. 9) 2
2   Upper parts black having three dime-sized white spots, spectacular ears 45–50 mm from inner notch to tip .... *Euderma maculatum*
2 ' Lacking white spots, ears less than 43 mm 3
3   Ears long (23–37 mm), blunt pig-like snout, dorsal fur pale yellowish or creamy yellow .... *Antrozous pallidus*
3 ' Not as above 4
4   Long ears (33–39 mm) with two large fleshy lumps on nose .... *Plecotus townsendi*
4 ' Ears less than 25 mm and not as above 5
5   Fur uniformly black and many of the hairs distinctly silver-tipped, dentition i. 2/3; c.1/1; p.2/3; m3/3 .... *Lasionycteris noctivagans*
5 ' Fur not silver-tipped, fur not black, dentition not as in 5 6
6   Dorsal surface of uropatagium completely furred 7

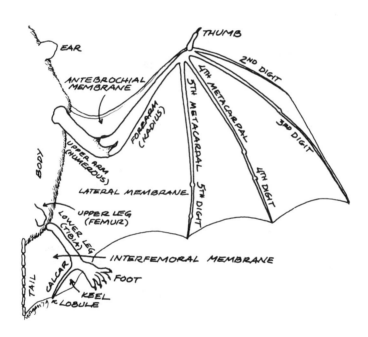

Figure 9. Skull of a big brown bat (upper). Anatomy of a bat's wing (lower). The interfemoral membrane is also called the uropatagium.

6' Dorsal surface of uropatagium only furred on anterior half 8
7 Ears conspicuously black-edged, with patches of yellowish hair scattered inside them, fur hoary .... *Lasiurus cinereus cinereus*
7' Ears not conspicuously black-edge ("frosted"), bare or at most scant-hair inside, fur red-orange .... *Lasiurus borealis*
8 Foot less than 8 mm, third metacarpal less than 30.5 mm, fur pale light tan .... *Myotis ciliolabrum ciliolabrum*
8' Foot more than 8.5 mm, fur dark 9

9 Total length more than 106 mm, dentition i. 2/3; c. 1/1; p. 1/2; m. 3/3, from side view, the first premolar visible to naked eye behind the upper canine approximately half as high as the canine and in contact with it at the base, forearm more than 40 mm (Fig. 9) .... *Eptesicus fuscus*

9 ' Total length less than 106 mm, dentition not as in 9, and from a side view, there is a gap between the canine and first premolar visible to the naked eye behind the canine 10

10 Ear when gently laid forward extending more than 2 mm beyond tip of nose; ear more than 16 mm 11

10 ' Ear when gently laid forward extending less than 2 mm beyond tip of nose; ear less than 16 mm 13

11 With a conspicuous (to naked eye) fringe of hairs projecting backward from the posterior edge of the uropatagium *Myotis thysanodes pahasapensis*

11 ' Without a conspicuous fringe of hairs projecting backwards from the uropatagium 12

12 Ears pitch black, opaque, 20–25 mm .... *Myotis evotis evotis*

12 ' Ears dark, 17–19 mm, but not dark black *Myotis keeni septentrionalis*

13 Distinct keel on calcar visible to naked eye 14

13 ' No keel on calcar visible to naked eye 15

14 Foot over 8.5 mm, forearm usually more than 34 mm, underside of wing furred from knee to elbow .... *Myotis volans interior*

14 ' Foot less than 8.5 mm, forearm usually less than 34 mm *Myotis californicus*

15 Greatest length of skull usually less than 14 mm, fur usually dull .... *Myotis yumanensis*

15 ' Greatest length of skull usually more than 14 mm, fur brassy-glossy .... *Myotis lucifugus*

ORDER LAGOMORPHA—Pikas, Rabbits and Hares

1 Hind legs slightly longer than forelegs; hind foot less than 40 mm in length; supraorbital process on frontal absent; nasals widest anteriorly; five cheekteeth above .... OCHOTONIDAE

1 ' Hind legs noticeably longer than forelegs; hind foot more than 40 mm in length; supraorbital process present; nasals widest posteriorly; six cheekteeth above .... LEPORIDAE

FAMILY OCHOTONIDAE—Pikas

.... *Ochotona princeps*

FAMILY LEPORIDAE—Rabbits, Hares and Jackrabbits

1 Interparietal fused with parietals; hind foot often more than 105 mm; in juveniles, interpterygoid space wider than 7.0 mm .... *Lepus*

1 ' Interparietal not fused with parietals; hind foot often less than 105 mm; in juveniles, interpterygoid space narrower than 7.0 mm .... *Sylvilagus*

Species of *Sylvilagus*

1 Tail small, fluffy, buffy underneath .... *Sylvilagus idahoensis*

1 ' Tail not as above 2

2 Greatest diameter of esternal auditory meatus less than 4.9 mm
.... *Sylvilagus floridanus*

2 ' Greatest diameter of external auditory meatus more than 4.9 mm 3

3 Ear usually longer than 70 mm; prominent upturned supraorbital processes; greatest diameter of external auditory meatus often more than 6.0 mm .... *Sylvilagus audubonii*

3 ' Ear usually shorter than 70 mm; small supraorbital processes with abrupt anterior point; greatest diameter of external auditory meatus usually less than 6.0 mm .... *Sylvilagus nuttallii*

Species and Subspecies of *Lepus*

1 Tail black above; upper parts never white in winter; known only from southeastern part of state .... *Lepus californicus melanotis*

1 ' Tail not black above; upper parts of most individuals white in winter; known throughout most of state 2

2 Tail all white lacking narrow, dorsal, gray line; summer pelage pale and brassy colored .... *Lepus townsendii campanius*

2 ' Tail not all white; summer pelage dark and brassy colored or pale and lacking brassy color 3

3 Tail all white excepting narrow, longitudinal, dorsal gray line; upper parts in summer pale and grayish or golden instead of brassy or buffy .... *Lepus townsendii townsendii*

3 ' Tail bicolored, concolor with back above and white below; upper parts in summer dark and flecked with golden or brassy color 4

4 Upper parts grayish and reddish golden; nasals nearly straight-sided as seen in dorsal view .... *Lepus americanus bairdii*

4 ' Upper parts grayish and flecked with yellowish-golden hairs; nasals markedly convex anteriorly in dorsal view .... *Lepus americanus seclusus*

ORDER RODENTIA — Rodents

1 Body and tail provided with quills; infraorbital foramen larger than foramen magnum .... ERETHIZONTIDAE

1 ' Body and tail lacking quills; infraorbital foramen smaller than foramen magnum 2

2 Tail flattened or depressed dorsoventrally, scaly; teeth having 8–10 transverse ridges .... CASTORIDAE

2 ' Tail not flattened dorsoventrally; teeth lacking 8–10 transverse ridges 3

3 External fur-lined cheek pouches present 4

3 ' External fur-lined cheek pouches lacking 5

4 Tail much shorter than head and body; front feet larger than hind; tympanic bullae not evident in dorsal view of skull .... GEOMYIDAE

4 ' Tail usually longer than head and body; front feet smaller than hind; tympanic bullae evident in dorsal view of skull ...... HETEROMYIDAE

5 Cheek teeth more than three 6

5 ' Cheek teeth three in normal individuals 7

Figure 10. Grinding surface of upper molars in *Peromyscus* (left) with two longitudinal rows of cusps, and *Mus musculus* (right) with three longitudinal rows of cusps.

6   Postorbital processes absent .... ZAPODIDAE

6 ' Postorbital processes present .... SCIURIDAE

7   Upper molariform teeth having three longitudinal rows of cusps (Fig. 10) .... MURIDAE

7 ' Upper molars having only two longitudinal rows of cusps or showing numerous triangles and transverse folds in occlusal view (Fig. 10) .... CRICETIDAE

FAMILY SCIURIDAE — Squirrels

1   Membrane present between forelimbs and hind limbs modified for gliding .... *Glaucomys*

1 ' Membrane lacking between forelimbs and hind limbs 2

2   Antorbital canal lacking, the antorbital foramen piercing the zygomatic plate of the maxillary; head striped .... *Tamias*

2 ' Antorbital canal present; head not striped 3

3   Zygomatic breadth more than 48 mm; anterior lower premolar having paraconulid .... *Marmota*

3 ' Zygomatic breadth less than 48 mm; anterior lower premolar lacking paraconulid 4

4   Tail less than one-fourth total length .... *Cynomys*

4 ' Tail more than one-fourth total length 5

5   Zygomata converging anteriorly; tail short usually; often striped or spotted .... *Spermophilus*

5 ' Zygomata nearly parallel; tail long and well-haired; lacking spots and/or stripes 6

6   Baculum well-developed; third premolar well developed .... *Sciurus*

6 ' Baculum spiculelike; third premolar vestigial or absent .. *Tamiasciurus*

Species of *Tamias*

1   Dorsal stripes obscure; upper parts grayish .... *Tamias dorsalis*

1 ' Dorsal stripes distinct; upper parts tawny (not grayish) 2

2   Venter yellowish or buff; tip of baculum more than 30 percent of length of shaft; shaft now widened at base .... *Tamias amoenus*

2 ' Venter white; tip of baculum less than 29 percent of length of shaft or if as much as, or more than, 29 percent, shaft widened at base 3

3   Size small to medium; greatest length of skull less than 34 mm; shaft of baculum not widened at base; outermost dorsal dark stripe never obsolete .... *Tamias minimus*

3 ' Size large; greatest length of skull rarely less than 34 mm; shaft of baculum widened at base; outermost dorsal dark stripe often obsolete, never strongly evident .... *Tamias umbrinus*

Species of *Spermophilus*

1 Upper parts usually having 13 longitudinal stripes (some stripes break up into distinct spots) .... *Spermophilus tridecemlineatus*
1 ' Upper parts lacking 13 stripes, although either stripes or spots may be present 2
2 Lateral stripes present .... *Spermophilus lateralis*
2 ' Lateral stripes lacking 3
3 Metaloph on P4 continuous; upper parts uniform grayish or brownish, often dappled with fine, obscure spots 4
3 ' Metaloph on P4 not continuous; upper parts reddish dappled, usually with distinct spots .... *Spermophilus spilosoma*
4 Underside of tail grayish; nasals deflected ventral anteriorly
.... *Spermophilus armatus*
4 ' Underside of tail buffy or orange; nasals nearly straight-sided
.... *Spermophilus elegans*

Species of *Cynomys*

1 Tail tipped with white, black fur around eye and on forehead
.... *Cynomys leucurus*
1 ' Tail tipped with black .... *Cynomys ludovicianus*

FAMILY GEOMYIDAE — Pocket Gophers

1 Pale yellowish tan fur, incisors distinctly grooved on anterior (front) faces .... *Geomys lutescens*
1 ' Pale yellowish buff to dark brown fur, incisors smooth or only grooved by indistinct line on anterior faces 2
2 Hind feet longer than 25 mm .... *Thomomys talpoides*
2 ' Hind feet less than 25 mm 3
3 Occurring in Sweetwater or Carbon counties .... *Thomomys clusius*
3 ' Occurring in Uinta, Lincoln or Sublette counties *Thomomys idahoensis*

FAMILY HETEROMYIDAE — Pocket Mice

1 Soles of hind feet well haired, hind foot more than 35 mm *Dipodomys ordii*
1 ' Soles of hind feet naked or furred to palm only, hind foot less than 35 mm 2
2 Total length more than 200 mm, fur harsh to the touch, hairs on end of tail usually longer than hairs at base of tail .... *Perognathus hispidus*
2 ' Total length less than 200 mm, fur soft to the touch, hairs on end of tail usually as long as hairs at base of tail 3
3 Tail more than half total length .... *Perognathus parvus*
3 ' Tail less than half total length 4
4 Upper parts olive brown .... *Perognathus fasciatus*
4 ' Upper parts light yellow (buff) or creamy 5

5   Light pale patch of fur behind ear indistinct and only as long as ear
.... *Perognathus flavescens*
5 ' Light pale patch of fur behind ear distinct and twice as long as ear
.... *Perognathus flavus*

FAMILY CASTORIDAE — Beavers

.... *Castor canadensis*

FAMILY CRICETIDAE — New World Mice

1   Cheek-teeth cusped; no occlusal lakes of dentine surrounded by enamel 2
2   Tail less than 60 percent of length of head and body; coronoid process more
     than 1 1/2 times as high as wide .... *Oncyhomys leucogaster*
2 ' Tail more than 60 percent of length of head and body; coronoid process
     less than 1 1/2 times as high as wide 3
3   Anterior faces of incisors grooved; total length of animal less than 150 mm 4
4   Total length less than 125 mm; length of tail less than 55 mm; pelage pale
     except middorsally; pinna of ear having two spots one above
     the other .... *Reithrodontomys montanus*
4 ' Total length more than 125 mm; length of tail more than 55 mm; pelage
     dark agouti as in *Mus;* pinna of ear lacking spots *Reithrodontomys megalotis*
3 ' Anterior faces of incisors smooth; total length of animal more than
     150 mm 5
5   Tail as long as head and body (rarely less, usually more) 6
6   Tooth-row usually shorter than 4 mm; pinna of ear shorter than
     hind foot .... *Peromyscus crinitus*
6 ' Tooth-row longer than 4 mm; pinna of ear longer than hind
     foot .... *Peromyscus truei*
5 ' Tail shorter than head and body 7
7   Tail not sharply bicolored; hind foot 22 mm or longer *Peromyscus leucopus*
7 ' Tail sharply bicolored; hind foot usually shorter than 22 mm
     .... *Peromyscus maniculatus*
1 ' Cheek-teeth lack cusps; occlusal lakes of dentine surrounded by enamel 8
8   Tail bushy; ears nearly naked (scantily haired) .... *Neotoma cinerea*
8 ' Tail not bushy; ears haired 9
9   Total length more than 480 mm; tail compressed laterally and
     scaly .... *Ondatra zibethicus*
9 ' Total length less than 480 mm; tail round and haired 10
10   Molars rooted in adults (Fig. 11) 11
11   Upper parts reddish; in lower molars inner re-entrant angles little if any
     deeper than outer re-entrant angles (Fig. 12) ... *Clethrionomys gapperi*
11 ' Upper parts buffy gray; in lower molars inner re-entrant angles deeper than
     outer re-entrant angles (Fig. 12) .... *Phenacomys intermedius*
10 ' Molars rootless in adults (Fig. 11) 12
12   Tail shorter than 27 mm; m3 having at least 4 prisms; auditory bullae
     cancellous .... *Lemmiscus curtatus*

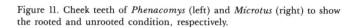

Figure 11. Cheek teeth of *Phenacomys* (left) and *Microtus* (right) to show the rooted and unrooted condition, respectively.

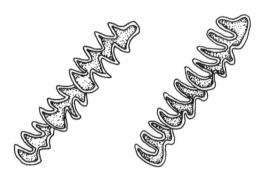

Figure 12. Grinding surface of lower cheek teeth of *Microtus* and *Clethrionomys* (left) to show inner and outer angles about equal and centered. In *Phenacomys* (right), with unequal angles, the line where enamel folds meet is distinctly off-center.

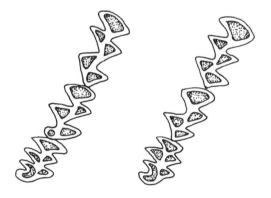

Figure 13. Grinding surface of upper teeth of *Microtus pennsylvanicus* (left) and *Microtus montanus* (right) showing (in second molar) five and four dental lakes, respectively. Anterior to top, lingual to left.

12' Tail longer than 27 mm; m3 having fewer than 4 prisms; auditory bullae noncancellous 13
13 Tail less than 30 percent of head and body 14
14 Venter washed with ochraceous or cinnamon; upper parts reddish brown .... *Microtus ochrogaster*
14' Venter usually whitish; upper parts brownish or grayish 15
15 Venter occasionally washed with cinnamon; upper middle molar having fifth posterior loop (Fig. 13) .... *Microtus pennsylvanicus*
15' Venter whitish, upper middle molar lacking fifth loop (Fig. 13) .... *Microtus montanus*
13' Tail about 30 percent of head and body or longer 16
16 Tail longer than 70 mm; hind foot longer than 25 mm; pelage dark .... *Microtus richardsoni*
16' Tail usually shorter than 70 mm; hind foot shorter than 25 mm; pelage olivaceous-brown; sides pale gray .... *Microtus longicaudus*

FAMILY MURIDAE — Old World Mice

1 Hind feet longer than 25 mm, tail longer than 115 mm *Rattus norvegicus*
1' Hind feet shorter than 25 mm, tail shorter than 115 mm *Mus musculus*

FAMILY ZAPODIDAE — Jumping Mice

1 Palatal breadth at M_3 less than 4.2 mm, total length less than 225 mm .... *Zapus hudsonius*
1' Palatal breadth at M_3 less than 4.2 mm, total length more than 225 mm .... *Zapus princeps*

FAMILY ERETHIZONTIDAE — Porcupines

.... *Erethizon dorsatum*

ORDER CARNIVORA — Carnivores

1 Hind foot five-toed 2
2 Three lower molars; length of head and body more than 104 mm URSIDAE
2' Two lower molars; length of head and body less than 104 mm 3
3 Teeth, 40; tail annulated .... PROCYONIDAE
3' Teeth fewer than 40; tail not annulated .... MUSTELIDAE
1' Hind foot four-toed 4
4 Four digits on forefoot; claws non-retractile; teeth, 42 .... CANIDAE
4' Five digits on fore foot; claws retractile; teeth, 28–30 .... FELIDAE

FAMILY CANIDAE — Foxes, Coyotes and Wolves

1 Basilar length usually less than 147 mm; frontals concave dorsally (dished) (Fig. 14) 2
2 Back of pinna of ear blackish; tail lacking dorsal black stripe; inferior margin of mandible lacking prominent step 3

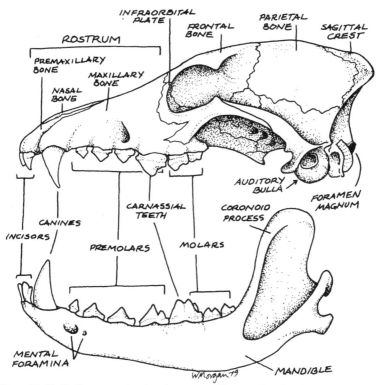

Figure 14. Skull of a coyote showing the names of bones referred to in the key.

3   Tip of tail white; ears black on outer surface of pinna; upper parts red-
     dish .... *Vulpes vulpes*
3 ' Tip of tail blackish; ears grayish on outer surface of pinna; upper parts
     yellowish gray intermixed dorsally with golden buff .... *Vulpes velox*
2 ' Back of pinna of ear reddish or rufous; tail having continuous dorsal black
     stripe; inferior margin of mandible having prominent step
     .... *Urocyon cinereoargenteus*
1 ' Basilar length usually more than 147 mm; frontals not concave dorsally 4
4   Anteroposterior length of upper canine less than 11 mm; upper carnassial
     shorter than 23.4 mm .... *Canis latrans*
4 ' Anteroposterior length of upper canine more than 11; upper cranassial usual-
     ly longer than 23.4 mm .... *Canis lupus*

FAMILY URSIDAE—Bears

1   Upper parts grizzled with golden buff; mane or "roach" of long hair on
     shoulders; upper M2 longer than 30 mm .... *Ursus arctos*
1   Upper parts not grizzled with golden buff; mane lacking; upper M2 shorter
     than 30 mm .... *Ursus americanus*

FAMILY PROCYONIDAE—Raccoons, Ringtail Cat

1   Tail longer than body; hard palate extends posteriorly about as far as last
    upper molar; hind foot less than 80 mm .... *Bassariscus astutus*
1 ' Tail shorter than body; hard palate extends posteriorly behind last upper
    molar for a distance of more than combined lengths of M1 and M2; hind
    foot more than 90 mm .... *Procyon lotor*

FAMILY MUSTELIDAE—Weasels

1   Premolars 4/4 2
2   Obscure brownish stripes laterally .... *Gulo gulo*
2 ' Stripes lacking ....: 3
3. Tail more than 290 mm; M1 more than 11 mm .... *Martes pennanti*
3 ' Tail less than 290 mm; M1 less than 11 mm .... *Martes americana*
1 ' Premolars fewer than 4/4 4
4   Premolars 4/3 .... *Lutra canadensis*
4 ' Premolars 3/3 5
5   Talonid of M1 trenchant .... *Mustela*
5 ' Talonid of M1 basined or dished 6
6   Single whitish longitudinal stripe on top of head and neck; basilar length
    more than 80 mm .... *Taxidea taxus*
6 ' Single white neck stripe lacking; basilar length less than 80 mm 7
7   Upper parts black with broken white stripes or spots 8
7 ' Upper parts black with continuous white stripes (two) or entirely black ex-
    cept white on top of head .... *Mephitis mephitis*
8   Tail is solid black except for white tip ... *Spilogale putorious interrupta*
8 ' Tail is white on underside for one-half its length ...... *Spilogale gracilis*

Species of *Mustela*

1   Length of upper tooth-row less than 20 mm in males and 17.8 mm in
    females 2
2   Postglenoidal length of skull more than 47 percent of condylobasal
    length 3
3   Tail without black pencil tip with at most a few black hairs at extreme tip,
    in both sexes mastoid breadth usually more than breadth of braincase, caudal
    vertebrae 11–16 .... *Mustela nivalis*
3 ' Tail with black tip, in females mastoid breadth usually less than breadth
    of braincase, caudal vertebrae 16–19 .... *Mustela erminea*
2 ' Postglenoid length of skull less than 47 percent of condylobasal
    length .... *Mustela frenata*
1 ' Length of upper tooth-row more than 20 mm in males and 17.8 mm in
    females 4
4   Abdomen white, face with black mask, M1 lacking even trace of metaconid,
    distance between upper canines more than width of basioccipital as mea-
    sured between foramina situated midway along medial sides of typanic
    bullae .... *Mustela nigripes*

4 ′ Abdomen dark brown like back, face uniformly brown without black mask, M1 with incipient metaconid, distance between upper canines less than width of basioccipital as measured between foramina situated midway along medial sides of typanic bullae. Length of upper molar–premolar tooth row less than 20 mm .... *Mustela vison*

FAMILY FELIDAE — Cats

1 Tail more than 30 percent of total length; 3 upper premolars present on each side .... *Felis concolor*
1 ′ Tail less than 30 percent of total length; 2 upper premolars present on each side 2
2 Tail tipped with black; tail less than 1/2 length of hind foot *Felis lynx*
2 ′ Tail tipped withi black above but white below; tail more than 1/2 length of hind foot .... *Felis rufus*

ORDER ARTIODACTYLA — Even Toed Hoofed Mammals

1 Horn sheaths have bony cores; horns present in both sexes (occasionally absent in females of *Antilocapra*) 2
2 Horns not branched or forked; lateral hooves present .. BOVIDAE .. 3
3 Tail longer than 150 mm 4
4 Length of skull less than 350 mm; length of maxillary tooth-row less than 120 mm .... *Oreamnos americanus*
2 ′ Horns in males branched or forked; lateral hooves lacking .... ANTILOCAPRIDAE, *Antilocapra americana*
1 ′ Bony antlers present; antlers in males only .... CERVIDAE .. 5
5 Antlers palmate; pendulous "bell" suspended from throat .. *Alces alces*
5 ′ Antlers not palmate; bell lacking 6
4 ′ Length of skull more than 350 mm; length of maxillary tooth-row more than 120 mm .... *Bison bison*
3 ′ Tail shorter than 150 mm .... *Ovis canadensis*
6 Posterior narial cavity not completely divided by vomer; canines present above .... *Cervus elaphus*
6 ′ Posterior narial cavity divided by vomer; canines lacking above 7
7 Antlers having one main beam on each side from which tines rise vertically; metatarsal gland less than 25 mm long; tail brown above, fringed with white .... *Odocoileus virginianus*
7 ′ Antlers branch dichotomously; metatarsal gland more than 25 mm long; tail tipped with black above .... *Odocoileus hemionus*

LITERATURE CITED
AND PARTIAL BIBLIOGRAPHY
OF WYOMING MAMMALS

ABLES, E. D.
  1974.   Ecology of the red fox in North America, pp. 148–163 in M. W. Fox, ed., The Wild Canids. Van Nostrand Reinhold Co., New York. 508 pp.
ALTMANN, M.
  1959.   Group dynamics in Wyoming moose during the rutting season. J. Mamm. 40:420–424.
ANDERSEN, B. B., and L. A. MILLER.
  1977.   A portable ultrasonic detection system for recording bat cries in the field. J. Mamm. 58:226–229.
ANDERSON, E., S. C. FORREST, T. W. CLARK, and L. RICHARDSON.
  1986.   Paleobiology, biogeography, and systematics of the black-footed ferret, *Mustela nigripes (Audubon and Bachman), 1851.* Great Basin Nat. Mem. 8:11–62.
ANDERSON, S.
  1954.   Subspeciation in the meadow vole, *Microtus montanus,* in Wyoming and Colorado. Univ. Kans. Mus. of Nat. Hist. Publ. 7:489–506.
ANDERSON, S., and J. K. JONES.
  1984.   Orders and Families of Recent Mammals of the World. John Wiley, New York. pp. 317–321.
ARMSTRONG, D. M.
  1972.   Distribution of Mammals in Colorado. Univ. Kans. Mus. Nat. Hist. Monog. No. 3.
ARMSTRONG, D. M.
  1975.   Rocky Mountain Mammals. Rocky Mtn. Nature Assoc., Rocky Mtn. Nat. Park. Colo.
ARMSTRONG, D. M., and J. K. JONES.
  1971.   *Sorex merriami.* Mammalian Species 2:1–2.
BALPH, D. F., and A. W. STOKES.
  1963.   On the ethology of a population of Uinta ground squirrels. Amer. Midl. Nat. 69:106–126.
BALPH, D. F.
  1984.   Spatial and social behavior in a population of Uinta ground squirrels: Interrelations with climate and annual cycle, pp. 336–352 in The Biology of Ground-Dwelling Squirrels, ed. by J. O. Murie and G. R. Michener. Univ. Neb. Press, Lincoln.
BARBOUR, R. W., and W. H. DAVIS.
  1969.   Bats of America. Univ. Kentucky Press, Lexington. 286 pp.
BARNES, V. G., and O. E. BRAY.
  1967.   Population characteristics of black bears in Yellowstone National Park. Colo. Coop. Wildl. Res. Unit and Colo. State Univ., Ft. Collins. 199 pp.
BATZLI, G. O., L. L. GETZ, and S. S. HURLEY.
  1977.   Suppression of growth and reproduction of microtine rodents by social factors, J. Mamm. 58:583–591.
BEE, J. W., G. E. GLASS, R. S. HOFFMANN, and R. R. PATTERSON.
  1981.   Mammals in Kansas. Univ. Kans. Mus. Nat. Hist. Public Educ. Ser., 7:1–300.
BEKOFF, M. C.
  1977.   *Canis latrans.* Mammalian Species 79:1–9.
BEKOFF, M. C.
  1982.   Coyote, pp. 447–459 in Wild Mammals of North America. Johns Hopkins Univ. Press, Baltimore. 1147 pp.
BEKOFF, M. C., and M. C. WELLS.
  1980.   Social ecology and behavior of coyotes. Sci. Amer. 242:130–148.

BELAN, I., P. N. LEHNER, and T. W. CLARK.
1978. Vocalizations of the American pine marten. *Martes americana.* J. Mamm. 59:871–874.

BELITSKY, D. W.
1981. Small mammals of the Salt Wells-Pilot Peak planning unit. BLM, Rock Springs, Wyo. 104 pp.

BELL, G. P.
1982. Behavioral and ecological aspects of gleaning by a desert insectivorous bat, *Antrozous pallidus* (Chiroptera, Vespertilionidae). Behav. Ecol. Sociobiol. 10:217–223.

BERGER, P. J., N. C. NEGUS, E. H. SANDERS, and P. D. GARDNER.
1981. Chemical triggering of reproduction in *Microtus montanus.* Science 214:69–70.

BIRNEY, E. C., W. E. GRANT, and D. D. BAIRD.
1976. Importance of vegetative cover to cycles of *Microtus* populations. Ecology 57:1043–1051.

BOGAN, M. A.
1974. Identification of *Myotis californicus* and *M. leibii* in southwestern North America. Proc. Biol. Soc. Wash. 87:49–56.

BOGAN, M.
1975. Geographic variation ion *Myotis californicus* in the southwestern United States and Mexico. U.S. Fish and Wildl. Serv. Wildl. Res. Rep. 3:1–33.

BOYCE, M. S.
1974. Beaver population ecology in interior Alaska. M. S. Thesis, Univ. Alaska, College. 161 pp.

BOYCE, M. S.
1980. First record of the fringe-tailed bat, *Myotis thysanodes,* from southeastern Wyoming. Southwest Nat. 25:114–115.

BOYCE, M. S., and L. D. HAYDEN-WING, eds.
1979. North American Elk: Ecology, behavior, and management. Univ. Wyo. Press, Laramie, 294 pp.

BRITT, L.
1972. Some aspects of the ecology of *Perognathus flavus, Dipodomys ordii,* and *Dipodomys merriami.* Ph.D. Dissert., Univ. New Mex., Albuquerque. 75 pp.

BROADBOOKS, H. E.
1970. Populations of the yellow-pine chipmunk, *Eutamias amoenus.* Amer. Midl. Nat. 83:472–488.

BROWN, L. N.
1965. Status of the opossum, *Didelphis marsupialis,* in Wyoming. Southwest. Nat. 10:142–143.

BROWN, L. N.
1967. Ecological distribution of mice in the Medicine Bow Mountains of Wyoming. Ecology 48:677–680.

BROWN, L. N.
1967. Ecological distribution of six species of shrews and comparison of sampling methods in the central Rocky Mountains. J. Mamm. 48:617–623.

BROWN, L. N.
1970. Population dynamics of the western jumping mouse *(Zapus princeps)* during a four year study. J. Mamm. 51:651–658.

BROWN, L. N., and D. METZ.
1966. First record of *Perognathus flavescens* in Wyoming. J. Mamm. 47:118.

BUCHLER, E. R.
1976. Use of echolocation by wandering shrews. Anim. Behav. 24:858–873.

BUNNELL, S. D., and D. R. JOHNSON.
1974. Physical factors affecting pika density and dispersal. J. Mamm. 55:866–869.

BURT, W. H., and R. P. GROSSENHEIDER.
1964. A field guide to the mammals. Houghton Mifflin Co., Boston. 284 pp.

Burns, J. C., J. R. Choate, and E. G. Zimmerman.
1985. Systematic relationships of pocket gophers (Genus *Geomys*) on the central Great Plains. J. Mamm. 66(1):102–118.

Camenzind, F. J.
1974. Territorial and social behavior of coyotes *(Coyotes latrans)* on the National Elk Refuge, northwestern Wyoming. J. Colo.-Wyo. Acad. Sci. 7:56.

Cameron, D. M., Jr.
1967. Gestation period of the golden-mantled ground squirrel *(Citellus lateralis)*. J. Mamm. 48:492–493.

Campbell, T. M., III, and T. W. Clark.
1981. Colony characteristics and vertebrate associates of white-tailed and black-tailed prairie dogs in Wyoming. Amer. Midl. Nat. 105:269–276.

Cambell, T. M., T. W. Clark, and C. R. Groves.
1982. First record of pygmy rabbits *(Brachylagus idahoensis)* in Wyoming. Great Basin Nat. 42:100.

Cary, M.
1917. Life-zone investigations in Wyoming. N. Amer. Fauna 42:1–95.

Carroll, L. E., and H. H. Genoways.
1980. *Lagurus curtatus*. Mammalian Species 124:1–6.

Casey, D. E., and T. W. Clark.
1978. An analysis of the journal literature on Wyoming mammals. Northwest Sci. 52:272–275.

Casey, D. E., J. A. Duwaldt, and T. W. Clark.
1986. An annotated bibliography of the black-footed ferret. Great Basin Nat. Mem. 8:185–208.

Chapman, J. A.
1978. *Sylvilagus nuttalli*. Mammalian Species 56:1–3.

Chapman, J. A.
1978. *Sylvilagus audubonii*. Mammalian Species 106:1–4.

Chapman, J. A., J. G. Hockman, and M. M. Ojeda.
1980. *Sylvilagus floridanus*. Mammalian Species 136:1–8.

Clark, T. W.
1968. Food uses of the Richardson ground squirrel *(Spermophilus richardsoni elegans)* in the Laramie Basin of Wyoming. Southwest Nat. 13:243–251.

Clark, T. W.
1970a. Richardson's ground squirrel *(Spermophilus richardsoni elegans)* in the Laramie Basin, Wyoming. Great Basin Nat. 30:55–70.

Clark, T. W.
1970b. Early growth, development, and behavior of Richardson ground squirrel *(Spermophilus richardsoni elegans)*. Amer. Midl. Nat. 83:197–205.

Clark, T. W.
1971a. Notes on the biology of the thirteen-lined ground squirrel in the Laramie Basin, Wyoming. Southwest. Nat. 15:465–505.

Clark, T. W.
1971b. Ecology of the western jumping mouse in Grand Teton National Park. Northwest Sci. 45:229–238.

Clark, T. W.
1973. Distribution and reproduction of shrews in Grand Teton National Park, Wyoming. Northwest Sci. 47:128–131.

Clark, T. W.
1977. Ecology and ethology of the white-tailed prairie dog. Milwaukee Pub. Mus. Publ. in Biol. and Geol. No. 3. 97 pp.

Clark, T. W.
1978. Current status of black-footed ferrets in Wyoming. J. Wildl. Manage. 42:128–143.

Clark, T. W.
1981. Some spatial and behavioral features of the thirteen-lined ground squirrel. Great Basin Nat. 41:243–246.

CLARK, T. W.
    1984a. Analysis of pine marten population organization and regulatory mechanisms in Jackson Hole, Wyoming. Natl. Geog. Soc. Res. Rept. 1975:131–143.
CLARK, T. W.
    1984b. Biological, sociological, and organizational challenges to endangered species conservation: the black-footed ferret case. Human Dimensions in Wildl. Newsl. 3:10–15.
CLARK, T. W.
    1984c. Strategies in endangered species conservation: a research view of the ongoing black-footed ferret conservation studies. Pp. 145–154. *In* Symp. on issues in technology and management of impacted western wildlife. November 1982. Steamboat Springs, Colorado.
CLARK, T. W.
    1985. Black-footed ferret recovery: Just a question of time? Endangered Species Tech. Bull. 2:1–3.
CLARK, T. W.
    1986. Black-footed ferret on the edge. Endangered Species Technical Bull. 3:1–4.
CLARK, T. W., and D. D. SKYRJA.
    1969. Postnatal development and growth of the golden-mantled ground squirrel *(Spermophilus lateralis lateralis)*. J. Mamm. 50:627–629.
CLARK, T. W., R. S. HOFFMANN, and C. F. NADLER.
    1971. *Cynomys leucurus.* Mammalian Species 7:1–4.
CLARK, T. W., and T. M. CAMPBELL.
    1977. Population organization and regulatory mechanisms of pine martens in Grand Teton National Park, Wyoming. 1st Conf. Res. in Natl. Parks, USGPO. Pp. 293–295.
CLARK, T. W., and C. RUSSELL.
    1977. Agonistic behavior in Uinta ground squirrels. Northwest Sci. 51:36–42.
CLARK, T. W., V. A. SAAB, and D. CASEY.
    1980. A partial bibliography of Wyoming mammals. Northwest Sci. 54:55–67.
CLARK, T. W., and J. L. WEAVER.
    1981. Mammals. Pp. 50–64 in Rare and endangered vascular plants and vertebrates of Wyoming, 2nd. ed., ed. by T. W. Clark and R. D. Dorn. Copies available from Box 2705, Jackson, WY 83001.
CLARK, T. W., and R. D. DORN, EDS.
    1981. Rare and endangered vascular plants and vertebrates of Wyoming, 2nd ed. Copies available from Box 2705, Jackson, WY 83001. 66 pp.
CLARK, T. W., T. M. CAMPBELL III, D. G. SOCHA, and D. E. CASEY.
    1982. Prairie dog colony attributes and associated vertebrate species. Great Basin Nat. 42:472–582.
CLARK, T. W., T. M. CAMPBELL III, M. H. SCHRODER, and L. RICHARDSON.
    1984a. Handbook of methods for locating black-footed ferrets. Wyoming Bur. Land Mgmt. Tech. Bull. 1:1–55.
CLARK, T. W., L. RICHARDSON, D. CASEY, T. M. CAMPBELL III, and S. C. FORREST.
    1984b. Seasonality of black-footed ferret diggings and prairie dog burrow plugging. J. Wild. Manag. 48:141–144.
CLARK, T. W., S. C. FORREST, L. RICHARDSON, D. CASEY, and T. M. CAMPBELL III.
    1986a. A description and history of the Meeteetse black-footed ferret environment. Great Basin Nat. Mem. 8:72–84.
CLARK, T. W., L. RICHARDSON, S. C. FORREST, D. CASEY, and T. M. CAMPBELL III.
    1986b. Descriptive ethology and activity patterns of black-footed ferrets. Great Basin Nat. Mem. 8:115–134.
CONAWAY, C. H.
    1952. Life history of the water shrew *(Sorex palustris navigator)*. Amer. Midl. Nat. 48:219–248.
CONLEY, W.
    1976. Competition between *Microtus:* A behavioral hypothesis. Ecology 57:224–237.

COOPER, S. V.
1975. Forest habitat types of northwestern Wyoming and contiguous portions of Montana and Idaho. Ph.D. Dissert., Wash. State Univ., Pullman. 190 pp.
COPPOCK, D. L., J. F. ELLIS, J. K. DETLING, and M. I. DEYER.
1983. Plant-herbivore interactions in a North American mixed grass prairie. I. Effects of black-tailed prairie dogs on intraseasonal above ground biomass and nutrient dynamics and plant species diversity. II. Response of bison to modification of vegetation by prairie dogs. Oecologia 56:1–15.
CRAIGHEAD, F. C., JR.
1979. Track of the grizzly. Sierra Club Books, San Francisco. 261 pp.
CRAIGHEAD, J. J.
1973. Home ranges and activity patterns of nonmigratory elk of the Madison drainage herd as determined by biotelemetry. Wildl. Monogr. 33:1–50.
CRAIGHEAD, J. J., G. ATWELL, and B. W. O'GARA.
1972. Elk migration in and near Yellowstone National Park. Wildl. Monogr. 29:1–48.
CRAIGHEAD, J. J., J. R. VARNEY, and F. C. CRAIGHEAD, JR.
1974. A population analysis of the Yellowstone grizzly bears. For. and Conserv. Exp. Sta., Sch. For., Univ. Mont., Missoula. Bull. No. 40.
CRANFORD, J. A.
1978. Hibernation in the western jumping mouse (Zapus princeps). J. Mamm. 59:496–509.
CROWE, D. M.
1974. Some aspects of reproduction and population dynamics of bobcats in Wyoming. Ph.D. Dissert., Univ. Wyo., Laramie. 191 pp.
CROWELL, K. L., and S. L. PIMM.
1976. Competition and niche shifts of mice introduced onto small islands. Oikos 27:251–258.
DAVIDSON, D. W., J. H. BROWN, and R. S. INOUYE.
1980. Competition and the structure of granivore communities. BioScience 30:230–238.
DAVIS, W. B.
1939. The Recent mammals of Idaho. Caxton Printers, Caldwell, Idaho. 400 pp.
DEEMS, E. F., JR., D. PURSLEY, EDS.
1978. North American furbearers: Their management, research, and harvest status in 1976. Univ. Maryland press, College Park. 171 pp.
DIERSING, V. E.
1980. Systematics and evolution of the pygmy shrews (subgenus Microsorex) of North America. J. Mamm. 61:76–101.
DIERSING, V. E., and D. F. HOFFMEISTER.
1977. Revision of the shrews Sorex merriami and a description of a new species of the subgenus Sorex, J. Mamm., 58:321–333.
DORN, R. D.
1986. The Wyoming Landscape, 1805–1878. Mountain West Publ. Co., Cheyenne, Wyo. 94 pp.
DOUGLAS, C. L.
1969. Comparative ecology of pinyon mice and deer mice in Mesa Verde National Park, Colorado. Univ. Kans. Mus. Nat. Hist. Publ. 18:421–504.
DOUGLASS, R. J.
1976. Spatial interactions and micro-habitat selections of two locally sympatric voles. Microtus montanus and Microtus pennsylvanicus. Ecology 57:346–352.
DURRANT, S. D.
1952. Mammals of Utah: Taxonomy and distribution. Univ. Kans. Mus. Nat. Hist. 6:1–549.
EGOSCUE, H. J.
1962. The bushy-tailed woodrat: A laboratory colony. J. Mamm. 43:328–337.
EGOSCUE, H. J.
1964. Ecological notes and laboratory life history of the canyon mouse. J. Mamm. 45:387–396.

EGOSCUE, H. J.
1979. *Vulpes velox.* Mammalian Species 122:1–5.
FARENTINOS, R. C., P. J. CAPRETTA, R. E. KEPNER and V. M. LITTLEFIELD.
1981. Selective herbivory in tassel-eared squirrels: Role of monoterpenes in ponderosa pines chosen as feeding trees. Science 213:1273–1275.
FENTON, M. B., and G. P. BELL.
1979. Echolocation and feeding behavior in four species of *Myotis* (Chiroptera). Can.J. Zool. 57:1271–1277.
FENTON, M. B., and M. R. BARCLAY.
1980. *Myotis lucifugus.* Mammalian Species 142:1–8.
FENTON, M. B., and G. P. BELL.
1981. Recognition of species of insectivorous bats by their echolocation calls. J. Mamm. 62:233–243.
FINDLEY, J. S.
1951. Habitat preferences of four species of *Microtus* in Jackson Hole, Wyoming. J. Mamm. 32:118–120.
FINDLEY, J. S.
1954. Competition as a possible limiting factor in the distribution of *Microtus.* Ecology 35:418–420.
FINDLEY, J. S., A. H. HARRIS, D. E. WILSON, and C. JONES.
1975. Mammals of New Mexico. Univ. New. Mex. Press, Albuquerque. 360 pp.
FINLEY, R. B.
1958. The wood rats of Colorado: Distribution and eoclogy. Univ. Kans. Mus. Nat. Hist. Publ. 10:213–552.
FISLER, G. F.
1971. Age structure and sex ratios in populations of *Reithrodontomys.* J. Mamm. 52:653–662.
FITCH, J. H., and K. A. SHUMP.
1979. *Myotis keenii.* Mammalian Species 121:1–3.
FLATH, D. L.
1981. Vertebrate species of special concern. Mont. Dept. Fish. Wildl. and Parks. 74 pp.
FLINDERS, J. T., and R. M. HANSEN.
1973. Abundance and disperson of leporids within a shortgrass ecosystem. J. Mamm. 54:287–291.
FORREST, S. C., T. W. CLARK, L. RICHARDSON, and T. M. CAMPBELL III.
1985. Black-footed ferret habitat: some management and reintroduction considerations. Bur. Land Mgmt, Cheyenne, Wyoming, Wildl. Tech. Bull. 2:1–49.
FRANZMANN, A. W.
1981. *Alces alces.* Mammalian Species 154:1–7.
FRASE, B. A., and R. S. HOFFMANN.
1980. *Marmota flaviventris.* Mammalian Species 135:1–8.
FRITZELL, E. K., and K. J. HAROLDSON.
1982. *Urocyon cinereoargenteus.* Mammalian Species 189:1–8.
FORBES, R. B.
1964. Some aspects of the life history of the silky pocket mouse, *Perognathus flavus.* Amer. Midl. Nat. 72:439–444.
FOSTER, J. B.
1961. Life history of the *Phenacomys* vole. J. Mamm. 42:181–198.
FULLARD, J. H., and M. B. FENTON.
1979. Jamming bat echolocation: The clicks of arctiid moths. Can. J. Zool. 57:647–649.
GARRETSON, M. S.
1938. The American bison: The story of its extermination as a wild species and its restoration under federal protection. New York Zool. Soc., New York. 254 pp.
GEIST, V.
1971. Mountain sheep: A study in behavior and evolution. Univ. Chicago Press, Chicago. 383 pp.

GEIST, V.
1981.   Behavior: Adaptive strategies in mule deer, pp. 157–223 in Mule and black-tailed deer of North America, ed. by O. C. Wallace. Univ. Neb. Press, Lincoln. 494 pp.
GLOVER, D. G., M. H. SMITH, L. AMES, J. JOULE, and J. M. DUBACH.
1977.   Genetic variation in pika populations. Can. J. Zool. 55:1841–1845.
GLOVER, F. A.
1942.   A population study of weasels in Pennsylvania. M.S. Thesis, Penn. State Univ., University Park, 210 pp.
GOLIGHTLY, R. T., and R. D. OMHART.
1978.   Heterothermy in free-ranging Abert's squirrels *(Sciurus aberti).* Ecology 59:897–909.
GOLLEY, F. B., K. PETRUSEWICZ, and L. RYSZKOWSKI, EDS
1975.   Small mammals: Their productivity and population dynamics. IBP 5. Cambridge Univ. Press, London. 451 pp.
GORDON, K.
1936.   Territorial behavior and social dominance among Sciuridae. J. Mamm. 17:171–172.
GRANT, P. R.
1976a. Competition between species of small mammals, pp. 38–51 in Populations of small mammals under natural conditions, ed. by O. P. Snyder. Univ. Pittsburgh Pymatuning Lab. Ecol., Spec. Publ. Ser. 5:1–237.
GRANT, P. R.
1976b. An 11-year study of small mammal populations at Mont St. Hilaire, Quebec. Can. J. Zool. 54:2156–2173.
GREEN, J. S., and J. T. FLINDERS.
1980.   *Brachylagus idahoensis.* Mammalian Species 125:1–4.
GREENHALL, A. M.
1982.   House bat management. U.S. Fish and Wildl. Serv. Res. Publ. 143:1–33.
GREENHALL, A. M., and J. L. PARADISO.
1968.   Bats and bat banding. U.S. Fish and Wildl. Serv. Bur. Sport Fish. & Wildl. Res. Publ. 72:1–40.
GRINNEL, J., J. DIXON, and J. M. LINSDALE.
1937.   Fur-bearing mammals of California, v. 2. Univ. Calif. Press, Berkeley.
GROSS, J. E., L. C. STODDART, and F. H. WAGNER.
1974.   Demographic analysis of a northern Utah jackrabbit population. Wildl. Monogr. 40:1–68.
GROSS, J. E., Z. WANG, and B. A. WUNDER.
1985.   Effects of food quality and energy needs: changes in gut morphology and capacity of *Microtus ochrogaster.* J. Mamm. 66:661–667.
HALFPENNY, J. C., and C. H. SOUTHWICK.
1982.   Small mammal herbivores of the Colorado alpine: A festschrift for John W. Marr. Univ. Colo. Inst. Arctic and Alpine Res. Occas. Pap. No. 37.
HALL, E. R.
1981.   The mammals of North America, 2nd ed., 2 v. John Wiley and Sons, New York. 1175 pp.
HALL, E. R., and K. KELSON.
1959.   The mammals of North America. Ronald Press, New York, 2 v. 1083 pp.
HART, E. R.
1971.   Food preferences of the cliff chipmunk, *Eutamias dorsalis* in northern Utah. Great Basin Nat. 31:182–189.
HART, E. R.
1976.   Life history notes on the cliff chipmunk, *Eutamias dorsalis,* in Utah. Southwest Nat. 21:243–246.
HART, E. B.
1982.   The raccoon, *Procyon lotor,* in Wyoming. Great Basin Nat. 42:599–600.

HAWES, M. L.
1977. Home range, territoriality and ecological separation in sympatric shrews, *Sorex vagrans* and *Sorex obscurus*. J. Mamm. 58:354–367.

HEANEY, L. R., and R. M. TIMM.
1983. Relationships of pocket gophers of the genus *Geomys* from the central and northern Great Plains. Univ. Kansas Mus. Nat. Hist. Misc. Publ. 74:1–59.

HELLER, H. C., and D. M. GATES.
1971. Altitudinal zonation of chipmunks *(Eutamias)*: Energy budgets. Ecology 52:424–433.

HENDERSON, F. R., P. F. SPRINGER, and R. ADRIAN.
1969. The black-footed ferret in South Dakota. S. Dak. Dept. Game, Fish and Parks, Tech. Bull. 4:1–37.

HENNINGS, D., and R. S. HOFFMANN.
1977. A review of the taxonomy of the *Sorex vagrans* species complex from western North America. Univ. Kans. Mus. Nat. Hist. Occas. Pap. 68:1–35.

HERMANSON, J. W., and T. J. O'SHEA.
1983. *Antrozous pallidus*. Mammalian Species 213:1–8.

HILL, J. E., and C. W. HIBBARD.
1943. Ecological differentiation between two harvest mice *(Reithrodontomys)* in western Kansas. J. Mamm. 24:22–25.

HILLMAN, C. N., R. L. LINDER, and R. B. DAHLGREN.
1979. Prairie dog distribution in areas inhabited by black-footed ferrets. Amer. Midl. Nat. 102:185–187.

HILLMAN, C. N., and T. W. CLARK.
1980. *Mustela nigripes*. Mammalian Species 126:1–3.

HOAK, J. H., J. L. WEAVER, and T. W. CLARK.
1982. Wolverines in western Wyoming. Northwest Sci. 56:159–161.

HOAK, J. H., T. W. CLARK, and J. L. WEAVER.
1984. Of grizzly bears and commercial outfitters in Bridger-Teton National Forest. Intern. Conf. Bear Res. and Manage. 5:110–117.

HOFFMAN, G., and R. R. ALEXANDER.
1977. Forest vegetation of the Bighorn Mountains, Wyoming. A habitat type classification. USDA For. Serv. Res. Pap. RM-170. 38 pp.

HOFFMANN, R. S., and D. L. PATTIE.
1968. A guide to Montana mammals: Identification, habitat, distribution and abundance. Univ. Mont. Printing Serv., Missoula. 113 pp.

HOFFMANN, R. S., P. L. WRIGHT, and F. E. NEWBY.
1969. The distribution of some mammals in Montana. I. Mammals other than bats. J. Mamm. 50:579–604.

HOFFMANN, R. S., and R. D. FISHER.
1978. Additional distributional records of Preble's shrew *(Sorex preblei)*. J. Mamm. 59:883–884.

HOFFMANN, R. S., and J. G. OWEN.
1980. *Sorex tenellus* and *Sorex nanus*. Mammalian Species 131:1–4.

HOFFMEISTER, D. F.
1981. *Perognathus truei*. Mammalian Species 161:1–5.

HOOVEN, E. F.
1973. Notes on the water vole in Oregon. J. Mamm. 54:751–753.

HORNOCKER, M.
1976. Cougars up close. Nat. Wildl. 14:42–47.

HOUSTON, D. B.
1968. The Shiras moose in Jackson Hole, Wyoming. Grand Teton Nat. Hist. Assoc. Tech. Bull. 1:1–110.

HOUSTON, D. B.
1974. The northern Yellowstone elk, v. 1 & 2: History and demography. U.S. Nat. Park Serv., Mammoth, Wyo. 185 pp.

HOUSTON, D. B.
    1978.   Cougar and wolverine in Yellowstone National Park. Yellowstone Nat. Park Res.
            Note 5.
HOWARD, W. E.
    1949.   Dispersal, amount of inbreeding and longevity in a local population of prairie
            deer mice on the George Reserve, southern Michigan. Univ. Mich. Lab. Vert.
            Biol. Contrib. 43:1–50.
INGLES, L. G.
    1941.   Natural history observations on the Audubon cottontail. J. Mamm. 22:227–250.
INGLES, L. G.
    1961.   Home range and habits of the wandering shrew. J. Mamm. 42:455–462.
JACKSON, H. H. T.
    1961.   Mammals of Wisconsin. Univ. Wisc. Press, Madison. 504 pp.
JANNETT, F. J.
    1978.   The density-dependent formation of extended maternal families of the mon-
            tane Microtus montanus nanus. Behav. Ecol. Sociobiol. 3:245–263.
JANNETT, F. J.
    1981.   Sex ratios in high-density populations of the montane vole, Microtus montanus,
            and the behavior of territorial males. Behav. Ecol. Sociobiol. 8:297–307.
JENKINS, S. H., and P. BUSHER
    1979.   Castor canadensis. Mammalian Species 120:1–8.
JONES, J. K.
    1964.   Distribution and taxonomy of mammals of Nebraska. Univ. Kans. Mus. Nat.
            Hist. Publ. 16:1–365.
JONES, J. K.
    1982.   [Book review of] The mammals of North America, 2nd ed., by E. R. Hall. J.
            Mamm. 63:717–718.
JONES, J. K., D. C. CARTER, H. H. GENOWAYS, R. S. HOFFMANN, and D. W. RICE.
    1982.   Revised checklist of North American mammals. Texas Tech. Univ. Mus. Oc-
            cas. Pap. 80:1–22.
JONES, J. K., D. M. ARMSTRONG, R. S. HOFFMANN, and C. JONES.
    1983.   Mammals of the northern Great Plains. Univ. Nebraska Press, xii + 379 pp.
JONES, J. K., D. M. ARMSTRONG, and J. R. CHOATE.
    1984   Guide to Mammals of the Plains States. Univ. Neb. Press, Lincoln. 371 pp.
JUNGE, J. A., and R. S. HOFFMANN.
    1981.   An annotated key to the long-tailed shrews (genus Sorex) of the United States
            and Canada, with notes on middle American Sorex. Univ. Kans. Mus. Nat. Hist.
            Occas. Pap. 94:1–48.
KAMAMICHI, T.
    1976.   Hay territory and dominance rank of pikas (Ochotona princeps). J. Mamm.
            57:133–148.
KEITH, J. O.
    1965.   The Abert's squirrel and its dependence on Ponderosa pine. Ecology 46:150–163.
KILGORE, D. L.
    1969.   An ecological study of the swift fox (Vulpes velox) in the Oklahoma Panhan-
            dle. Amer. Midl. Nat. 81:512–534.
KING, J. A., ED.
    1968.   Biology of Peromyscus. Amer. Soc. Mamm. Spec. Publ. No. 2.
KOEPPL, J. W., and R. S. HOFFMAN.
    1981.   Comparative post natal growth of four ground squirrel species. J. Mamm.
            62:41–57.
KOFORD, C. B.
    1958.   Prairie dogs, white faces and blue grama. Wildl. Monogr. No. 3.
KORTLUCKE, S. M.
    1984.   Variation in Bassariscus (Mammalia: Procyonidae). Doctoral Thesis, Univ. Kan-
            sas, Lawrence. 115 pp. + appendix.

KRITZMAN, E. B.
1974. Ecological relationships of *Peromyscus maniculatus* and *Perognathus parvus* in eastern Washington. J. Mamm. 55:172–188.
KUNZ, T. H.
1982. *Lasionycteris noctivagans.* Mammalian Species 172:1–5.
KUNZ, T. H., and R. A. MARTIN.
1982. *Plecotus townsendii.* Mammalian Species 175:1–6.
KURTEN, B., and E. ANDERSON.
1980. Pleistocene mammals of North America. Columbia Univ. Press, New York. 442 pp.
LARRISON, E. J.
1976. Mammals of the northwest. Seattle Audubon Society, Seattle. 256 pp.
LARRISON, E. J., and D. R. JOHNSON.
1981. Mammals of Idaho. Northwest Naturalist Books, Univ. Ida. Press, Moscow. 166 pp.
LECHLEITNER, R. R.
1969. Wild mammals of Colorado: Their appearance, habits, distribution, and abundance. Pruett Publ. Co., Boulder, Colo. 254 pp.
LEE, D. S., and J. B. FUNDERBURG.
1982. Marmots, *in* Wild Mammals of North America, ed. by J. A. Chapman and G. A. Feldhamer. Johns Hopkins Univ. Press, Baltimore. 1147 pp.
LILLEGRAVEN, J. A., Z. KIELAN-JAWOROWSKA, and W. A. CLEMENS, EDS.
1979. Mesozoic mammals. Univ. Calif. Press, Berkeley. 311 pp.
LONG, C. A.
1965. The mammals of Wyoming. Univ. Kansas Publ. Mus. Nat. Hist. 14(18):493–758.
LONG, C. A.
1973. *Taxidea taxus.* Mammalian Species 26:1–4.
LONG, C. A., and W. C. KERFOOT.
1963. Mammalian remains from owl pellets in eastern Wyoming. J. Mamm. 44:129–131.
LONG, C. A., and D. CRONKITE.
1970. Taxonomy and ecology of sibling chipmunks in central Colorado. Southwest. Nat. 14:283–291.
LOTZE, J., and S. ANDERSON.
1979. *Procyon lotor.* Mammalian Species 119:1–8.
LOY, R. R.
1981. Ecological investigations of the swift fox *(Vulpes velox)* in Pawnee National Grasslands, Colorado. M.S. Thesis, Univ. North. Colo., Greeley.
MACKIE, R. J.
1970. Range ecology and relations of mule deer, elk, and cattle in the Missouri River Breaks, Montana. Wildl. Monogr. 20:1–79.
MACKIE, R. J.
1976. Interspecific competition between mule deer, other game animals and livestock, pp. 49–54 in Mule deer in the West: A symposium. Utah State Univ. Agric. Exp. Sta., Logan.
MADISON, D. M.
1980. Space use and social structure in meadow voles, *Microtus pennsylvanicus.* Behav. Ecol. Sociobiol. 7:65–71.
MADSON, S., J. GILBERT, J. HINCKS, C. FRENCH, and J. PARKS.
1980. Small mammal inventory of the Grass Creek Resource Area. BLM-USDI, Worland, Wyo.
MARTIN, A. C., H. I. ZIM, and A. L. NELSON.
1951. American wildlife and plants. Dover Publ., New York. 484 pp.
MASTER, L. L.
1977. The effect of interspecific competition on habitat utilization by two species of *Peromyscus.* Ph.D. Dissert., Univ. Mich., Ann Arbor. 179 pp.

Maxell, M. H., and L. N. Brown.
   1968.   Ecological distribution of rodents on the high plains of eastern Wyoming. Southwest. Nat. 13:143–158.
McCarty, R.
   1978.   *Onychomys leucogaster.* Mammalian Species 87:1–6.
McCracken, G. F.
   1984.   Communal nursing in Mexican free-tailed bat maternity colonies. Science 223:1090–1091.
McHugh, T.
   1972.   The time of the buffalo. Alfred A. Knopf, New York. 339 pp.
McManus, J. J.
   1974.   *Didelphis virginiana.* Mammalian Species 40:1–6.
Meagher, M. M.
   1973.   The bison of Yellowstone National Park. U.S. Nat. Park Serv. Sci. Monogr. Ser. 1:1–161.
Mech, L. D.
   1970.   The Wolf. Natural History Press, Garden City, New Jersey. 384 pp.
Mech, L. D.
   1974.   *Canis lupus.* Mammalian Species 37:1–6.
Melquist, W. E., and M. G. Hornocker.
   1979.   Methods and techniques for studying and censusing river otter populations. Univ. Ida. For., Wildl., and Range Exp. Sta. Contrib. No. 154. 17 pp.
Merritt, J. F.
   1981.   *Clethrionomys gapperi.* Mammalian Species 146:1–9.
Meserve, P. L.
   1971.   Population ecology of the prairie vole, *Microtus ochrogaster,* in the western mixed prairie of Nebraska. Amer. Midl. Nat. 86:417–433.
Meserve, P. L.
   1977.   Three-dimensional home ranges of cricetid rodents. J. Mamm. 58:439–558.
Meslow, E. C., and L. B. Keith.
   1968.   Demographic parameters of a snowshoe hare population. J. Wildl. Manage. 32:812–834.
Messick, J. P.
   1981.   Ecology of the badger in southwestern Idaho. Ph.D. Dissert., Univ. Idaho, Moscow. 127 pp.
Metzgar, L. H.
   1980.   Dispersion and numbers in *Peromyscus* populations. Amer. Midl. Nat. 103:26–31.
Mickey, A. B.
   1961.   Record of the spotted bat from Wyoming. J. Mamm. 42:401–402.
Mickey, A. B., and C. N. Steele.
   1947.   A record of *Sorex merriami merriami* for southeastern Wyoming. J. Mamm. 28:293.
Miller, R. S.
   1964.   Ecology and distribution of pocket gophers (Geomyidae) in Colorado. Ecology 45:256–272.
Morgan, J.
   1980.   Mammalian Status Manual. Linton Publ. Co., Eastham, Mass. 43 pp.
Murie, A.
   1960.   Aquatic voles. J. Mamm. 41:273–275.
Murie, A.
   1948.   Cattle on grizzly bear range. J. Wildl. Manage. 12:7–72.
Murie, O. J.
   1974.   A field guide to animal tracks. Houghton Mifflin Co., Boston. 375 pp.
Nadler, C. F., R. S. Hoffmann, and K. R. Greer.
   1971.   Chromosomal divergence during evolution of ground squirrel populations (Rodentia: *Spermophilus*). System. Zool. 20:298–305.

NASH, D. J., and R. N. SEAMAN.
1977. *Sciurus aberti.* Mammalian Species 80:1-5.

NEGUS, N. C.
1950. Habitat adaptability in *Phenacomys* in Wyoming. J. Mamm. 31:351.

NEGUS, N. C., and J. S. FINDLEY.
1959. Mammals of Jackson Hole, Wyoming. J. Mamm. 31:371-381.

NELSON, Z. C., J. R. HIRSCHFIELD, D. O. SCHREIWEIS, and M. J. O'FARRELL.
1977. Flight muscle contraction in relation to ambient temperature in some species of desert bats. Comp. Biochem. Physiol. 56A:31-36.

NICHOLSON, A. J.
1941. The homes and social habits of the wood-mouse *(Peromyscus leucopus noveboracensis)* in southern Michigan. Amer. Midl. Nat. 25:196-223.

O'FARRELL, M. J.
1981. Status report: *Euderma maculatum* (J. A. Allen). U.S. Fish and Wild. Serv. Off. of Endangered Species, Albuquerque.

O'FARRELL, M. J., and W. G. BRADLEY.
1970. Activity patterns of bats over a desert spring. J. Mamm. 51:18-26.

O'FARRELL, M. J., and D. O. SCHREIWEIS.
1978. Annual brown fat dynamics in *Pipistrellus hesperus* and *Myotis calfornicus* with special reference to winter flight activity. Comp. Biochem. Physiol. 61A:423-426.

O'FARRELL, M. J., and E. H. STUDIER.
1980. *Myotis thysanodes.* Mammalian Species 137:1-5.

O'FARRELL, T. P.
1965. Home range ecology of snowshoe hares in interior Alaska. J. Mamm. 46:406-418.

O'FARRELL, T. P., R. J. OLSON, R. O. GILBERT, and J. D. HEDLUND.
1975. A population of Great Basin pocket mice, *Perognathus parvus,* in the shrub-steppe of south-central Washington. Ecol. Monogr. 45:1-28.

O'GARA, B.
1978. *Antilocarpa americana.* Mammalian Species 90:1-7.

OLIN, G.
1971. Mammals of the southwest mountains and mesas. Southwest Parks and Monuments Assoc., Globe, Ariz. 102 pp.

PARKER, M., F. J. WOOD, B. H. SMITH, and R. G. ELDER.
1985. Erosional downcutting in lower order riparian ecosystems: Have historical changes been caused by removal of beaver? *In* Riparian ecosystems and their management. First North American Riparian Conf. USDA For. Serv. Gen. Tech. Rept. RM-120. 523 pp.

PATTIE, D. L., and N. A. M. VERBEEK
1967. Alpine mammals of the Beartooth Mountains. Northwest Sci. 41:110-117.

PEARSON, O. P., M. R. KOFORD, and A. K. PEARSON.
1952. Reproduction in the lumped-nosed bat *(Corynorhinus rafinesquii)* in California. J. Mamm. 33:273-320.

PEFAUR, J. E., and R. S. HOFFMANN.
1971. Merriam's shrew and hispid pocket mouse in Montana. Amer. Midl. Nat. 86:247-248.

PETERSON, R. L.
1955. North American moose. Univ. Toronto Press, Toronto. 380 pp.

PFISTER, R. D.
1982. Designing succession models to meet management needs, pp. 44-53 in Forest succession and stand development research in the northwest, ed. by J. E. Means. Ore. State Univ. For. Res. Lab.

PILS, C. M., and M. A. MARTIN.
1978. Population dynamics, predator-prey relationships and management of the red fox in Wisconsin. Wisc. Dept. Nat. Res. Rep. 105:1-56.

PIMLOTT, D. H.
1967. Wolf predation and ungulate populations. Amer. Zool. 7:267-278.

POCHE, R. M.
  1981.   Ecology of the spotted bat *(Euderma maculatum)* in southwest Utah. Utah Dept.
          Nat. Res. Div. Wildl. Res. Publ. 81:1–63.
PORTER, C. L.
  1962.   Vegetation zones in Wyoming. Univ. Wyo. Publ. 27:6–12.
POWELL, R. A.
  1979.   Ecological energetics and foraging strategies of the fisher *(Martes pennanti).*
          J. Anim. Ecol. 48:195–212.
POWELL, R. A.
  1981.   *Martes pennanti.* Mammalian Species 156:1–6.
PRINCE, L. A.
  1940.   Notes on the habits of the pygmy shrew *(Microsorex hoyi)* in captivity. Can.
          Field Nat. 54:97–100.
REED, R. M.
  1969.   A study of vegetation in the Wind River Mountains, Wyoming. Ph.D. Dissert.,
          Wash. State Univ. Pullman. 77 pp.
REICH, L. M.
  1981.   *Microtus pennsylvanicus.* Mammalian Species 159:1–8.
RICHARDS, R. E.
  1976.   The distribution, water balance, and vocalizations of the ringtail, *Bassariscus
          astutus.* Ph.D. Dissert., Univ. North. Colo., Greeley. 104 pp.
RICHARDSON, L., T. W. CLARK, S. C. FORREST, and T. M. CAMPBELL III.
  No   Winter ecology of the black-footed ferrets *(Mustela nigripes)* at Meeteetse, Wyo-
  Date   ming. American Midl. Nat. *In press.*
RIDDLE, B. R., and J. R. CHOATE.
  1986.   Systematics and biogeography of *Onychomys leucogaster* in western North
          America. J. Mamm. 67:233–255.
RIDEOUT, C. B., and R. S. HOFFMANN.
  1975.   *Oreamnos americanus.* Mammalian Species 63:1–6.
ROBINSON, J. W., and R. S. HOFFMANN.
  1975.   Geographical and interspecific cranial variation in big-eared ground squirrels
          (Spermophilus): A multivariate study. System. Zool. 24:79–88.
ROOP, L.
  1971.   The Wyoming lion situation. Wyo. Wildl. 35:16–21.
ROTHWELL, R., G. SKUTCHES, J. R. STRAW, C. SAX, and H. HARJU.
  N.D.   A partial bibliography of the mammals of Wyoming and adjacent states with
          special reference to density and habitat affinity. BLM and Wyo. Game and Fish
          Dept., Contract No. YA-512-CT8-126.
RUSSELL, K. R.
  1978.   Mountain lion, pp. 207–225 in Big game of North America, ed. by J. L. Schmidt
          and D. L. Gilbert. Stackpole Books, Harrisburg, Penn. 494 pp.
SCHNEIDER, B.
  1977.   Where the grizzly walks. Mountain Press Publ. Co., Missoula, Mont. 191 pp.
SCHREIBER, K. R.
  1978.   Bioenergetics of the Great Basin pocket mouse, *Perognathus parvus.* Acta Theriol.
          23:469–487.
SCHULLERY, P.
  1980.   The Bears of Yellowstone. Citron Printing, Denver, Colo. 176 pp.
SEIDENSTICKER, J. C., IV, M. G. HORNOCKER, W. V. WILES, and J. P. MESSICK.
  1973.   Mountain lion social organization in the Idaho Primitive Area. Wildl. Monogr.
          35:1–60.
SEVERINGHAUS, W. D.
  1977.   Description of a new subspecies of prairie vole, *Microtus ochrogaster.* Proc. Biol.
          Soc. Washington 90(1):49–54.
SHAFFER, M. L.
  1978.   Determining minimum viable population size: A case study of the grizzly bear
          (Ursus arctos L.). Ph.D. Dissert., Duke Univ., Durham, N. Car. 190 pp.

SHAW, W. T.
1924. Alpine life of the heather vole *(Phenacomys olympicus)*, J. Mamm. 5:12–15.
SHELDON, W. G.
1953. Returns on banded red and gray foxes in New York State. J. Mamm. 34:125.
SHUMP, K. A., and A. U. SHUMP.
1982. *Lasiurus borealis.* Mammalian Species 183:1–6.
SHUMP, K. A., and A. U. SHUMP.
1982. *Lasiurus cinereus.* Mammalian Species 185:1–5.
SKRYJA, D. D.
1974. Some aspects of the ecology of the least chipmunk *(Eutamias minimus operarius)* in the Laramie Mountains of southeastern Wyoming. M.S. Thesis, Univ. Wyo., Laramie. 104 pp.
SMITH, A. T.
1974. The distribution and dispersal of pikas: Consequences of insular population structure. Ecology 55:1112–1119.
SMITH, C. C.
1970. The coevolution of pine squirrels *(Tamiasciurus)* and conifers. Ecol. Monogr. 40:349–371.
SMITH, C. F.
1936. Notes on the habits of the long-tailed harvest mouse. J. Mamm. 17:274–278.
SMITH, C. F.
1948. A burrow of the pocket gopher *(Geomys bursarius)* in eastern Kansas. Trans. Kans. Acad. Sci. 51:313–315.
STEELE, R., S. V. COOPER, D. M. ONDOV, and R. D. PFISTER.
1979. Forest habitat types of eastern Idaho and western Wyoming. USDA For. Serv. Intermtn. For. and Range Exp. Sta., Ogden, Utah, Gen. Tech. Rep., Rev. Draft. 182 pp.
STREUBEL, D. P., and J. P. FITZGERALD.
1978a. *Spermophilus tridecemlineatus.* Mammalian Species 103:1–5.
STREUBEL, D. P., and J. P. FITZGERALD.
1978b. *Spermophilus spilosoma.* Mammalian Species 101:1–4.
STROM, G. L., R. D. ANDREWS, R. L. PHILLIPS, R. BISHOP, D. G. SINIFF, and J. B. TESTES.
1976. Morphology, reproduction, dispersal, and mortality of midwestern red fox populations. Wildl. Monogr. 49:1–82.
STROMBERG, M. R.
1975. Habitat relationships of the black-tailed prairie dog (*Cynomys ludovicianus*): Vegetation, soils, comparative burrow structure. M.S. thesis. Univ. Wisc. Madison. 175 pp.
STROMBERG, M. R.
1978. Subsurface burrow connections and entrance spatial patterns of prairie dogs. Southwestern Nat. 23:173–180.
STROMBERG, M. R.
1979a. Field identification of *Peromyscus leucopus* and *P. maniculatus* with discriminant analysis. Trans. Wisc. Acad. Sci., Arts and Letters 67:159–164.
STROMBERG, M. R.
1979b. Experimental analysis of habitat performance and direct observations of deer mice *(Peromyscus)* in southern Wisconsin. Ph.D. Dissert., Univ. Wisc.-Madison. 224 pp.
STROMBERG, M. R.
1982. New records of Wyoming bats. Bat Res. News 23:42–44.
STROMBERG, M. R., D. E. BIGGINS, and M. BIDWELL.
1981. New record of the least weasel in Wyoming. The Prairie Natur. 13:45–46.
STROMBERG, M. R.., R. L. RAYBURN, and T. W. CLARK.
1983. Black-footed ferret prey requirements: An energy balance estimate. J. Wildlife Manag. 47:67–73.
STROMBERG, M. R., and M. S. BOYCE.
1986. Systematics and conservation of the swift fox, *Vulpes velox,* in North America. Biol. Conserv. 35:97–110.

STRUHSAKER, T. T.
   1967.   Behavior of elk *(Cervus canadensis)* during the rut. Z. Tierpsychol. 24:80–114.
TELLEEN, S. L.
   1978.   Structural niches of *Eutamias minimus* and *E. umbrinus* in Rocky Mountain National Park. M.S. Thesis, Univ. Colo., Boulder. 141 pp.
TERRY, C. J.
   1978.   Food habits of three sympatric species of Insectivora in western Washington. Can. Field Nat. 92:38–44.
THAELER, C. S.
   1972.   Taxonomic status of the pocket gopher, *Thomomys idahoensis* and *Thomomys pygmaeus* (Rodentia: Geomyidae). J. Mamm. 53:417–428.
THAELER, C. S.
   1979.   *Thomomys clusius,* a rediscovered species of pocket gopher. J. Mamm. 60:480–488.
THAELER, C. S.
   1980.   Chromosome number and systematic relations in the genus *Thomomys* (Rodentia: Geomyidae). J. Mamm. 61:414–422.
THAELER, C. S.
   1983.   Personal communications.
THOMPSON, L. S.
   1977.   Dwarf shrew *(Sorex nanus)* in north-central Montana. J. Mamm. 58:248–250.
THOMPSON, L. S.
   1982.   Distribution of Montana amphibians, reptiles and mammals. Montana Audubon Council, Helena. 24 pp.
TRAPP, G. R.
   1978.   Comparative behavioral ecology of the ringtail and grey fox in southwestern Utah. Carnivore 1:3–32.
TRIPPENSEE, R. E.
   1953.   Wildlife management. Vol. 2: Furbearers, waterfowl, and fish. McGraw-Hill, New York. 572 pp.
TURNER, R. W.
   1974.   Mammals of the Black Hills of South Dakota and Wyoming. Univ. Kans. Mus. Nat. Hist. Misc. Publ. 60:1–178.
UDVARDY, M. D. F.
   1969.   Dynamic zoogeography with special reference to land animals. Van Nostrand, Reinhold Co., New York. xviii + 445 pp.
U.S. FISH AND WILDLIFE SERVICE.
   1985.   Northern Rocky Mountain Wolf Recovery Plan. Agency review draft. Denver, Colorado. 84 pp.
VAN ZYLL DE JONG, C. G.
   1979.   Distribution and systematic relationships of long-eared *Myotis* in western Canada. Can. J. Zool. 57:987–994.
VAN ZYLL DE JONG, C. G.
   1980.   Systematic relationships of woodland and prairie forms of the prairie shrew *Sorex cinereus cinereus* Kerr and *S. c. haydeni* Baird, in the Canadian prairie provinces. J. Mamm. 61:66–75.
VAN ZYLL DE JONG, C. G.
   1982.   An additional morphological character useful in distinguishing two similar shrews, *Sorex monticolus* and *Sorex vagrans.* Canadian Field Nat. 96:349–350.
VAN ZYLL DE JONG, C. G.
   1984.   Taxonomic relationships of Nearctic small-footed bats of the *Myotis leibii* group (Chiroptera: Vespertillionidae). Canadian J. Zool. 62:2519–2526.
VAN ZYLL DE JONG, C. G.
   1985.   Handbook of Canadian Mammals. 2. Bats. Nat. Mus. Nat. Sci. Ottawa, Can. 210 pp.
VAUGHAN, T. A.
   1967.   Food habits of the northern pocket gopher on shortgrass prairie. Amer. Midl. Nat. 77:176–189.

VAUGHAN, T. A.
1969. Reproduction and population densities in a montane small mammal fauna, pp. 51–74 in Contributions in mammalogy, ed. by J. K. Jones, Jr. Univ. Kans. Mus. Nat. Hist. Misc. Publ. 51:1–428.

WADE-SMITH, J., and B. J VERTS.
1982. *Mephitis mephitis.* Mammalian Species 173:1–7.

WALKER, D.
1983. Late Pleistocene/Holocene environmental changes in the northwestern plains of the United States: The vertebrate record; in Late Pleistocene-Holocene environmental changes in the High Plains: The vertebrate record, ed. by H. A. Senken, Jr., and R. W. Graham. Ill. State Mus. Rep. of Investigations. (In Press)

WATKINS, L. C.
1977. *Euderma maculatum.* Mammalian Species 77:1–4.

WEAVER, J. L.
1977. Coyote-food base relationships in Jackson Hole, Wyoming. M.S. Thesis, Utah State Univ., Logan. 88 pp.

WEAVER, J. L.
1978. The wolves of Yellowstone. U.S. Nat. Park Serv. Nat. Res. Rep. 14:1–38.

WEBSTER, W. D., and J. K. JONES.
1982. *Reithrodontomys megalotis.* Mammalian Species 167:1–5.

WECKER, S. C.
1963. The role of early experience in habitat selection by the prairie deer-mouse, *Peromyscus maniculatus bairdi.* Ecol. Monogr. 33:307–325.

WESTON, M. L.
1982. A numerical revision of the genus *Ochotona* (Lagomorpha: Mammalia) and an examination of its phylogenetic relationships. Doctoral Thesis, Univ. British Columbia.

WHELAN, J. A., and L. A. RIGGS.
1981. A selected bibliography of Wyoming mammals. U.S. Fish and Wildl. Serv. Denver Wildl. Res. Center. 120 pp.

WHITAKER, J. O.
1972. *Zapus hudsonius.* Mammalian Species 11:1–7.

WHITAKER, J. O.
1980. Field guide to North American mammals. Alfred A. Knopf, New York. 745 pp.

WIGAL, R. A., and V. L. COGGINS.
1982. Mountain goat, pp. 1008–1020 in Wild mammals of North America, ed. by J. A. Chapman and G. A. Feldhamer. Johns Hopkins Univ. Press, Baltimore. 1147 pp.

WILLIAMS, D.
1971. The systematics and evolution of the *Perognathus fasciatus* group of pocket mice. Ph.D. Dissert., Univ. New Mex. 174 pp.

WILLIAMS, D.
1978. Karyological affinities of the species group of silky pocket mice (Rodentia, Heteromyidae). J. Mamm. 59:599–612.

WILLIAMS, D., and J. FINDLEY.
1968. The plains pocket mouse *(Perognathus flavescens)* in New Mexico. J. Mamm. 49:771.

WILLIAMS, D. F., and G. H. GENOWAYS.
1979. A systematic review of the olive-backed pocket mouse, *Perognathus fasciatus* (Rodentia, Heteromyidae). Ann. Carnegie Mus. Nat. Hist. 48:73–102.

WILLNER, G. R., G. A. FELDHAMER, E. E. ZUCKER, and J. A. CHAPMAN.
1980. *Ondatra zibethicus.* Mammalian Species 14:1–8.

WIRSING, J. M., and R. R. ALEXANDER.
1975. Forest habitat types on the Medicine Bow National Forest, southeastern Wyoming: Preliminary report. USDA For. Serv. Gen. Tech. Rep. RM-12. 12 pp.

WOODS, C. A.
1973. *Erethizon dorsatum.* Mammalian Species 29:1–6.

Wright, W. H.
1909. The Grizzly Bear. Univ. Neb. Press, Lincoln. 274 pp.
Wrigley, R. E., J. E. Dubois, and H. W. R. Copland.
1979. Habitat, abundance and distribution of six species of shrews in Manitoba. J. Mamm. 60:505–520.
Wyoming Game and Fish Department.
1978. The mule deer in Wyoming. Wyo. Game and Fish Dept. Bull. 15:1–149.
Wyoming Game and Fish Department.
1981. Working draft of Wyoming Mammal Atlas. Wyo. Game and Fish Dept., Cheyenne. 20 pp.
Young, S. P.
1951. Part I. Its history, life habits, economic status, and control. Pp. 1–226 in The Clever Coyote, S. P. Young and H. H. T. Jackson. Stackpole, Harrisburg, Penn. 411 pp.

INDEX TO SCIENTIFIC AND COMMON NAMES
OF MAMMALS